GOD SPEAKS

Perspectives on Hearing God's Voice

GOD SPEAKS

Perspectives on Hearing God's Voice

AMY AXBY • JESSE BIRKEY • ROB COSCIA • HOLLY CUSATO
CHERYL FRITZ • MATT HALLOCK • GLEN HARTLINE
LAURIE BRUESEHOFF HILGERS • TONI IMSEN
CHRISTINA KLOVER INMAN • MARLON KATSIGAZI
J.D. KING • MICHAEL C. KING • HAZEL MAY LEBRUN
FAITH LIVING • CYNDI MILLETT • ANONYMOUS MOTH
LORI ORLANDO • MELODY PAASCH • NORTHWEST PROPHETIC
CHARIS PSALLO • CHERIEANN RADIANT
KATIE REGAN • SENECA SCHURBON • TANYA VEZZA
GINNY WILCOX • KEVIN E. WINTERS
AND
PRAYING MEDIC

INKITY PRESS™

Copyright © 2017 Inkity Press LLC

All rights reserved. No part of this collective work may be reproduced, distributed, or transmitted in any form or by any means, including photocopying, recording, or other electronic or mechanical methods, without the prior written permission of the publisher, except in the case of brief quotations embodied in critical reviews and certain other noncommercial uses permitted by copyright law.

Copyright for this anthology/collective work is owned by the publisher, Inkity Press LLC. Contributing authors have granted permission to publish their essays in this book.

Each contributing author is the sole copyright owner of their own contributed essay and retains all rights to their essay except for those expressly granted to the publisher, Inkity Press LLC. Contributing authors may reproduce their individual essays elsewhere with proper copyright notice and acknowledgment of this collaborative publication, *God Speaks* by Inkity Press LLC, as outlined in their agreement with Inkity Press LLC.

Contributing Authors: Amy Axby, Jesse Birkey, Rob Coscia, Holly Cusato, Cheryl Fritz, Matt Hallock, Glen Hartline, Laurie Bruesehoff Hilgers, Toni Imsen, Christina Klover Inman, Marlon Katsigazi, J.D. King, Michael C. King, Hazel May Lebrun, Faith Living, Praying Medic, Cyndi Millett, Anonymous Moth, Lori Orlando, Melody Paasch, Northwest Prophetic, Charis Psallo, Cherieann Radiant, Katie Regan, Seneca Schurbon, Tanya Vezza, Ginny Wilcox and Kevin E. Winters.

Unless otherwise noted, all scripture quotations are taken from the New King James Version®. Copyright © 1982 by Thomas Nelson, Inc. Used by permission. All rights reserved.

For permission requests, write to the publisher at the address below or send an email request to: admin@inkitypress.com

Inkity Press, LLC
137 E. Elliot Road #2292
Gilbert, AZ 85234

This book and other Inkity Press titles can be found online at: PrayingMedic.com and InkityPress.com. Available from Amazon.com, CreateSpace.com, and other retail outlets. For more information visit our website at www.inkitypress.com or email us at admin@inkitypress.com or admin@prayingmedic.com

ISBN-13: 978-0998091235 (Inkity Press)
ISBN-10: 0998091235

Printed in the U.S.A.

Acknowledgments

I'd like to thank the contributors to this book. Some are my long-time friends, some are new friends, but they have all graciously shared their personal understanding of hearing God, and even their intimate experiences with God, for this collaborative project. It's been a pleasure learning from and growing with you.

I'm grateful to my friend and editor, Lydia Blain, for her assistance as the primary editor. Working with over two dozen authors at one time is no simple endeavor—yet she managed to recognize each writer's voice and allowed their unique writing styles to be maintained along the way.

I'd like to thank my wife for the many hours she spent reviewing the manuscript, formatting the interior files and developing the cover art. This book would not have been possible without her contribution.

Table of Contents

	Introduction 9
1.	Our Father's Invitation .... 11 Matt Hallock
2.	Does God Still Speak? .... 19 Jesse Birkey
3.	My Secret Times with God .... 27 Northwest Prophetic
4.	Gifting versus Relationship .... 33 Michael C. King
5.	Enigma: Following the Clues .... 41 Charis Psallo
6.	Is It God or Is It Me? .... 53 Praying Medic
7.	Light or Darkness .... 59 The Anonymous Moth
8.	Listening for God's Humor .... 69 Hazel May Lebrun
9.	Cultivating God's Communication .... 77 Marlon Katsigazi
10.	The Comforter Speaks .... 95 Rob Coscia
11.	A First Encounter with Sound .... 103 Amy Axby
12.	Healing for Hearing God .... 107 Toni Imsen
13.	Morning DJ .... 125 Seneca Schurbon
14.	Experiencing God's Voice .... 129 Ginny Wilcox

15. Birthing the Supernatural through the Five Senses 137
    J. D. King

16. Hearing God 153
    Christina Klover Inman

17. I Hear the Voice of God 159
    Faith Living

18. You Can Hear God's Voice Clearly 171
    Kevin E. Winters

19. Sensitive People 181
    Lori Orlando

20. Hearing God's Voice 189
    Glen Hartline

21. Hearing the Voice of God 201
    Melody Paasch

22. Hearing God for the Basics but Not Much More 207
    Cheryl Fritz

23. God Speaks One Way and Then Another 211
    Cyndi Millett

24. Table for Three Please 217
    Holly Cusato

25. How the Lord Talks to Us 227
    Tanya Vezza

26. Hearing from God 237
    Katie Regan

27. Hearing God in "Knowing" 249
    Laurie Brueshoff Hilgers

28. You <u>Can</u> Hear Dad's Voice 259
    Cherieann Radiant

Introduction

A FEW YEARS AGO, I had a dream where I was collaborating with friends on a book about hearing God's voice. If you follow my website, PrayingMedic.com, or read my books, you may know that I pay close attention to my dreams—especially when I understand that God is directing me through them. This dream intrigued me because I happen to have many friends who are writers. Some have published books, and others are bloggers, but they're all passionate about God. And each one has a unique message. When I floated the idea of a compilation book to them, the response was overwhelming. Two years have passed since this book project was first born. Now, you're holding in your hands a book that is literally a dream come true.

I'd like to bring to your attention to a few issues that are unique to this collection of writings.

It's not unheard of for an author to write under a fictitious name, but it seems even more common in publishing today. Many writers are connecting with their readers through the Internet, and having a presence online can bring security concerns. Out of a desire for privacy, some of the contributors to this book have chosen to write under pen names.

The contributors to this book come from all walks of life. Some are pastors, but others don't regularly attend church meetings. They come from many denominations, but a few would deny any denominational affiliation. Some of the authors are American, but others are Brits and Canadians. You'll find not just denominational but cultural and linguistic distinctions from one author to the next.

In some essays, you may find phrases and words with which you're not familiar. Christian sects and denominations are well-known for their religious jargon that mystifies outsiders. Keep in mind the context of a term, and you'll probably arrive at a good guess at its meaning. You can always use a search engine to look up a word or phrase if you're not sure. (Consider it an opportunity to broaden your horizons.)

Because each contributor has different experiences with God, you'll find many different names used for Him. Some refer to Him as The Lord, but others refer to him as Father, Daddy, Papa, Abba, Jehovah, or Creator. Rest assured, regardless of the personal name used, each writer is referring to the same God of the Bible.

You may notice here and there that the views of one author may seem to contradict those of another. Rather than demonstrating significant theological conflicts, I see these differences as merely a reflection of each writer's personal experiences. As you read, ask the Holy Spirit to show you the truth that each writer has to share—and what the Lord is speaking to you through them.

Now that you have an idea of what to expect, it's time to dive in. Whether you're a seasoned believer or a newbie, you'll find something in these essays that will challenge you to experience God in ways you've never dreamed. Happy reading!

~ Praying Medic

Our Father's Invitation
Matt Hallock

GOD'S VOICE IS NEAR. It is accessible. It is ready. It is intimate.

The first time I remember hearing God speak to me was during the summer before my senior year of high school. It had been about six years since I had last seen my dad, and I was depressed, feeling alone in my struggle to become a man. Without my dad, I was afraid of life, afraid of failing, afraid of being found out as a phony Christian. I was under so much accusation from the enemy, and I believed most of it.

But I had made a habit of spending time seeking God. Granted, I did so out of desperation, trying to earn my sonship. I hoped that if I asked enough, He would take the time to invest in me the way my dad had not. But God, not caring as much about me getting it right as He did about being close with me, met me there.

One night I was in my bed, depressed as usual, reading my Bible. I came to Isaiah 64:8, which says:

But now, O LORD, you are our Father;
We are the clay, and you are our potter;
We are all the work of your hand.

All of a sudden, it was as if the world all around me stopped and heaven descended into my room. I broke down sobbing. I couldn't contain it.

I didn't hear any words with my ears or even in my thoughts. This time I didn't need any. Holy Spirit had ripped this verse right out of my Bible and poured it all over me like oil and water and fire and wind. God was indeed my Dad. He would teach me how to be a man. He would give me my worth and my security. I didn't need to fear failure or the opinion of other men or feel like I didn't measure up because my Dad in heaven thought the world of me.

GOD'S VOICE IS SIMPLE

After this night, I started hearing God's voice more regularly—yes through Bible verses, but also in my thoughts. Holy Spirit was conversing with me, as a friend. Simple. It didn't always result in pivotal life-shattering moments, but it was no less precious to me.

Over the next few years, as I grew in discerning God's thoughts from my own thoughts, our relationship became much more intimate and real than it had ever been before. I treasured His thoughts and really lived by them. So many times He would give me direction while I'd be praying. He'd gently urge me to give away $100, only to send me $100 back the next day. He'd tell me to ride my bike downtown to talk to a homeless man who needed His love. Or He'd just tell me what He thinks about me.

The funny thing about so many of us who wish we could hear God's voice is that we think we need to hear it with our ears. Or we assume that whatever inaudible voice God uses will be obviously and unmistakably from Him. So we can get stuck thinking He just doesn't speak to us, and we assume that hearing from Him is only for the select few, the elite, the ones who cracked the code and figured out a way into the kind of Christianity that we all want but don't really think is possible anymore.

Most of what I heard from God wasn't painfully obvious to me. It took faith. I had to choose to believe that these thoughts were from Him and not me. Yes, they were distinct in that they seemed to be dropped in my mind rather than generated from within it. But it's so hard to be certain of that distinction. It really does take a child's faith to grow in hearing God speak. But it's better to believe that it's God and be wrong than to never step out and break the paralysis of our own reasoning.

GOD'S VOICE IS RISKY

At one point, during the summer before my junior year of college, I was spending time with God at a river close to my house and He spoke to me in gentle conviction. If I wanted to propose to my girlfriend, I needed to tell her about my struggle with pornography.

What?! Okay, so apparently hearing God's voice is risky. It can cost us. It can cost us the right to cower in fear, the right to direct our own lives, the right to protect ourselves. None of these bring life anyway. Following God's voice always brings life, even after death to myself.

So, pornography huh? God, you really want me to confess that to her?

Yeah, you can't build a solid marriage on that foundation.

What followed was nearly an entire year of me refusing to do what I had clearly heard God say—a year full of conviction. I heard His voice almost all the time, gently reminding me of what He had asked. He spoke through sermons in church and on the radio, through songs, and through His voice in my mind.

It was never accusatory or guilt-inducing, but it was sobering and convicting, to be sure. Humbling, absolutely. God would always meet me as my loving Dad whenever I sought Him. Even though I was currently not obeying what I had heard Him say, He didn't withdraw. He blessed our times together and fought against Satan's accusing voice with His own affirmation. He kept me in fellowship even when my own actions should have broken it.

And when I finally did obey and tell my girlfriend, who had now become my wife, God released His freedom, His washing, His complete clearing of my conscience. And He blessed me even more with a wife who showed me the most complete and compassionate and Christ-like forgiveness I have ever experienced.

GOD'S VOICE IS MIRACULOUS

I still battle doubt at times, at which point God meets me again. Like the time He told us to move across the country from California to New York. My wife and I had just graduated college and we were considering going to a seminary out in New York. After two months of praying and waiting for Him to tell us yes or no, He finally told us to go.

One evening, I was listening to a sermon on the Internet, and just like that first night several years ago, everything around me stopped. Heaven descended into our little apartment, and I just knew that God was telling us to go to New York. He didn't use words, other than the words in the sermon. He just connected with my spirit—outside of words and understanding.

Once He told us to go to New York, I started questioning whether I had really heard Him or not. We were about to completely uproot ourselves and move three thousand miles to a place where we knew no one. It felt foolish. It looked foolish to those close to us. To many, it seemed like we were moving on a whim. But to us, well, we were just following God's voice—we hoped.

I came back to God one day, asking, "Is this really you, Father? I mean, I feel like I'm about to lead us all the way across the country because of thoughts in my head. The only way this is going to work is if you are actually the one leading us. Otherwise, it's crazy."

This is what He countered with: "Okay, I'll give you a sign so that you know it's from me. Before the year is over, Corrie will be pregnant. Then you can know that you are hearing my voice."

Okay! Now I know I am making it all up! God had spoken to me so many times before, but this was just too specific, too prophetic, too readily "testable." This was actually Him telling me about the future. If it panned out, that would be great. But if not, I'd know it was from me, not Him.

The tricky thing about this was that there was still no way for me to know for sure right now! It was brilliant of God actually. He was giving us a sign that would anchor our faith, but for right now, we still had to have faith to take any action. We had to obey before the fulfillment of the promise.

So we moved believing—hoping, really—that this was God. Today, our seven-year-old daughter is the fulfillment of that promise, born in New York that same year. God spoke, and God delivered.

That's the beautiful thing about hearing God's voice. The Bible itself cannot speak to our specific situations. Move to New York. Don't move to New York. This or that event is going to happen. Pursue this or that dream. But Holy Spirit, whether through the Bible or not, can and does speak into the very specifics of our lives.

God doesn't expect us to navigate on our own. In fact, He quite repeatedly and emphatically tells us to NOT rely on our understanding, to walk after the Spirit, that we'll hear a voice saying, "This is the way, walk in it."

IT'S ALL ABOUT RELATIONSHIP

Why would God, who wants more than anything to have an intimate relationship with each of us, limit that relationship to reading about Him and then inferring for ourselves what we should do in life? Why would He not breathe life into His word and then, with that same life, by His Spirit speak to us about all things?

It would be so sad if I were the kind of dad that we sometimes assume God to be. Imagine me sitting at the kitchen table, working, when my daughter trots over to me.

"Dad? Do you have any ideas about what I can do to help mommy today?"

Silence.

"Dad? Dad?!"

What if I thought to myself, *Doesn't she realize I wrote all this down for her four years ago in her comprehensive life letter? There's a whole section on how she can be helpful to her mom. I said everything in there that I would say right now, so I'm not going to say anything about it anymore. She'll hopefully remember to go read that.*

I would be a cold, heartless, and frankly lifeless dad if I treated my daughter like that. But we put this same thing on our Father all the time. For some reason, it just doesn't feel as absurd. We think that if we ask Him a question that might have an answer already written in the Bible, then we are somehow wrong for asking. We should already know, or at least know to go read. Of course, we should be devouring the written word of God in order to know His heart and His ways, but does that replace our need and His passion for relationship?

There's absolutely no relationship happening when I sit silently at the table waiting for my daughter to go read what I wrote years ago. That's just not our Father, our Dad. At the very least he'll speak up and remind us what he's written. Or maybe he's less legalistic and more loving than we think, and he'll just tell us directly.

Or let's say my daughter's question was more trivial.

"Dad? What color should I make my Lego house? Green or blue? Dad? Dad?!"

Well, now. This is a pointless question. It doesn't matter at all whether the house is green or blue. It literally makes no difference. Either way she will be fine, the Lego house will be fine. I will be fine. So I'm not even going to answer her question. I will just stay quiet until she realizes I have no opinion on the matter. That would be best for her.

Again, absurd. But it hurts my heart when I think of the prevailing presumption in much of Christianity that puts this same attitude on God. It says that God cares mostly about the deep, important issues of morality, obedience, holiness, and converting sinners. But if we need His help deciding what career we should pursue, then we're on our own. It doesn't matter in light of eternity, and so God is not going to speak to it.

But if my daughter asked me what color her Lego house should be, I wouldn't just sit quietly. At the very least I would say, "You know. I think you should choose between green or blue. Both are going to be absolutely beautiful."

But I believe most "trivial" matters have more eternal weight than we realize, and that God has more opinions than we think. He might actually answer with something like, "Well, green is my favorite color. And I love when you make green things. It brings out who you really are, and it blesses my heart and the world around you. I'd love for you to make the Lego house green."

The point is, regardless of His specific opinion on the specific situation, God speaks to us. He is a more loving, more caring, more intimate and involved Dad than we will ever be. If we would speak, then He definitely speaks.

My history of hearing God's voice from that first night back in high school when He told me He is my Dad, to Him convicting me of my sin, to Him leading my wife and me to New York, to now, has shown me more than anything that God wants to be intimately involved in our lives. He wants a deep, passionate, vibrant relationship with each of His children.

When we limit Him to any one form of speaking or to not speaking at all, we are containing Him in a box that He will never fit into. And we are cheating ourselves out of a powerful, living experience of our powerful, living God. But when we abandon ourselves to our Father and let Him do whatever He wants, to speak however He wants, even if it shakes us up and makes us uncomfortable, then we get to know just how wide, how high, and how deep His love for us is. We get to watch dry bones come to life. We get to know the character and kingdom of this great Dad who, with a word, infuses every corner of our being with His light.

Matt Hallock is the husband of a beautiful, powerful, and passionate wife, the dad of two precious princesses, and a son of the Father. While developing his career as an author, Matt runs a kingdom-centered tutoring business, where he prays for healing for his students and delivers God's heart to them while helping them overcome school challenges.

Much of Matt's inspiration and revelation for his writing has come out of his own body's battle with chronic disease and his family's journey into the promised land, taking hold of every bit of the inheritance that Jesus purchased for all of us.

Matt and his wife have both been writers for the last several years and are passionate about pointing others to a more intimate, real, power-filled walk with Jesus than they ever imagined to be possible. They want to see Jesus bring massive restoration to broken marriages, broken bodies, and broken souls in their community in Santa Cruz, California.

Web: www.matthallock.co
Email: matt@pleasurepointchurch.com

Does God Still Speak?
Jesse Birkey

THERE'S SO MUCH we can talk about when discussing how we can hear God, but it's still good to start at the basics. I remember trying to teach my son the importance of walking before running when it came to sports. He proceeded to ignore me and continue heaving the basketball the way he wanted. We see so much of ourselves in our kids, don't we?

But running ahead of God can lead us right over a cliff. Many times I've fallen victim to my zeal and limped back licking my wounds. I'll never forget when God asked me, *why are you running? Who are you trying to keep up with?*

So, one of the most basic questions is, *Does God speak to us?*

I was a skinny little 15-year-old when my youth pastor prayed for me to receive the gift of prophecy. A few days later, I was praying for a man when images sprung into my mind. They were dark shadows creeping around a room that I guessed was his.

I blinked and studied the guy as a few words fluttered across my mind. *Fear of death.* I wasn't sure if the words came from my own imagination or God, but they seemed to fit the image I'd seen. I shifted my weight and muttered something about how the guy didn't need to fear death.

His bald head lifted to reveal wide eyes. He explained that he'd feared death ever since his wife passed away. Dry lips trembled as he told me how oppressed he feels in his room at night. I glanced toward the front of the room. The leader was busy so I blurted what anyone would. "Okay, see ya." I had a lot of maturing to do.

Flash forward 19 years to Easter Sunday and I'm sitting in church. The pastor had preached about halfway through the message when I had to use the bathroom. I uttered apologies and squirmed out of the pew.

When I exited the restroom I decided to stand in the foyer instead of returning to my seat. The pastor was wrapping up and I figured staying out would be better than distracting people from his closing comments.

I wasn't alone. There were mothers and toddlers everywhere. It was like a mom group with a child overflow. But what caught my eye was a woman standing in the library. Her eyes were down as she scribbled something on a piece of paper. It wasn't long before I felt my spirit begin to stir.

I took another look and it was as if her eyes were selected and zoomed in. I watched them transform into the eyes of an eagle. Then the Lord began to explain.

I've given her eyes like an eagle. Keen eyes that see into the hearts of people around her to reveal and bring life to circumstances that seem dead. They are eyes that can see how to encourage and lead others to victory and freedom.

A smile tugged on the corner of my mouth as my heart filled. I stepped to the counter. "Hey, I'm Jesse."

Does God Still Speak?

I saw her eyes search through her facial recognition software and come up empty. "Hi," she replied and shook my hand.

"Hey, listen," I gushed. "Sometimes the Lord lays things on my heart for others. I feel like He has something for you. Would it be okay if I shared that with you?"

Her eyebrows raised a notch and her voice was soft. "That would be fine."

I smiled. "Do you operate in the prophetic gifting?"

Her eyes grew wide as plates. She considered me for a long moment before slowly nodding like she was sharing the details of a deep secret.

I explained what I saw in the vision God gave me. Tears rolled down her cheeks like raindrops as the Lord spoke words about her worth and value.

Don't be afraid of the gifts I've given you, He told her. *I am growing the gifting within you and will increase the amount of those being watered by the words I give you to speak.*

By this time she was groping for paper towels stacked on the counter and another woman close by was getting emotional as well. All I could do was smile and squeeze her shoulder as we were both coated by the incredible love of God.

After the service, she caught up to me and informed me that when I walked up she was writing a note to a friend with cancer who'd asked her if God was really there. "I've got goose bumps," she squeaked.

I grinned. "That's Jesus loving on you." I joined my family and I'm sure she joined hers.

I use these "bookend" testimonies to make the point that there has never been a period in my life in which I can say God stopped talking. Even before my first experience with prophecy, I can remember times in which God spoke. And I have no reason to doubt he'll continue speaking in the days ahead.

But sometimes it feels like He goes quiet. For some, those experiences can be long and drawn out. We wring our hands desperately searching for some kind of reason it would make sense for God to leave us alone. Many times we let our shoulders slump and resign to the assumption God is letting us suffer in order to teach us some kind of lesson. "It's so I'll learn how to trust Him," we parrot to anyone who questions. "If He was always around I'd never need to trust Him for anything." But I challenge this line of thinking.

The entire foundation of my argument against this common mindset is love. It's the kind of perfect love God is supposed to be. The kind of love Jesus lived out. We know from one of the most famous chapters in the Bible that love is kind, patient, and longsuffering. It bears all, believes all, hopes all, and endures all. It doesn't delight in the suffering of others even though it could produce a positive outcome. Okay, I added that last part.

Seriously though, try this hypothetical example on for size. My 11-year-old son comes to me and says, "Dad, it's late and I haven't eaten all day. I'm really hungry. My stomach is, like, eating itself. Can I have some food?"

"Ooh, sorry," I reply. "Can't do it."

He eyes the full pantry and tosses me a confused look. "But there's a ton of food in there."

I cross the kitchen and place my hand on his shoulder. "If I let you eat now you won't trust that I'll have breakfast ready for you in the morning. But I want you to know that I love you."

He goes to bed hungry, confused, and angry. Not to mention the fact that love is now tied to the cause of suffering. And since God is love, it rings true that God is cool with us suffering as long as it produces some kind of beneficial result. And the perceived silence of God has certainly been a point of suffering for many of us.

But we've got to start lining our perceptions of God next to Jesus. Jesus is the exact representation of God. He is the fullness of God's character. When God shines it looks like Jesus (Col 1:15, Heb 1:3,

Jn 17:26). So, Jesus continually went out of His way to give the people what they needed. Whether that be physical healing, emotional, spiritual, or whatever else, Jesus met their needs. He didn't withhold Himself in order to teach them some kind of lesson about trust.

I don't trust a silent God. I don't love a silent God. I fear a silent God because I don't know Him. There's no relationship and no intimacy. So, it seems that a period of silence would be extremely counterproductive if we are the objects of His affection and He desperately, as I believe He does, wants intimacy with us.

> *Therefore my people shall know my name: therefore they shall know in that day that I am he that doth speak: "behold, it is I."*
> ISA 52:6 KJV

God is always speaking. I said earlier that I couldn't say there's ever been a time in which I felt God stopped chatting with me. But that doesn't mean there weren't times in which I couldn't hear Him or that I wasn't listening at all.

One night, I was sitting with a small group of friends thinking about the different ways I'd heard God for others. But then a thought struck my heart like a whip. *Why can't I hear God speak to me about me?* Tears filled my eyes. I quickly blinked them back, but continued to ponder it the rest of the night. Never had the question been so loud. Like a splinter in a sock, my desire to hear God talk to me about me had only occasionally poked me. It was too painful to think about so I'd ignore it. I would tell others the beautiful things God spoke about them, but I rarely heard Him say things like that to me.

Later that night I fell on the floor ready to have it out with God. "Alright," I cried out. "I believe that you *want* to speak to me. Why can't I hear you?" The Lord began to rip away a veil, exposing that I didn't come to Him ready to hear words for *me*. I only came to Him looking for His words to *others*. I rocked back. He was right, of course, but I couldn't figure out why. "Why don't I want to hear you talk about me?" The answer came swiftly, *because you don't think I want to tell you how I feel about you. You're afraid you won't hear anything at all and then your suspicions would be right.*

Tears leaked out onto my cheeks. The truth revealed the lie for the ugly mess it was. The rest of the night was spent pulling it down and destroying the stronghold. Truth rose from the rubble and I instantly began hearing God speak the wonderful things I'd been missing. It was water for my parched soul. That part of me hasn't been dry since.

You may have a story like mine. But lies like what I believed aren't the only things that can keep us from hearing God. Sin is an ugly word producing a wide range of emotions, but the fact is that it separates us from God (Isaiah 59:2). God doesn't leave; we push Him away. The things we choose to do matter. Sin is like a hook that drags our ears toward the voice of our adversary and away from God. Our character is defined and formed by the choices we make. The more we make poor decisions, the harder it is to hear the soft voice of God. The noise of the world often acts like Dre's *beats,* canceling out the sounds of the kingdom. Satan is a loud-mouthed, roaring lion looking to fill our heads with nothing but His song (1 Peter 5:8). I'm certainly not going to spend any time talking about how bad electronics are in all their glorious forms. They're useful and entertaining. But there's a point in which they become what we serve. And to the extent we serve them, we won't serve God.

One of my best friends and mentor, Richard Mull, travels around the country talking about how God isn't a mute. He reports that the percentage of people who don't feel like they hear God often is very high. But by the end of the conference, everyone reports hearing something. It's no coincidence that the conference material deals with misunderstandings and wrong perceptions about God and His desire to talk to us. Jesus said that His sheep hear His voice (John 10:27). If there's a problem with communication, consider that it's the sheep having the issue and not the shepherd. He loves us more than we can grasp and wants us to hear and believe His beautiful thoughts toward us. He *is* talking. Let's start listening.

A Common Question:
How do you start hearing God and how do you know it's Him?

I can only answer out of my own experience and revelation I feel God has shared with me. Hearing God takes practice. It takes an invested effort into developing a relational intimacy with God. I think two essential elements in this are journaling and accountability.

Go to a quiet place if that's best for you, or some like to play soft music. We're all different so just build an environment where you can focus. Then just tell God you're ready to hear Him. I sometimes ask, "What are you saying, Lord?"

When learning to hear the voice of God it's important not to filter anything that goes through your mind. Write it all down including pictures, colors, and whatever else. Then you can send it to some people you feel can hear God well so they can help discern what's Him and what's not. Doing this can help you discover the way He speaks and what He sounds like.

However, you're not going to be able to completely eliminate trial and error. Sometimes you'll just have to step out in what you feel God has spoken and see where the chips fall. It can be hard to learn this way, but just remember that God's arms are open, not crossed. You get unlimited chances to get it right. Mess-ups don't equal disqualification. Learn from the experience, let God love on you and heal any wounds, and move on to the next opportunity.

Just remember that God *wants* to talk to you. It's not an act of obligation to Him. He's ready to tell you all sorts of things. There's an excitement in His eyes when we say, "I'm ready to hear." It's what love is.

Jesse Birkey is the author of *Life Resurrected, Extraordinary Miracles Through Ordinary Miracles.* He grew up as a pastor's kid and received the gift of prophecy through an extraordinary encounter when he was 15. He struggled through the next 11 years until a dramatic experience unfolded in his Chevy Blazer. Jesse came to life with Jesus that day and searched out mentors to help him hear God's voice and deepen his relationship with Him. As a Firefighter/Paramedic, he began to prophesy to his patients and saw the dead raised and lives changed by the words God laid on his heart. Jesse and his wife founded **Reflect Ministry** through which they look for ways to help people hear God's voice and find life again.

Web: www.jessebirkey.com
Email: jbirkey@jessebirkey.com

My Secret Times with God
Northwest Prophetic

For quite a while, I've wanted to write about "my times with God" because this was how I developed a real relationship, a friendship with God, and how I learned to hear and to recognize His voice.

But how do you write about such private experiences, and how do you hold up such intimate times for others to read and perhaps to learn from them? Good gracious, that's intimidating!

This was my regular, disciplined practice for decades. I say, "disciplined" because it was discipline that developed this routine, and for many years, discipline maintained it; this is what obedient churchmen do, and so I needed to maintain these sorts of devotions.

I've since developed an opinion that discipline alone is insufficient for a real relationship, especially for a real friendship. In hindsight,

I realized that I treasured the unusual times, the times where something personal and intimate broke through the discipline to touch me. I often didn't even recognize that this had happened until I put down my pen and closed my journal with a sigh.

I recognized a bit of His presence here, I glimpsed a bit of His heart there, I came away knowing who He really is a little bit better; these were the things that kept me going in this practice, and in truth, still keep me going. In fact, doing your devotions out of discipline is fine, but it's probably not enough to keep you going. And it's certainly not as much fun as connecting with God.

Let me share with you some of the secrets of my secret times with God, and some of how I learned to recognize His voice. If you like, you're welcome to glean from this for your own times with Him.

My goal was to set aside an hour or more to spend with God and my Bible. I've never been real good about doing the same thing at the same time every day, but mornings became my preference because there were fewer distractions then. Sometimes I took an hour before retiring for the night.

More often, I just grabbed an hour or so wherever I could. I remember many mornings spent in an unlocked church building near where I lived, or at my dining room table, in an empty classroom, or lunchroom, or conference room, or a table at the local library. Often times I parked my car for a while in a rest stop or even some wide spot in the road between here and there. (Can you tell I'm an introvert? I love my solitude!) I tried to find (or make) time for us every day, but I didn't worry too much if I missed a day.

The first thing I did after I sat down was almost always just to sigh. I'd just sit there quietly for a few moments, quieting my soul from all the noise and chatter of a busy day. Then I'd open my knapsack or reach to my bookshelf and pull out three things: my Bible, my journal, and a mechanical pencil. (My personal Bible always has cross references, but is never a "Study Bible." I don't want to hear what other people think. I want to discover what God thinks, and see if I can make my own thinking line up with that.)

I figure the best way to learn from *any* book is to cheat, to ask the author about it. So before I opened either book, we'd talk. "Hi Dad. Love you! I'm looking forward to what you're going to show me today. Help me to see, OK? Help me to recognize what you're showing me, what you're doing, please. Thanks. You're awesome!" And I'd open both books at the ribbon bookmark. The longer I practiced this pattern, the more the sense of anticipation grew; I get to hang out with God! How cool is that!

In my Bible, I was often working my way through one of the Gospels, or one of the New Testament letters, section by section. Most translations have headings dividing up the text; I'd tackle no more than the text between one heading and the next, typically only a couple of paragraphs.

In my journal, I listed the date and the day's Bible passage, and then pushed that book out of my way for a bit, while I devoted my attention to the Bible. (I should add that I used my journal for other purposes, processing my thoughts and emotions, reflecting on my day or a particular event. In these times, it had another purpose.)

I read the passage through. You know the way you read a textbook assignment that you don't love? Yeah, this was **not** that. Here, I read carefully through my few sentences slowly enough that my attention didn't drift. If I could, I'd read it out loud, even if only under my breath. It says (Romans 10:17) that "faith comes by hearing," so I wanted to hear the text as much as see it. Besides, I was learning to hear my Daddy's voice. I listened to myself as I read, and I imagined, "He's talking to me!"

Listening to myself reading, I turned my imagination loose to walk among these people I read about, to hear the sounds and smell the smells of the story as I read. This was the fun part, exploring! If I was reading an epistle, I'd listen for the apostle's tone of voice, and I'd imagine how the people it was addressed to felt as they read it. If I felt like it, I'd look at a few cross references, but I guarded against bunny trails. Then when I finished, I'd read through it again, and then again.

While I read, I'd often underline the verbs, using a set of markings I developed for myself after years of this. I started the habit to keep my mind from wandering, but I discovered that I learned much more if my pencil was active. I often circled the verbs, and underlined modifying words. If there were three or four things listed, I'd number the points. Sometimes I'd ask questions, of the text or of Father, about what was going on. Sometimes I'd memorize a verse or two, and that wasn't always intentional. But everything I did was just keeping me involved with the text until the light went on.

Invariably, one bit would eventually catch my attention, sometimes as if it were highlighted to me. Usually, it didn't happen until the third or fourth or seventeenth time I read through the passage. When that happened, it was as if my Father were pointing to a spot, and saying, "Look here, son." Sometimes it was just a word, or a phrase, sometimes a whole verse. Maybe it was a repeated word. Occasionally, it was an idea that never actually made it into the words of the text.

When that happened, it was like I had arrived at the X on a treasure map. It meant, "Dig here." That was the real assignment. Now I reached for my journal as the really good stuff showed up.

The first part of digging was to write (legibly) the verse or phrase that stuck out to me into my journal. And then I go to work to focus my attention on that verse, that passage, and to dig for treasure in that spot.

I need to digress for a moment because this is an intensely personal and intimate exercise. But because it's so personal, it is therefore incredibly difficult to describe. The tools are the tools of study, but the process is one of adventure, of love, of discovery.

For example, really often, when in the moment, I found that I had real difficulty identifying "the target" that God was drawing my attention to. In practice, it was often a tentative thing; "Well, I sure can't tell what God is pointing out!" Sometimes, I had the sense that he'd pointed it out, but often, I'd really struggle to identify a target at all. And on other days, I'd have two or three candidates and no way to pick between them. (Sometimes, I'd just choose the shorter one, as it would take less time to write it in my journal.)

Let's pick an example. One time when I was reading through Mark, chapter eight, I was caught by verse 31:

And He began to teach them that the Son of Man must suffer many things and be rejected by the elders and the chief priests and the scribes, and be killed, and after three days rise again.

This day, I found myself outlining what I saw in that verse. Here is what I wrote in my journal:

What are the "many things" He would suffer? (I listed several that I could think of, and added a note to look at Matthew 20:19 for more details.)

Who rejected Him? (I listed the people who rejected Him, including references, if it was convenient.)

He said that He would be killed: He doesn't say by whom. Is that significant?

He'd rise again after three days.

And as I was writing the outline, I realized that I was thinking *most* about something I'd never noticed; a fact that Jesus had never discussed before. We're 20 chapters into the book, and he's only *now* free to talk about these things; only after verse 29, only after they realized that He was, in fact, the Messiah they were looking for. Only *now* could He describe the hell He was heading into, which they would have to witness.

I wrote most of a page of reflections on what it must have felt like, knowing that this terrible stuff was coming, and not having anybody, not a single person on the planet, that He could have talked to about it before this moment.

Then I meditated (that's Christianese for "I thought about it") for a while on how He Himself must have learned the details of His gruesome death. Since He had been born as a normal baby (see Philippians 2 and Hebrews 4:14, 15), He had to learn all this stuff in His own private conversations with Father. I reflected on what that first conversation might have been like, when Father described what needed to happen. There must have been a lot of tears that day.

And only then, I realized that Jesus got His direction from, more or less, from the same thing that I was doing just now.

And I was done. Either I was out of time, or "the anointing lifted," or something else. And that's the point; I'm not looking to write a pretty article from my hour or so with God. I'm not looking for some big and powerful conclusion.

The big conclusion isn't the point of this experience. The point is that Father and I have time together in His Word. Years later, I realized that He was training me, through these times, to hear His voice, and that it was remarkably effective. But even that training wasn't the point. The point was our time together, our relationship.

Now, why have I just told you all this? It's because of something I heard in our time together; I had the sense that some folks are pretty well grounded in hearing Father's voice, but others are still scratching their heads and wondering how to do that.

If you want to learn how to hear Father's voice well, this practice, or one like it, is one way to learn. It has an additional benefit of giving you a pretty healthy grounding in the Bible.

If you decide to follow this trail, you have my blessing, and more important, you have Father's. May you have as much fun in your time with Father on this trail as I have! I know he'll enjoy His time with you!

Northwest Prophetic is an elder saint who writes about the adventure we call "the Kingdom of God." Raised in a denominational church, born again in the Jesus People Movement, he's spent his life since then pursuing two questions: "What is God doing *now*?" and "How can I be a part of it?"

In recent years, he's been trying to help others answer these same questions for themselves. That's where Facebook, Twitter and his blog (The Pilgrimgram) come in. Feel free to join in the conversations.

Web: www.pilgrimgram.com

Facebook: www.facebook.com/northwestprophetic

GIFTING VERSUS RELATIONSHIP
Michael C. King

WHEN PEOPLE WANT to hear God more clearly, most turn to spiritual gifts, as they can be very useful to hear and discern the voice of the Lord. While learning to engage the prophetic gifts is important, there can be an over-emphasis on these gifts to the detriment of a much deeper calling—knowing the Person of God in His three aspects—Father, Jesus, and Holy Spirit. I have run into this in my own life, partly because it is easy for this to happen. A combination of excitement about the supernatural, zeal for God, a burning desire for His power and goodness to manifest and transform the Earth, and a whole lot of striving to make it happen are a wonderful recipe for an overemphasis on spiritual gifts, as well as a quick ticket to spiritual burnout.

Nevertheless, it is possible to live in such a way and keep the main goal in focus without missing out on the fun and excitement of spiritual gifts. One of the things I used to believe was that those who just "sought after God" and didn't pay attention to the gifts of the spirit would rarely operate in such gifts and would just love God a lot. I still believe that we need to responsibly cultivate the gifts of the spirit, but at the same time I no longer think that ONLY loving God is as much of a waste as I used to. "Lovers make better workers than workers do" is a rough quote from Mike Bickle of IHOP in Kansas City, and I believe this is true. My wife is far more willing to go the extra mile for me in life than anyone I hire to help out with yardwork. Likewise, God is the same way. If we want to go deeper in the prophetic gifts we need to become much more closely acquainted with the Person of God and not just with the cool prophetic stuff He gives us.

For those who are unfamiliar with the prophetic gifts as found in scripture, 1 Corinthians 12:8-10 speaks about them in a list among nine gifts of the spirit. These spiritual gifts are supernatural empowerments designed to help us destroy works of darkness, and the prophetic gifts are a subset of those nine: prophecy, word of knowledge, word of wisdom, and discernment of spirits. Opinions vary, but tongues and interpretation of tongues can act like prophecy when used together and can be counted among the prophetic gifts. All of these spiritual gifts involve receiving divine revelation—which is basically getting information downloaded into our minds from heaven that share with us things we could not otherwise know in the natural. Prophecy is usually for encouragement, building up and strengthening of one another, and comfort (1 Corinthians 14:3). The word of wisdom and word of knowledge are somewhat self-explanatory, giving either wisdom or factual information to help move a situation forward. Discernment of spirits is one of the more controversial of the prophetic spiritual gifts, to the point that some would not include them in this category. I have found the versatility of this spiritual gift goes beyond what the common understanding is, which is to know whether someone is speaking from their own mind, God's heart, or the devil's. Discernment allows us to discover the presence of angels and demons, to see clearly into what God and the enemy are doing in a given moment, and can have significant impact in deliverance and inner healing, intercession, and more.

While I have divided the prophetic gifts into neat little categories based on scripture, the truth is that they all run together when actually putting them to use. When I receive divine revelation about someone and begin to prophesy about current life events, is it prophecy, or maybe a word of knowledge at work? Or maybe I am discerning something spiritual that God is doing. The truth is that for functional daily use it almost doesn't matter which gift I operate out of as long as I know how to flow in the prophetic as a whole, but this comes with practice over time.

In my own life, I have come to a place where I can actually differentiate between when God is speaking or communicating with me directly, or when He is using a spiritual gift to communicate something. While this may seem strange, it is the difference between operating out of a spiritual gift and living out of a relationship. When I pray for someone, it is usually easy for me to operate in the prophetic and get some sort of information for or about them through prophetic gifts. This can be very helpful when trying to figure out how and what to pray for, but it's not foolproof. There are other times where in spite of my confidence and experience level in this area, I hear and perceive nothing. When that happens, I have learned to use my fallback plan; have a conversation with God out of our relationship.

Some find it odd that I refer to the relationship as the fallback plan, because one would think that relationship typically trumps use of a gift. It's not that I will use gifts exclusively and then *only* engage the relationship if that fails, but rather that I am comfortable knowing that even if the gifts fail me that God Himself lives in me, and whether gifts are active or not we can chat with each other and still continue the task at hand. It is *very* rare that I have been unable to hear God talk to me even if gifts aren't working, and even then it's not so much that God wasn't talking but that my ability to hear and perceive clearly wasn't very effective in that moment. God and I literally have back and forth conversations inside my mind and spirit. The point of saying this isn't to brag about myself as though I'm somehow special, but to open up the idea that there is another possibility many may not have considered, a "deeper" means of communing with God.

God is a person with a personality, and who has His own hopes and desires. Oftentimes those hopes and desires are inextricably linked with ours, but He cares about an awful lot of things. If we choose to take time, even a little time here and there, to talk to Him and hear about

His heart and mind, we cannot help but have our hearts transformed to become like His. In these times of talking and relating we can do more than just share information. We do this by going a step further and receiving His love and in turn sharing it with those around us. Much like a relationship with other people, it grows stronger the more contact we have with each other. Long times apart don't necessarily strain a relationship, but they do mean that we have to do some "catching back up" to see what the other has been up to since we parted last. God always knows what we are doing, but our own hearts must remain sensitized toward Him so we can continue to walk in that deep communion.

In the beginning, Adam had a face-to-face relationship with God where they walked in the garden that God planted in the city of Eden, and God's desire has been to have that same relationship with each of us ever since. Talking to God is simple, but hearing God is the next step. It involves knowing God wants us to have ongoing communion—not the kind with the bread and wine but an ongoing intimate relationship where we communicate with Him daily. Brother Lawrence, whose writings make up *The Practice of the Presence of God* was familiar with this, as were many of the Christian mystics, whose simple devotion to communion with God resulted in signs, wonders, miracles, and a high level of accuracy in the prophetic gifts.

Prophetic gifts are fantastic and a great tool that we all can make use of, but intimate relationship is really the foundation that the prophetic needs to build upon, not the means by which we believe we have a relationship. Gifts can dry up when the power behind them isn't as strong as it once was, but there isn't a "power source" behind a relationship other than love. As long as we are loved by God, there will be a steady flow of power into the relationship to keep it going, and God's love is immutable, inexhaustible, and infinite.

Knowing it is possible to have a one-on-one relationship with God, *how* do we engage that relationship? How do we engage *any* relationship? Time and communication. I personally find it hard at times to wrap my brain around communing with an invisible omniscient and omnipresent being that I can neither see nor touch, but the more I simply choose in my heart to desire to know Him more, I can feel His love flowing in. It's as simple as "draw near to God and He will draw near to you." (James 4:8a) The more I choose to engage my heart in gratitude, love, and interest toward God, I find that I experience the same from Him. As I talk to Him about my life and then stop talking out loud as well as silencing my mental chatter, I begin to hear that still, small voice speaking inside my mind. For me it's not a matter of "will God talk to me," but "am I really even listening?" There are times when the conversation is extremely short, when God only says one or two things to me, none of which are earth-shattering revelations, but the truth is they don't have to be. Life doesn't usually consist of constantly having our understanding blown to smithereens by a tidal wave of deep revelatory experiences, but by the steady drip-drip of gentle communication over time, occasionally punctuated with larger, grander encounters.

As we are faithful in the small things, in those simple, daily encounters with God, there is a natural progression. Those infrequent grand encounters begin to be more frequent. That revelation which seemed so small and insignificant starts to take on a higher level of impact, touching our hearts and those around us at a deeper level than before. As we get to know God better, literally by taking time with Him and getting quiet in our hearts to let Him speak, the relationship grows. This doesn't mean that the outside world has to resemble a Tibetan Monastery with its austerity and silence, but that regardless of whether we are riding a busy train full of people or are sitting in the middle of a call center with phones ringing off the hook, our internal space is turned toward the Prince of Peace and we are able to commune with Him regardless of external circumstances.

I want to end with a short story about an experience I once had, because He wants to do the same type of thing with every reader. Many years ago I worked as a temp laborer at a factory making piezokinetic products; lead-based ceramic parts for various machines. I stood there for hours on end each day cleaning sand off of small fired ceramic rings, then covering unfired rings with sand to put them in the kiln, to pull them out hours later to clean the sand off again. I was physically busy but my mind was barely engaged at all, so I got permission to listen to CDs with a portable CD player. As my drug of choice was preaching and teaching, I listened to a series by Todd Bentley about the Holy Spirit and how He wants us to have an intimate relationship with

Him. Todd shared a series of experiences he had that were similar to ones that Benny Hinn shared in his books *Good Morning, Holy Spirit* and *The Anointing*. As I listened, my heart was stirred with desire for this same level of personal friendship with God and not just a distant obeisance of worship as a servant or slave to an untouchable deity.

As I listened to these messages, I very simply asked God if He would be willing to be my friend. I felt like He said "Yes" inside my head, but I didn't know where to go from there, so I just kept listening to the messages with my heart burning inside. As I drove home that afternoon after work, I was talking to God again about being His friend and I looked up in the sky and saw a portion of a rainbow reflected in a cloud. There wasn't a rainbow in the whole sky, but just this single cloud itself was rainbow-tinted. Holy Spirit has always represented Himself to me as a rainbow, and when I saw that I heard Him say in my mind "I will show you signs in the heavens and wonders on the Earth." When I heard this I was filled with joy because I felt Him confirming that He indeed wanted to be my friend as I had asked Him.

Even as I write this I am reminded of the simplicity of that day because I knew without a doubt that God WANTED to talk to me and it excited me. I am reminded that even now I need to step back into that place of communion on a deeper level than I have before. I also know that in the same way that God wants me to know Him more, this level of relationship is available to every reader. God does play favorites, but He can get away with it because everyone is His favorite. Now is the time to ask God to be your friend, and now is the time to let your heart overflow with love for Him. I encourage the reader to set this book down and take a few minutes to commune with God. Get quiet in your heart, close your eyes if it helps, and ask God to be your friend. Ask Him what He is happy about today, what He likes about you, even what His favorite color is and why. Open up your heart to the possibility that there is a whole new side of God you have never met before, and even if you know God as a friend already, go a bit deeper. Let God rearrange your heart with His goodness and take you to another level. As you do this, know that prophetic gifts are still available to you and are very useful, but nothing can sever that relationship you are building in your heart even now, and no being, whether person or spirit, can remove your ability to commune with God and hear Him speaking to you.

For I am convinced that neither death nor life, neither angels nor demons, neither the present nor the future, nor any powers, neither height nor depth, nor anything else in all creation, will be able to separate us from the love of God that is in Christ Jesus our Lord.
ROM 8:38-39

Michael C. King author of *Gemstones from Heaven, Faith to Raise the Dead,* and *The Gamer's Guide to the Kingdom of God,* is an avid writer and loves to explore all things spiritual. He has a love for miracles and strange phenomena, and is passionate about God's power helping us live abundant lives. A writer by day, he is a Registered Nurse by night, and is known by family and friends for his proficiency in healing prayer and energy work. Michael is married to a beautiful wife who also doubles as his professional editor. His blog focuses mainly on spirituality with a hint of health-related topics.

Blog: www.thekingsofeden.com

ENIGMA: FOLLOWING THE CLUES
Charis Psallo

I HAD NO IDEA who the guy was who came by my desk and asked me out for dinner. I worked at the university as a clerk in the physics department. I also studied voice, sang in the chorus of the city opera company, and volunteered at my church. I didn't have time for dating.

Well, that was my excuse. The truth is I was still smarting from the last dating experience. It turns out the potential "Mr. Right's" first name was actually "Always."

"Thanks, but no thanks," I said, smiling politely.

He was not deterred. Over the next few weeks, he asked me out eight times. I turned him down eight times. By then I knew his name and the kind of research he was doing in the physics department. One day

I was handed a pile of files to update. The top folder file had his name on it. I peeked. It contained transcripts and professors' and teachers' comments going back to high school. They were all positive. Even though they and the people I worked with respected him, I still was not interested. But his persistence caught my attention.

No, I reasoned. He's nearly eight years older, he's finishing his Ph.D. in a field I don't understand, he's not a Christian, and besides, he looks like his mother dresses him, except for the pocket protector and horn-rimmed glasses. Even a mother wouldn't accessorize like that. My friends would not approve.

The eighth time he asked I said, "No. Sorry, I'm busy tonight." As he walked away with slumped shoulders I impulsively added, "But try Thursday."

He didn't turn around. Instead, he tossed and caught his keys a couple of times on his way out the door.

"I'll pick you up at seven."

"But you don't know where I live." I shouted after him.

"You live next door to the department administrator," he called from the hallway. "You used to babysit for him."

"How did you know…" but he was gone.

Wait a minute. The department head's wife, Mrs. Johnson, was always encouraging me to aim high. She was the one who urged her husband to hire me. Hmm.

On Thursday evening I changed my outfit three times trying for a look between sophisticated and unenthused. I heard my father get the door.

"I'm not interested in insurance or encyclopaedias or whatever you are selling," he said.

"Dad," I said, rushing to the foyer, "This is my friend, Alex."

He scrutinized the man in the entry and looked at me with a raised eyebrow.

"He doesn't look like any of your other friends."

I don't think any of my guy friends even owned a suit, let alone an overcoat.

"Nice to meet you, Sir," Alex said, extending his hand. "I promise to bring your daughter home safely at a reasonable hour."

Dad shook his hand reluctantly.

"Make sure you do."

As we went out into the cool winter air I heard Dad shout up the stairs, "Honey, did you know about this?" I think I also saw the curtains part a little at the house next door.

"I'm only going out with you to prove that we have nothing in common and this will be a colossal bore," I told him when he opened the car door for me.

"How do you know? Tell me what interests you. What are you reading? What music do you listen to? Who do you look up to? I can talk about more than physics, you know," he said.

We talked for hours. He treated me like I had a brain and could keep up. I looked up a couple of words in the dictionary when I got home, but I enjoyed the challenge. Amongst his many interests was a shared passion for classical music.

We went for coffee a few times after that, but I had heard all the lectures on the dangers of dating non-Christians, so I became "busy" again.

"Let me know when you have an opening in your calendar," he said. "You can explain bel canto to me and maybe I can turn you on to the Russian composers. I'd love to show you my record collection."

A few weeks later I held in my hand an embossed invitation from the Opera Guild president who also sang in the chorus with me. I read it eagerly. A concert by a famous opera singer with private reception to follow! It was addressed to me and my escort. I couldn't think of a single male friend I could drag to such an event, except maybe this guy. He knew a lot about classical music, so I asked him if he would accompany me. I really, really wanted to go. I asked him in the elevator at work. He agreed. I hoped I wouldn't regret my decision.

At the reception, the elaborately coifed woman who sent the invitation pulled me aside while he was getting us some punch.

"How did you snag a Gold Key man?" she asked.

She knew him as a recipient of a prestigious award for outstanding service to the university. She showed me an aspect of him I didn't know about. Apparently, in her eyes, I just went up a rung on the social ladder. After the reception, my escort and I sat in the car and talked late into the night.

We also talked the next night and the next... We often talked about God and faith. I told him my belief in Jesus Christ was not negotiable.

"I am a scientist. My beliefs are based on evidence, but for you, I'll look into this religion stuff," he promised.

When I went to the UK to study, he wrote to me every day, sometimes twice a day after he heard we received morning and afternoon postal delivery. He sent jokes and riddles and told me stories of his past, about what he was thinking in the present, and his dreams for the future. He bragged about the carpentry skills he developed building a fence with my Dad.

He read the Phillips translation New Testament I gave him before I left and in the process of examining it, he encountered the Writer himself. He scoffed through Matthew, cried through John, marveled through Acts, shook through Romans, and by Revelation was trusting Jesus Christ and talking to God Himself. Two months after I returned to Canada we were married.

He has been stalwart in his faith in Jesus Christ for over forty years. I have never had a moment's doubt that he loves the Lord or that he loves me. We still talk in the car for hours, but now it is while we are on our way to visit our grandchildren.

Why am I telling you this in an essay on hearing God's voice? Because hearing God is all about relationship. Because there are similarities in this story with learning to hear God's voice. It's hard to hear Him when we don't know who He is, or when we have defensive walls up, or when we are too busy, or when we are influenced by critics and not open to seeing Him as more experienced believers do, no matter how many overtures He makes. Relationship requires response. We can learn about who He is through written words, but as we come to trust Him and recognize His character, we want to spend more time in His presence. Just reading about Him is not enough. We long to listen to Him, respond to Him, and do things together.

A few years ago, after I spent a lot of time talking to God about my struggles with depression and going through the process of forgiving old offences, not only did the depression lift, but I began to have dreams. These dreams were more than the ordinary jumble of events of the previous day emptied out and scrambled up like pocket contents on the dresser. Sometimes the dreams came true within days. Sometimes I was told what scripture passages to read. Sometimes lines from songs answered questions I asked the Lord before bedtime. I realized He was talking to me.

I come from a culture that holds the Bible in high regard. Up until then, I believed that God spoke only through scripture and perhaps through ordained people expounding on that scripture. This kind of communication was new to me. I am grateful now for grounding in the scriptures that allow me to test if something I think is from God lines up with His principles the Bible, but I began to wonder, What if there is more to this relationship than study? What if prayer is a two-way conversation?

I have friends who hear God's voice very clearly. He tells them which scarf to wear, which shop to go into, and not to buy the first lawn mower in the store because it's a lemon. Maybe someday I will rid my heart of distractions enough to be able to hear the Lord's voice like they do, but so far, for me, it doesn't work that way.

God spoke to Moses through a burning bush in the desert. The danger in talking about how individuals experience God's voice is that we are tempted to ask, "What's wrong with me that I've never seen a burning bush that didn't burn up?" Maybe because you live in the Arctic? Many also think it's only for "special" people. We don't realize He speaks to each of us in words and images and situations we will understand. He's speaking all the time. God communicates in a language familiar to us, but not always in words. It's a matter of paying attention.

Since I am a musician, He frequently uses music to carry a message and I've learned to pay attention to the songs playing on repeat in my head, but that may not be the case for you. Jesus also said that when the Comforter came He would bring to mind the things Jesus had said. I am grateful now for all the scripture I had to memorize as a child. The Holy Spirit reminds me of those passages. I'm amazed that they are still filed somewhere in my cluttered brain, and they come to mind when I need them. Again, this may not be the case for you.

Sometimes I hear a quiet internal voice and on rare occasions an audible voice, and sometimes I see something like snapshots or short videos, but they don't always make sense right away. Usually, there is a pursuit involved. It's like God drops a trail of clues for me to follow, and the goal is Himself. Learning to hear is more about pursuing the question of who than how. He grabs my attention and gives me puzzle pieces in the form of scripture passages, dreams, nature, art, poetry, music, films, books, podcasts, sermons, random posts on social media, and even the observations of little children. He knows I like research and hides gems where I can find them, often via an Internet search.

Early one morning I heard an audible voice that sounded like a BBC announcer giving direction to a website. I heard: "Follow 228. Ban our tires."

I still wasn't fully awake, but it was so clear I wrote it down like a telephone message. I found the weird note later and did an Internet search, grateful no one could see me. Nothing meaningful showed up in the search, so I went away questioning my sanity.

A day or two later I remembered the British accent and searched again using the UK spelling of tyres. This time it led to an advertisement for a bicycle shop. Boxes in the margin displayed photos of items like tyres and Ray Ban glasses. The center box featured a sale item. It was a bicycle headlamp for serious endurance bicycle racers and cost £228. The caption read "Vision LED lamp." A company called Hope made it. Certain words popped out on the page and because of the way they were aligned this is what I read:

HOPE: VISION-LED ENDURANCE

I cried. You see that week we had received three very bad reports. Two involved serious degenerative diseases that meant my husband could end up in a wheel chair and our newly married daughter would be unable to have children. Then an email arrived telling us a betrayal by a partner in a business venture my husband had poured his heart into had literally sent the whole thing south.

Three dreams dashed all at once. I asked the Lord what hope meant in a situation like this, and He answered, but it required me to pay attention and pursue the clues.

Since then all three of those "disasters" have been to the glory of God as our daughter birthed three miracle babies, my husband's spinal cord is no longer threatened (he still runs six kilometers a day) and the skills he learned in the failed project have proven to be very useful in another successful venture. Hope meant we could endure because God gave us those visions and faithfulness is part of His character.

In another puzzling dream an angel handed me various articles: shoes, keys, books, a suitcase, and other items.

"Hold onto these. You're going to need them later," he said.

I am learning to use Mary's example and treasure these clues. Luke tells us that after Mary heard the shepherds' account of their encounter with an angel, accompanied by a multitude of the heavenly host who announced the Saviour's birth and praised God; she treasured up the details in her heart. She pondered them later. Sometimes I need to ponder over my collection of little treasures for a long time, but it's so exciting when the pieces come together!

I was surprised to read a margin note in my Bible—1 Corinthians 13. (Yes, the love chapter.) Beside verse 12, the verse about "seeing through a glass darkly," the tiny print read, "as in a riddle." J.B. Phillips translates it: "At present we are men looking at puzzling reflections in a mirror." The Greek word used here is *ainigma,* from which we derive the English word enigma.

I consulted a Koine Greek expert and he said *ainigma* does not refer to a completely unknowable mystery, but rather implies a riddle or puzzle that is solvable and worthy of study. I realized that the Lord invites me to take all the pieces He brings to my attention and try to fit them together. (In another dream Jesus sat on the floor with me like He was playing with a little kid. We fit complicated puzzle pieces together. Well, I tried. He did most of them.) This game we enjoy might drive other people nuts, but He made me this way, and I think He enjoys it too, like a dad who sets up a treasure hunt for His child. His hiding places can be quite interesting sometimes.

One of the most surprising places I heard God's voice coming from was out of the mouth of a tenor I worked with who had a reputation, and it wasn't for church attendance. He was hitting on me at the time (and every other soprano within range). He heard me say something about having trouble forgiving myself for a rhythm error in a performance.

"But that's why Christ died," he said looking right at me, "To offer you forgiveness."

Now the Lord had been telling me that all week, but I hadn't been listening. I stared at Mr. Hot Stuff incredulously. Talk about your Balaam's donkey moment. I knew it was God speaking though, because it lined up with scripture, and fit with the other puzzle pieces He had been giving me. His tone of voice was evident in the message.

After I started paying attention to the songs and dreams in the night, and the multiple coincidences during the day, they began to increase in frequency. I still had doubts that this was God. What if I just wanted to hear so badly that I was making it up? Did I need a tinfoil hat? And what about the times when I didn't understand and pushed an interpretation of a metaphor that turned out to be wrong? I talk about learning to hear God's voice, but honestly hearing a little bit leaves me feeling frustrated that I can't hear more. I want the unmistakable thunderous voice from the clouds giving me explicit directions. I know one fellow, equally frustrated during a period of unemployment, who stood under thunder clouds with a metal rake balanced on his head and shouted to God, "Talk to me!" I know the feeling.

On the other hand, the Bible tells the story of that time when God spoke in a loud booming voice from the sky. Some heard Him clearly, but others said all they heard was thunder (John 12:29).

The thing is, for His reborn, Spirit-filled sons and daughters, the Voice is no longer up in the sky. The Voice is in us. I asked for confirmation of what I was experiencing.

I had a dream. I saw people throwing huge lasso ropes into a city that was crumbling faster than a set for a sci-fi dystopia movie. One of them looped around a young man who was almost entirely buried in debris. I joined in pulling on the rope and hauled him out of the city of destruction. I recognized him as a zealous new believer I had been praying for who had more than a few rough edges. He stood up, brushed himself off, and began running.

"Hey you!" I yelled, "You're not cleaned up yet!"

He shouted over his shoulder, "Do you recognize Christ in you well enough yet to know that He has called me?" and kept running.

Then I saw a strange word written in large letters. It was obviously not in English since it began with "qo." I looked it up. My search led me to a strange-looking page in which the word appeared only once. I saw numbers interspersed with text and "2 Korintasve 13" printed at the top. I realized this was a page from Corinthians! Looking in my own Bible I found the verse which said, in part: "Or do you not recognize this about yourselves that Christ is in you…?"

My eyes fell on a phrase in verse three where Paul wrote, "…since you are seeking for proof of the Christ who speaks in me…"

That's what I remembered the young man say in the dream – "Do you recognize Christ in you?" I was asking for proof that I was hearing the voice of the Christ who speaks in me. I was amazed. It "resonated." I knew that familiar tone of voice and it gave me confidence.

And what is that tone? Voices surround us constantly—parents, teachers, friends, employers, and media. The loudest one of all may be our own. How do we pick out the Shepherd's voice in all this noise?

At one time I was totally rattled when I thought He was saying, "You are not good enough… you are a disappointment… you have sinned… you have failed to love… you don't belong here…" It threw me because it came through Christian people who are usually kind, and because it was true. I have failed. I have disappointed people. I have not even lived up to my own standards let alone Jesus' command to love. I felt overwhelmed with shame (not just that I did something wrong, but that I am something wrong).

Then, in His kindness, the Lord brought gentle words of correction into my life when I heard a podcast by Graham Cooke and when, at the same time, a page fell out of my journal. They both reminded me that this part of the journey I'm on is about learning to better discern God's voice for myself.

"The fruit of the Spirit," said the speaker, "characterizes the way the Holy Spirit speaks."

I understand that to mean that it's His fruit, not something I have to conjure up on my own. It is His character. He is love. He is peace. When He speaks He speaks with the voice of love, of kindness, of the reassurance of His faithfulness in seeing me through and He does not reject or condemn me. His tone is gentle, kind, patient, and full of peace, because that's who He is.

Here's a question: Even if the message was firm and pointed out a needed change in thinking and behaviour, did the voice that told you that you are a disappointment have a loving, peaceful, gentle, patient, kind, joyful tone? Did it agree with who the scriptures say you are in Christ? Did it invite you to a deeper relationship?

If not, it was not Him. Wrong voice.

If God is asking you to change the way you think so that it shows up in your choices, He gives you access to His patience and self-control. With every challenge that will help you grow there is a provision set aside, a spiritual blessing in the heavenly realms, a grace that will enable you to change. You need to keep your eyes on Him to access it.

Jesus seemed quite confident that we would be able to hear Him. He said:

> *"The gatekeeper opens the gate for Him, and the sheep listen to His voice. He calls His own sheep by name and leads them out. When He has brought out all His own, He goes on ahead of them, and His sheep follow Him because they know His voice. But they will never follow a stranger; in fact, they will run away from him because they do not recognize a stranger's voice."*
> JN 10:3-5

He is not just speaking to a few people with a public platform or a title. He's asking you to come closer, to listen to His heart for you.

He absolutely adores you, you know.

Charis Psallo is the pen name of a woman who is still learning. Her journey has taken her through mountain highs and valley lows but she has discovered that God is always good, even when it may not have looked like it at the time. Since retiring from teaching music she regularly sets off the smoke alarm while simultaneously cooking dinner and asking questions on the internet. When not seated at the computer she can be found, with her camera, contemplating the beauty of God and his creation on walks in the Canadian Rockies where she lives. Sometimes she gets around to painting, writing essays, poems, and songs, and blogging at *Charis: Subject to Change*

Blog: http://charispsallo.me

Is It God or Is It Me?
Praying Medic

ONE CONCERN YOU MIGHT HAVE about hearing God's voice is whether something you heard originated in your own mind or the mind of God. For some, there is too much uncertainty over knowing the origin of an idea that they prefer not to attempt to discern what God might be saying, for fear of being wrong. Determining the origin of revelation may seem like a daunting task, but there are a few simple steps we can take that will help us verify the source of any revelation. First, a review of the ways in which God communicates may be helpful.

A few (though not all) of the ways in which God speaks to us are visions, dreams, aromas, emotions, skin sensations, personal circumstances and thought impressions that carry messages to our mind. Rather than see them as divine communication, we often attribute these things to our imagination. I've noticed something about God's messages that can help us distinguish them from the workings of our own mind.

The believer has two spirits living inside them: their own spirit and the Spirit of God. These two spirits are the sources of two different kinds of thought or streams of revelation. Before we can know which thoughts are God's we must first know which belong to us. One problem many of us have is that we do not know our own thoughts the way we should. When we know ourselves well and understand clearly the ways in which our mind works, we can view our own thoughts like an objective observer. The better we know our own thoughts, the easier it is to discern the thoughts that are not ours, but God's, or those of a demon. The first step in learning to distinguish our thoughts from God's is becoming more aware of the nature of our own thought life.

In the more than half a century I've walked the earth I've come to know myself pretty well. I've learned to recognize the ways in which my own mind thinks. If someone copied and pasted one of my articles into an e-mail and sent it to me I would recognize it as mine. If someone hung one of my paintings on the wall of a restaurant, I would recognize the artist as myself. I recognize my own thoughts and the visual material of my own mind when I see them. And when I hear a thought that is unfamiliar to my way of thinking, I also recognize it as being "not from me." When I see a visual image that is foreign to my own creativity I recognize it as being "not mine."

While the thoughts of mortals are different, they are more or less of equal quality. The thoughts of God however, are infinitely higher and distinctly different from our own. God's thoughts are so much more sublime than my thoughts. They are full of love, life, wisdom, compassion, and mercy. Although I would like to think that my thoughts are like this, if I am honest with myself, I must admit that God's thoughts carry a certain quality that my thoughts do not have. If we're going to discern God's thoughts from ours, we must learn to be honest with ourselves about our thoughts. Otherwise, we deceive ourselves and we can't hope to distinguish God's thoughts from our own.

We know that every good and perfect thing comes down from the Father of Lights (James 1:17). Everything that is good in the world has its origin in God. I would like to think that the good thoughts I have originated in my own mind. But when I have a thought that is full of love or compassion or mercy—even though the thought seems to have sprung forth from within my own mind—I must conclude that it could not have come from me. I know its source must be the mind of God; for that is the origin of everything that is good and perfect.

We must remember that although God's voice is external to us, His Spirit resides in us. Because of this, when He speaks, we perceive His external voice to be an internal experience. We perceive His thoughts as our own thoughts. The way in which His thoughts come to us is so subtle it's often hard to recognize that they had their origin outside of us. But these brilliant, loving, compassionate thoughts are the thoughts of God being spoken by the Holy Spirit. The same is true for visual images that we receive from Him. Many times we think an image came from our imagination when it actually came from God. Half the battle of knowing that what you're seeing, feeling, or hearing is from God is simply a matter of knowing that it isn't from you.

Confirmation of the things we believe we've heard from God is important. But how do we begin to know if something is from God or from another source?

Our soul creates its own messages, including thoughts, impressions, emotions, and visual images. One difference between the ones that come from an external source and ones that come from our soul is that those which come from an external source are difficult or impossible to manipulate or change willfully. A message that is external to us cannot be changed by us. Whereas a message that originates in our soul can be changed by exerting our will over it.

There is another way in which we can distinguish the origin of revelation, but it is different (and contrary) to the way that is taught by many church leaders. Many people teach that anything we believe we've heard from God must line up with scripture in order for us to know with certainty that it's from God. If it does not line up with scripture, they say, we must toss it out. There's nothing wrong with searching the scriptures to see if something has a biblical basis, but many of the things God will reveal to us cannot be verified by the scriptures. I've had God speak to me about accepting a new job, turning down opportunities to speak at various churches, and many other personal issues, none of which could be conclusively verified by scripture alone.

A wise person takes their decisions before God and asks for His input. But whether something came from the heart of God or some other place is not determined by its inclusion in the Bible. The origin of wisdom and the source of any revelation can best be determined by evaluating the fruit it produces. Jesus taught that a polluted stream does not give pure water and that you do not gather grapes from thorn bushes or figs from thistles. The source of anything is always best determined by examining the fruit that it bears. False teachers and evil spirits can quote the scriptures, but the fruit that a thing produces will always reveal its source.

The Holy Spirit is called the Comforter, the Spirit of Grace, the Spirit of Peace, the Spirit of Wisdom, and the Spirit of Truth, because these are the things that His words produce. If anyone hears the words of the Spirit and acts on them, the same fruit will be produced in their life. The voice of the Spirit produces the fruit of the Spirit, which is love, joy, peace, longsuffering, kindness, goodness, faithfulness, gentleness, and self-control (Galatians 5:22). So if a person says they are hearing from God, and they act upon what they have heard, but the fruit produced is condemnation, fear, discord or any other negative quality, we can tell that this person was not hearing from God. I transport mentally ill patients frequently who hear voices that speak condemning and cruel words to them. These people often think they are hearing God's voice. I know that in most cases they are not hearing from God, because the fruit that comes from what they hear is not the fruit of the Spirit. These people tend to be filled with self-hatred, fear, anxiety, envy, and other attitudes that are inconsistent with the fruit of the Spirit.

My friend Shae Bynes once organized a retreat for entrepreneurs. She asked God what the theme for the retreat would be and she received no answer. She received many prompts from Him about logistics, but she registered attendees without telling them what they would be learning. As the time for the retreat drew near, she became concerned as she still didn't know what the retreat would be about. She recalled the day that God finally told her what the agenda would be:

> "I went to the hair salon to get my hair done and after my appointment, my husband asked me to meet him at Office Max. I drove over to Office Max, turned the car off, and was just about to open the car door when I felt

a heartache unlike I had ever felt before. I started to cry uncontrollably... I didn't even know why I was crying. My hair was looking fabulous and I was in a great mood just moments earlier. All I knew was at that moment my heart hurt... a lot."

Shae doesn't suffer from depression, yet she sobbed for what felt like no reason. She had never felt these kinds of emotions before. She contacted her business partner who suggested it might be a prophetic message about the subject of the retreat. During their chat, God revealed that the attendees would be delivered from bitterness and unforgiveness. At the retreat, she explained to the attendees that God wanted them to go through a process of forgiving people (former business associates as well as family members) for the pains they had caused them. The retreat turned into a mass exercise in deliverance and emotional healing.

Shae would never have known if the emotions she felt were really from God and if her interpretation of them was correct if she had not taken the risk of delivering a very unusual message to the group. The fact that the attendees responded to the message en masse, was the fruit that testified to the origin of the revelation. The kingdom of God is advanced when we take risks. Taking risks is one of the best ways we can learn to know if and how we are hearing from God. As we obey the revelation we receive and act upon it, producing fruit, we'll grow in confidence that we're hearing accurately from God.

> **Praying Medic** is a former atheist who worked as a paramedic for decades. After having a dramatic encounter where God told him He would use him to heal the sick, he began praying with his patients and with strangers and has seen thousands of them healed. Through dreams, online discussions, and hands-on experience, he has discovered the answers to some of the most common questions people have about the supernatural life. Praying Medic is the author of ***Divine Healing Made Simple*** and many other related books that have inspired thousands of readers to seek God for themselves. His books and his website are valuable resources for learning about the Kingdom of God.
>
> Web: www.prayingmedic.com
> Books: bit.ly/Praying-Medic

LIGHT OR DARKNESS
The Anonymous Moth

I AM NOT A PERSON who talks about how to hear God's voice.

No, I am a person who talks about how to avoid hearing the wrong voice, which is another way of saying I am an expert in going wrong.

The past few decades have seen me flitting around bright lights that look like the way out, and instead crashing into windows and getting caught in webs of despair and deception. I'm still trying to clean the sticky mess off my wings.

A LITTLE BACKGROUND

Many years ago, when my family first began trying to hear from God (I came to Jesus as an adult as a result of spiritual warfare—long story), we started hearing answers to our prayer questions. This was very exciting. The voices spoke of helping people and healing. But the emphasis slowly veered away from God and Jesus. Eventually, after some disastrous events, I discovered the spirits were teaching New Age doctrine. Let's just say now I don't like or trust New Age doctrine!

I came out more determined to get to know God and Jesus. My family gave up so I went solo. But the churches I went to seemed hollow. I remember going to one Christmas service excited to hear the joyous message of Jesus' birth and the love of God for humanity. But all I heard from the pulpit was fear and condemnation and resentment.

So churches didn't seem the way to go. You might think it odd that I didn't persist in this direction, but I was a new Christian with no Christian background at all. Supposedly "Christian" children had tormented me on the playground when I was younger. I discovered those same kids hadn't even read the Bible! Meanwhile, I, the agnostic kid, read the Bible cover to cover by myself, and to me, it was full of freaky, violent, scary stuff, like God commanding the killing of entire families. On top of this, I had easily seen through the preacher hypocrisy on television. When the mega church scandals hit the news, I wasn't surprised in the least. So I held out little hope for finding a place in mainstream Christianity.

I kept looking. I found God in quiet little places. A soup kitchen. The fellowship of friends who also didn't find God in many churches they'd tried. Praying for others online.

Times changed. My situation changed. My life story seemed to devolve into a series of mistakes, and I longed to hear from God directly, but could not seem to do so except on exceedingly rare occasions. I seriously needed inner healing and deliverance. I did talk to a deliverance counselor once, but later learned he was unstable. So much for that. I looked outside the church. Even while trying to avoid the New Age and looking for Jesus, I somehow ended up in things that turned out to be the New Age wearing various masks.

Eventually I found some churches, even though I had to switch when I realized some of them were more harmful than helpful because they didn't understand spiritual warfare in the least. I read a lot of books in healing and deliverance, even though the stuff in the books didn't work for me. I tried various healing and deliverance services and events, even though most did nothing, and some actually caused more anguish and pain.

Battle scars? I've got 'em. Got deceived? I even got the t-shirt. Learned to not believe every word and prophecy? You bet. Skeptical? Yup. Hopeful? Have to be. I still believe Jesus is salvation—that He came to save and rescue the lost, and He's not done with me. He's all I have, my only hope. I'm counting on Him.

Anyway, I have hope that my mistakes can be someone's gain. Here are some principles about hearing God that I've noticed over the many years. Talk to God about them, test them out, and discard if needed. I just hope these help others avoid some of my trials!

1. All Messages Should Encourage the Love of God

All supposed messages from God should point us back to God. If this sounds obvious, consider that every Christian church and even various cults seemingly all do this—yet, many of them can hardly stand to be in the same room with each other.

This is my opinion, but I don't think the message should be love of a "religious spirit" God. Remember how I read the Bible by myself as a kid and freaked out? Out of context and without the Holy Spirit's help, the Bible can be confusing. One thing I've realized is that I need to keep my eyes on Jesus Himself as my best example and teacher. He healed everyone who came to Him, forgave the lost, didn't stone people, and even welcomed little children. In other words, He presented an example of God as the rescuer, forgiver, healer, and loving parent. He also used a lot of symbolic language. (No one actually swallowed entire camels or got wooden beams in their eyes; not everything is meant to be literal.) I think we can, and probably should, check if any message points to God *as revealed by Jesus' words and actions,* not the rest of the world's interpretations. The world has used scripture to justify slavery and glorify money, but Jesus freed the oppressed and spoke against the pursuit of earthly riches.

On the other hand, the message can't be pointing to a wishy washy weak God, either. My experiences with the New Age give concrete examples of that sort of deception. But it's subtle! The messages are not often stamped with a "New Age" logo. Many New Age messages may even extol God's love and the leadership of Jesus, but the tone gradually, slowly shifts. God becomes an impersonal force, and Jesus becomes a teacher who had a "Christ Consciousness." Supposed angels or other spirits become intermediaries to God.

In fact, if an angel, prophet, minister, spirit guide, "Ascended Masters," "Higher Self," or anyone else steps into the spotlight instead of God, I would suggest running away—fast. Or, bind and cast out!

My opinion is that the message should glorify God alone—but not thunderbolt-throwing God, nor the Light Side of the Force—rather, the God who breaks chains, who rescues the lost sheep, who wants us healed and to come to Him.

2. Messages Need to Help Us Love Our Neighbors

I'm coming back to our hypothetical room full of different Christian churches. What did God really mean when He told us to love one another? This is where I think divisions really start to show up.

From what I can tell, He didn't tell us that love is standing up in judgment of each other. Ever been to a place where the leaders were mostly into accusing various people of sinning, and seemed to care more about religious regulations than relieving suffering? Jesus was in such a place. He called those leaders "Pharisees." He didn't actually support their actions. Instead, He went out of His way to heal the sick, cast demons out of dirty crazy people, and even dined with known sinners. When His disciples wanted to call fire down on a town in judgment, He rebuked them. When a disciple cut off someone's ear, He healed it. When soldiers nailed Him to the cross, He prayed forgiveness.

And this is why, when I hear messages mocking atheists, condemning people for their skin color or nationality, or denigrating people of opposing political parties as "fools" or "idiots," I start wondering who the inspiration really is. That kind of condemnation-based spirit pushed me toward atheism back in my younger days, and it continues to push many people away from Christianity. Why? I think it's because deep down in their hearts people are looking for divine love, and they sure aren't sensing any directed at them from those Christians!

Could a woman caught in adultery love a Jesus who would point His finger at her and say, "I'm sinless, so I'll cast the first stone"?

On the other hand, at the other extreme, there are Christians who genuinely try to help others, yet who are led astray by a culture of over-permissiveness. This is true especially of those not aware of the mechanics of spiritual warfare. I think it's great when churches don't cast stones at the lost sheep, such as the woman caught in adultery. However, it's not always enough until we are able to heal the inner pain of someone in that situation, cast out the demons encouraging the behavior, forgive, and give discipleship and wisdom. "Sin no more, lest something worse may happen to you" are not words of condemnation, but they *are* words of caution for someone previously unaware of soul-ties, doors to the demonic, and the effects of sin on loved ones and all of society. It seems to me that Jesus simply doesn't want people to suffer!

Because sin does cause suffering, even to innocent bystanders, good intentions need to be backed up by spiritual wisdom and a call to holiness, taking seriously Jesus' words not just about helping others, but also honoring God *and* each other through our actions, thoughts, and deeds.

3. Seek First the Fruit of the Holy Spirit, Not the Gifts

There are stories circulating on the Internet of people who got off track when they went "too far" into charismatic Christianity—led astray, demonized, and even possibly teaching falsehoods from the pulpit. Sadly, I think the stories are all too true and are likely to keep happening. What's going wrong? At least part of it is pretty clear to me, probably because I've gone down that road myself. I see the danger signs especially among people who walk in signs and wonders. The danger is in getting sucked into the desire for the gifts of the Spirit more than seeking the fruit of the Spirit. Of course we want to hear God! We want to be healed and to heal the sick! We want anointing and blessing and upgrades! We want to experience the Presence and get "whacked" as so many put it. But this can become exactly like a New Age adherent wanting spirit guides, Higher Self advice, healing powers, chakra alignment, and psychic abilities and visions. In the spiritual realm, I believe the intentions show up clearly, and the intentions of someone wanting New Age powers probably look surprisingly like someone wanting Christian divine upgrades.

You can even do a word for word translation:

I want psychic abilities (impartations and upgrades)! I want a message from my Higher Self (a word of knowledge)! I want interdimensional objects from my guides (divine gems, gold dust)! I want bliss (I want to get whacked)!

I want... I want... I want more stuff!

Notice a theme? These are fundamentally selfish, even if we are nominally there to get healing for ourselves or our families. It's still like a classroom of kids wanting the teacher's prizes for the right answers. I have been in rooms of both New Age and Christian persuasion where the greedy atmosphere was tangibly the same. People eagerly hoping. Hoping for gifts. Hoping for words of knowledge. Hoping for healing. Knowing others were there for the same reason, but hoping against hope. "Me first!" Oooh, pick me. Let me be a special one. Let me get a prize. I want. I want. (Yes, I've been there.)

And as a warning, just because we listen to music and sermons and say prayers that have words like "Jesus" and "Holy Spirit," does not necessarily mean we are on the right track when we start seeking spiritual phenomena. Some slave traders of the past have undoubtedly used the name "Jesus" to justify themselves. We can be deceived into thinking that our motivations are holy. To the spirit world, unfortunately, selfishness still looks like selfishness.

I believe Jesus gave us the correct prescription. We must be seeking *first* the Kingdom of God and God's righteousness. The greatest commandment is loving God Himself. And the second commandment is loving our neighbor, and seeking always to produce the fruit of the

Holy Spirit (against which, of course, there is no law). Yes, we are told to seek the gifts, too, but if our hearts are more about seeking upgrades and experiences rather than loving God and helping our neighbors, then we may find ourselves gradually listening more and more to the wrong spirit.

4. Messages Have Reasonable Brevity and Focus

I've read or at least looked at a number of texts that claim to be messages or words from God. Many even claimed to be from Jesus. But, frankly, the longer the message, the more I start to doubt.

From all that I understand, God's angels (messengers) are all about business; the business of God's Kingdom. They are on assignment. They don't stop to yak, make long theological discussions, talk about various planes of existence, or go on and on about this that and the other. Some messages also make me wonder when they seem more about scolding and condemning than giving specific information that increases the glory to God.

Jesus' words, as recorded in the New Testament, are short and to the point. His parables were crisp and concise. He talked about how to live in the here and now, even if always from a Heavenly point of view. Yes, He did have some harsh words, but even those were pretty concise and to the point.

Suffice to say, the more a messenger seems to like to hear himself talk, the less I trust the message. And the more a messenger wants to talk about things not at all useful to the here and now and the needs of people, the less I trust the message.

5. How Does It Make You Feel?

I've read a lot of deliverance books and sites. Many of them leave me with nasty images and a lot of fear floating through my mind, thanks to descriptions of evil acts, lists of horrible events, and warnings of how even the slightest mistake can lead to horrific things... this can be scary stuff. The authors usually have good intentions, and there is a lot of meat despite bones to spit out, but... I'll just mention I once got hit by a big demonic assault at a weak moment when I was reading something scary in a deliverance book. Go figure. So, at the risk of sounding touchy-feely, I do have to ask, "How does the message make you feel?"

Also, check for evidence of emotional manipulation. I've seen too many Christians posting or forwarding chain letters that promote feelings of self-righteousness, judgment of others, rage, and fear. (Even worse, usually the chain letter or post contains half-truths... which is another way of saying it's full of lies that nobody bothered to fact check.)

A worried person asking for prayers for a family member is one thing, but what about a preacher promoting worry and fear on a vast scale? How about leaders who promote finger-pointing and blame? Never mind the stuff that comes out of my own mouth—I wonder what comes out when I type messages for the public? Who benefits from encouraging Christians to feel things like rage, worry, fear, anxiety, blame?

Feelings aren't everything, of course. I know we are to operate by faith, not feelings. But feelings have an impact on us, and those who listen to us.

Personally, I'm looking for messages that inspire me to feel joy and awe of God, a renewed desire to do His will, and a peaceful knowing that His amazing will is to love, heal, save, rescue, and care for people and this beautiful creation, in the here and now. One of my favorite feelings leads to exactly this thought: How great are your works, Lord; how profound are your thoughts! And that's what I want to inspire in others, too.

6. Check Your Results

I remember receiving what I thought was a wonderful prophecy. Something awesome was going to happen within a week! I went home elated. I was so hopeful. The days slipped by.

A week came and went. Nothing happened. Another hope dashed.

Even worse are the hopeful prophecies for people who are battling serious illness which simply don't pan out. I've seen that happen, too.

There are many different thoughts on this topic, and many different failure points. It may be the people involved failed to follow through on something important. It may be the enemy found a way to block the prophecy through someone else. Or, it could be the person giving the prophecy delivered it poorly. Or... it could be it wasn't really a prophecy from God.

Sometimes it may even turn out the prophecy came true, just not in the manner expected!

I am not operating in the gift of prophecy right now, so I don't know what that's like. I have, however, seen the hurtful effects of prophecies that didn't come true. From that perspective, I think it would be nice if people did some following up, especially for any prophecy with a definite time frame. And if something has gone awry, pray into it. Maybe seek more training from mature, experienced believers who operate in prophecy. And perhaps remember to tell the people receiving the prophecy they have the right to exercise discernment. A lot of newcomers may not realize they have the right and responsibility to weigh messages for themselves, and even reject them as needed. Lastly, noted prophet Shawn Bolz advocates tracking words to learn where one's strong and weak prophetic areas are.

7. Test the Spirits

I've done a lot of research. I know there is a lot of deception out there, and a lot of confusion. We are supposed to test the spirits, but even that isn't necessarily straightforward. We may even have to test the spirits that are trying to influence how we test the spirits! For example, the New Testament tells us:

> *Every spirit that acknowledges that Jesus Christ has come in the flesh is from God, but every spirit that does not acknowledge Jesus is not from God.*
> 1 JN 4:2B-3A NIV

But different English translations use different words. Some claim that the phrase, "has come in the flesh" is past tense, but it must be present tense to be valid; "*is* come in the flesh." Otherwise deceptive spirits can squirm out of the test. But then again, some argue that *"has* come in the flesh" includes the present tense, that it means Jesus is still here, and hence it's totally okay; it's really just the English rendition of *"did* come in the flesh" that is totally wrong for testing spirits. Furthermore, I'm pretty sure I've heard people claim that this test was for that time and place, and that demons can lie their way past it nowadays no matter what. Meanwhile, a lot of people reading the Bible just have no idea about any of this in the first place.

So even with something as simple as one single line in the Bible, there is disagreement.

What does that say? I think we must always be watching, knowing the enemy is prowling like a hungry lion. For example, I believe that just because a message comes in the exact same manner as previous good messages may not mean it's trustworthy. I think we need the humility to be able to admit we *can* be wrong, confess if we actually do go wrong, and have the courage to change course—repent—and keep trying.

There is no doubt in my mind, though; we have to follow 1 John 4:1— the admonition to test every spirit—in the best way we know how, and be ready and willing to learn.

I'm still learning!

The Anonymous Moth is a writer and sometimes computer entertainment professional who is currently on a renewed quest of discovery and trying to level up quickly. There's nothing like lots of enemy action for fast XP, friends to twink one out with gear and advice, quest cheats written up in Kindle books, and one invisible but highly recommended Game Admin to help out in case of getting stuck in the physics!

LISTENING FOR GOD'S HUMOR
Hazel May Lebrun

THERE I STOOD, pacing back and forth like a cranky mama bear in front of a closed courtroom door. My daughter was involved in a custody case and my grandson's future hung in the balance. I was full of nervous energy and absolutely furious that the enemy of my soul would target my family and me in such a disgusting way.

This was time for some serious prayer, and I was a lean mean praying machine. I paced and paced and spoke in tongues, thankful to be in Canada where passersby would assume I was an immigrant speaking a foreign language. I decreed victory. I quoted scripture. I rebuked Satan, and released angels to do their assigned tasks in this situation.

And I sealed this prayer storm in the usual good religious Christian way and went all out. I said, "In the name of Yeshua Ha'Mashiach, Tsidkenu!" Take that, minions of hell!

Immediately after that invocation, God's voice broke through my prayer. What I am saying is... He interrupted me. You know how you tell your kids not to interrupt? God doesn't believe in that etiquette. This was His perfect cue to chime in.

He said, and I quote: "Is that like when one of your kids is in trouble and you use his full name when you call him?"

On one of the most stressful days of my life, God made me double over, laughing out loud. How could I help it? His comic timing is perfect. I replied, "Yes, it is just like that!"

We won the case. That is, the dad and mom ended up talking and working things out in a really short time and the custody case became a peace accord. So, God made me laugh *and* He answered my prayer.

I have been hearing God's voice since I was a little girl. Of course, I didn't always know it was Him. He speaks to me through dreams and visions, through people and His word, through songs and stories, through the news. He also speaks audibly once in a while, but a lot of times, I hear His voice inside me, encouraging me, teaching me, loving me and, yes, making me laugh.

God has a sense of humor. He invented humor.

God is a chatterbox. That is, He talks all the time. We are not always listening. When we do listen, what He says is often filtered through our preconceived idea of who He is and how He has to sound. I know people who think He is always speaking in an angry, scolding voice. Some think He is always speaking in King James English. Mainly, we need to let go and let God talk how He wants to. He will talk in a way you can understand Him and that is unique to your relationship with Him.

I have rarely ever heard God say anything to me that sounded angry. He has been so patient with me that I sometimes shake my head and can't believe it. I wouldn't be that patient with me. In fact, I'm not and sometimes God tells me to give myself a break. He says I need to forgive me while I'm forgiving others. What a kind and generous God.

I'm not pointing fingers when I say we need to let Him talk how He wants to. This has been a process for me too. My most frequent question to God has to be, "Is that really you?" I admit it. I question whether or not it's His voice. I know He tells us to test the spirits, but I'm hardcore. I could hear something so amazing, it could only be God, and I will still ask, "Is that you?"

I did that once too often, I guess, and one day, when I asked, "God, is that you?" I got a reply that went "Thou, therefore my son... there. Is that better?" I laughed, and stopped asking that question so often.

There are some basic ways to know if a voice is God or not. Anything that sounds like condemnation is not Him. If he's telling you to do something that is completely against His character, that's not Him. Seriously, if a voice tells you to kill people, hurt people, or generally do hateful things—that's not God. I wish I didn't have to clarify that, but I have known people personally who thought God wanted them to go around "killing His enemies, the devil worshippers." Oh yeah, I'm not kidding.

So, no special ops for Jesus will be taking people out, thank you very much. You are not the next Messiah or His right-hand man or woman and no, God is not telling you to take over a church, curse people, or otherwise do harm and act like Public Fruitcake Number One. If that's what you're hearing, do not act on what that voice says.

Rest assured that God is more interested in your growth as His son or daughter than He is in asking you to do some crazy thing that will take you farther away from Him. If something you are being told to do makes you seek God less or push away from Him, you can bet that the enemy put it in your path, even if it seems like a 'good' thing to do.

It is also important to note that, if you are hearing derogatory things about other people, then you are likely being spoken to by a religious spirit. If you hear something like, "See that girl? She's sinful!" God doesn't tend to talk that way. For one thing, that girl's sins are none of your business. For another thing, everything God says and does in regards to us is redemptive. He corrects us, but not in a way that makes us feel lower than dirt. He wants to lift us up, not put us down.

So if He did, for some reason, pick you to talk to about "that girl," He would be telling you so that you could pray for her or help her. God doesn't gossip. Let's say, for example, that "that girl" is hooked on drugs. God wouldn't say, "That girl is a useless junkie." He would want you to pray for her freedom, either directly or indirectly.

So if you feel pressured by a "word" you heard, if you feel compelled to go and tell someone their sins or somehow give them words that are condemning or scolding, that is not God pressuring you. That is a religious spirit and you can rebuke it and defeat it by deliberately decreeing blessings over the person it is targeting.

He often speaks about a person's strengths in juxtaposition to the person's weakness. For example, a prophetic man I know was given a vision of a man stabbing his pastor in the back. This is what the man was doing with his words all the time, but the prophetic man knew better than to just blurt out, "Hey. You're a backstabber!"

He asked God, "What do I say to this man?" The Lord had him prophesy in this way: "You are a supportive rock to your pastor. He can lean on you for strength. You intercede for this pastor and he can count on you." He prophesied things like that instead of the backstabbing vision and that man rose to the occasion and became what he prophesied, leaving his backstabbing ways behind him.

A less experienced person might have assumed that what he heard and saw from the Lord was meant to be just spoken out without checking with God to see what to do with it. Wisdom comes with experience and with practice.

One of the incidents in which I heard God speaking audibly to me happened in the mid-1990s. I am a singer/songwriter. I play guitar and write original tunes. At that time, all of my songs were what churches would call "worship music." I was on a worship team and the church that I attended used some of my songs for their Sunday morning services.

Since that time, I have ended up at folk festivals and other events. I write a variety of music now, led by the Holy Spirit to go outside church walls and change the atmosphere, but if you had told me 20 years ago that I would be doing that, I would not have believed you. I didn't realize that the secular and the sacred did not need a magical line drawn between them. Thank God He is erasing that line.

Anyway, I fell asleep one afternoon and when I awoke, it was like I had stepped into a conversation. I was in that groggy, sort of awake state. I was sitting up in bed and aware of my surroundings. I was not dreaming. I also could hear quite clearly God's audible voice having a chat with me—a chat! He was talking out loud. Not inside my heart. Not a thought in my head. He was talking rather loudly. Now, this was quite an occasion. I was thrilled. Who doesn't dream of the moment that God will talk to them out loud? Wouldn't you be delighted? Giddy? Gushing with happiness?

Do you want to hear the incredibly spiritual and holy sounding things that the Lord of Glory, my Heavenly Father, spoke to me out loud in my bedroom that day? Brace yourself for the key to the meaning of life. I dropped in on this riveting piece of advice.

God: "Don't treat your music like a ministry. Treat it like a business."

Me: "Why?"

God: "Because everybody will want to know what brand of toothbrush you buy."

And just like that, the loud, audible voice of God was gone. Vanished. He didn't even wait for me to say, "Right-O! Catch you later! Give my regards to Gabriel."

I hurried downstairs to tell my best friend (and roomie at the time) about this experience. We agreed that God was preparing me for something that was coming. Calling the music "a ministry" would constrict me, cage me in and bring scrutiny down on any money I earned. I do minister to people when I play, but I don't call it a ministry. I just sing and nobody questions that I can earn something from it because I didn't slap churchy sounding words on it that suggest I am a charitable organization.

My first audible communication was business advice. God has great wisdom and it doesn't always sound religious. He can advise you on what seems like the most mundane things. He once helped me bake a pie because I was having trouble with the crust. I asked Him to help me and started hearing, "A little more flour, mix it this way."

Not all of my conversations with God are jokes and humorous exchanges, but I do feel His joy. His word says that in His presence there is fullness of joy and at His right hand are pleasures forevermore. Laughter and humor were His ideas and if we let Him, God will bring us into His happy place and He will share His sense of humor with us. It makes me love Him even more.

He is the King and the Lord of Creation, yet, like any good Father, He will sing goofy songs, do silly things, and generally play with His children. It's a beautiful aspect of His nature. I can't get enough of it. I pray that you have an encounter with the Lord of Fun. No, I am not saying that there aren't serious things going on in the world, but in the midst of all of that, God wants us to play and He wants to heal us with laughter. Our joy is actually one of those weapons of our warfare. The ones that aren't carnal. We can pull down strongholds if we laugh along with God.

I will share one more example of God speaking to me in a funny way. I have had many encounters, especially in dreams, with spiritual beings. I'm talking about angels and demons. I used to see evil beings often and I don't consider myself a scaredy cat, but they stink. They look ugly. Their presence is uncomfortable. I would see them frequently and after a while, it bothered me to the point where I stopped seeing them.

But then, I stopped discerning certain things that I needed to discern too. So I finally said to God, "All right. I want to see if you are the one showing it to me, but I hate them. They're ugly. I don't like seeing them, but I ask you to reopen my eyes because I need the discernment that came along with the seeing."

That very night and the night after that, I had encounters with demonic spirits appearing in my dreams again, but this time, they were all in cartoon form. In fact, the whole first dream that night was a big cartoon and I was in it. I was in a sleigh flying in the sky and cartoonish bombs and artillery fire were going off all around me.

The horse that pulled the sleigh in the sky was actually an angel. It gave me a funny smile. I just knew it. The demonic things were cartoons. I saw all the spirit beings, but none of it was uncomfortable because it was all just silly looking animations. I woke up laughing and said, "I didn't mean you had to make the dream for kids!" But He kept doing that and I found it hilarious.

God loves me enough to make demons and angels look like cartoons and funny animals. He cares about every little detail of our lives. I know some people may think I'm off the beam. We do like to picture God like Zeus with a lightning bolt or like some cosmic priestly-looking being. To me, He is my Father, my God, my King, and the funniest person I have ever known. Joy is a fruit of the Spirit, and if the peel of that fruit happens to fall on the ground, God will slip on it and do a pratfall. Be prepared... He may tickle your funny bone when you least expect it. You need it and I need it. Ha ha hallelujah!

If you are wondering how to even begin to hear God's voice in this way (or in any way at all) I have a suggestion you can try yourself. It's not a formula. What works for you may be unique to you, but you can try some things and get ready for your encounters to begin or to become more frequent.

You can do this in a chair if you want to. Sometimes I use a chair, but I will sometimes lie on my back either on the floor or on my bed or on a sofa. Go someplace quiet. I like to do it outdoors when I can too, when I am alone in the middle of a field or somewhere secluded. Pick a place that you like.

Just put your hands in the air. Start telling God you love Him, that He is good, that He is faithful, that He is wonderful. Keep telling Him for a while. Tell Him that you love to hear His voice—that you love to be close to Him and hear His heartbeat.

And then... wait. Repeat. Wait again. Repeat. Wait again. And let peace come over you. Don't worry. Don't fear. Don't think, "But what if the enemy talks to me?" Relax and let go. Thoughts will come. God's tangible presence will manifest around you. You don't need to be scared. What if the enemy did talk to you? You tell him to leave. He has no claim on you. If you have given yourself to God, you belong to the Kingdom of Heaven. Hell has no rights to you.

God will talk. Sometimes He will sing. He will come and share time with you and you will feel His joy. You will start to be filled with it. Tell God that you want to hear His voice, that you want to tune in to His frequency, and He will help you dial in.

"My sheep hear my voice." That is what the Bible says. If you are His sheep, you can hear Him and He says the most wonderful, amazing and, yes, even humorous things.

Hazel May Lebrun is a Metis writer and singer/songwriter living in Ottawa, Ontario, Canada. When she is not writing and singing, she can be found either shopping for or spending time with her beautiful, spoiled grandchildren. Hazel May is currently shopping two fiction novels around to publishers and hopes to have both works in bookstores and online later this year.

Email: hazelmaylebrun64@gmail.com
Blog: https://hazelmaylebrun.wordpress.com

CULTIVATING GOD'S COMMUNICATION
Marlon Katsigazi

As CHILDREN OF GOD we are wired to hear His voice, because we are created for relationship with Him. Relationship is a two-way dynamic and involves communication. In communication there is an exchange of voices. Jesus said, "My sheep listen to my voice; I know them, and they follow me." God, our Good Shepherd, speaks to His sheep to lead and guide them and they know His voice.

> *When they heard the voice of the LORD God as he was walking in the garden during the breeze of the day, the man and his wife concealed themselves from the presence of the LORD God among the trees of the garden.*
> GEN 3:8 ISV

God's original blueprint in Genesis was to have a loving relationship with man. Adam and Eve heard God's voice in the cool of the day and this was an invitation for a deep relationship. Then, sin separated man from God, but through the redemptive work of Jesus, we are reconciled back to having a loving relationship with God. When Jesus became the atoning sacrifice for our sins on the cross, the veil was torn. There was no longer a separation between man and God because of sin. Man could now go through the door, Jesus, live beyond the veil, and commune with God. The envelope of intimacy is no longer concealed. This was always God's original intent from the creation of Adam and Eve.

> *And the LORD God formed man of the dust of the ground, and breathed into his nostrils the breath of life; and man became a living soul.*
> GEN 2:7 KJV

I believe the essence of God (breath of life) is in us and we are created in His image and after His likeness, therefore God comes in to commune with His very essence in us, which we call the spirit. We are comprised of spirit, soul, and body (1 Thessalonians 5:23). The Bible says that God is Spirit and we are to worship Him in spirit and truth (John 4:24). So when He comes to communicate with us, it is Spirit-to-spirit.

HOW TO STAY IMPLANTED IN THIS LOVE RELATIONSHIP

Sometimes in our walk with God we lose appetite for His presence because of certain things in life that may consume our heart and take away our focus on God, but an important key to regaining appetite is to ask for a hunger for God.

A relative of mine was struggling to relate with God and hear His voice. Then she prayed for a hunger for God, and her life was changed. God gave her a supernatural hunger for Him. She began to have a yearning for the things of God, like a deer that pants for water. Her relationship with God grew to new levels.

We can ask to have a hunger for God and seek His face. Being intentional is also significant. Know that you are wired to commune with God and expect to hear from Him.

Blessing for Hunger

May God give you the grace to hunger for Him. May your soul thirst for God as a thirsty land. May your mind be saturated with His goodness and may you be like David, one after the heart of God. May He fill you with a love for Him, and every day when you rise and sleep, may your mind be stayed on Him. As you draw closer to Him, may He draw closer to you. May the heavens be opened over you and may you always receive revelation from heaven that ensures your relationship with God goes from glory to glory. In Jesus' name. Amen.

As you grow in this loving relationship, you begin to understand the nature and person of God. He becomes a dear Friend to you and He begins to share with you mysteries and secrets which only enhance your relationship with Him. Just as you get to know the personality of your friend by spending time with them, the same applies to God. He is our Friend and wants to commune with us all the time. Enjoy your loving relationship with God.

GOD'S METHODS OF COMMUNICATION

God communicates to us in many ways. When your intimate relationship with Him grows, you begin to know in a deeper way the personal and unique way God speaks to you.

In my life I found out He communicates to me in these ways:

1. Revelation of His Word:

When I read the word of God, a scripture is "highlighted" by the Spirit of God and I feel like my heart leaps with excitement. This is when I know God is speaking to me; when the word of God comes out of the page and has a specific instruction or message that I would not have known without the help of the Holy Spirit; it comes alive. I call this "illumination of the word of God." If this has never happened to you, here's something you can do. Before you read the word, you can ask the Spirit of God to reveal to you what He wants you to see. He is faithful and will show you what is required for the season you're in. He is our ever present help who teaches us all things. Application of the revealed word brings solution to challenges.

Blessing to Receive Revelation of Truth from the Word

Open my eyes to see the wonderful truths in your instructions.
PS 119:18 NLT

May the Holy Spirit open your eyes to receive revelation of truth as you read the word. May the words become life and empower your soul. May the Holy Spirit reveal a word (a rhema word which is inspired/revealed by the Holy Spirit) that you can apply to your life and bring breakthrough, hope, liberation, and peace. May the word become a light to your path of destiny bringing understanding and divine order. As you read His word, may it become a love letter revealing the love of Abba to you. May His love comfort, heal, and restore your soul. May the word bring joy to your heart.

2. Dreams

God speaks to me frequently through dreams, and I absolutely love going to sleep. I have learned when you enter your bed with a heart of expectancy, knowing that God will speak to you, He reveals Himself. I look at my bed as a portal to the realms of heaven.

I remember in January 2013 I asked God, "I want to taste of your goodness and experience your reality." God is faithful and He will answer our questions. So I went on a journey to get to know God personally. I read about His character in the word of God and I embraced His awesomeness. Also at this time I was helping a friend, Isaac Leeward, write a book called *Encounters with the Supernatural.* In this book my friend had amazing encounters with God which stirred up my passion to experience God in a whole new way. My expectant heart wanted to experience the reality of God. So one day I was sleeping and I suddenly heard an audible voice, "My light is in your eyes." God announced Himself to me in a memorable way that will stick in my mind forever.

Cultivating God's Communication

A new walk of intimacy with God was birthed. I felt His presence and I was in awe when I heard His voice. After this encounter I began to have dreams regularly. His dreams brought so much encouragement and hope to me. I believe dreams from God reveal an aspect of His character which you experience during and after the dream—like hope, peace, love, and joy.

During this period I was dealing with fear. I was about to publish my first book and I was afraid, because I did not know how people would receive the book and it was a whole new journey. Then the Lord gave me a dream to encourage me.

In the dream God was narrating a story:

There was a son afraid of flying. He never entered a plane. But one day he decided to face his fear, using his will. He knew his dad loved traveling to Denver, Colorado to ski. This time he wanted to join the flight and go with his dad.

The son had a long conversation with his dad in the airport about memorable times together as a family.

Finally, his dad says, "I am ready to go." Then his son replied, "I want to go with you!"

His dad responds, "But you can't fly," with a chuckle. The son says, "I can fly. I will go with you and fly. I want to spend time with you and I won't let fear come in my way." Now his dad loved to fly, and he always wanted to fly with his son. When his dad heard this response, tears ran down his cheek. Tears of joy and love. He was finally going to have a moment he longed for with his dear son. To fly together and enjoy the Denver Mountains.

The son had a ticket he had bought the previous day after deciding to go on this triumphant journey of overcoming fear. He pulled out his ticket and embraced his dad saying, "Let us go in!" As soon as the son pulled out the ticket, the father was beaming with joy. This was the moment of victory, when the son pulled out his ticket and chose to fly. They entered the plane and they shared more intriguing family moments and their relationship grew even more after this. It was a new day, a new season, every year the son and father flew to Denver, Colorado to ski.

After overcoming this fear, a lot of gifts came out of the son. He always wanted to become a teacher of God's truth. He started a church with the help of his father. His messages were centered on overcoming fear and the love of God. His church grew in stature, power, and influence, going beyond the four walls and touching people around the world. God began using him in a mighty way to touch the nations.

This dream brought so much encouragement and I felt the love of God after the dream. This love overcame the fear and I was excited about becoming an author. It was a new journey I now faced with anticipation and joy.

The scripture reflects in Habakkuk 2:2-3 (NIV):

> *"Write down the revelation and make it plain on tablets so that a herald may run with it. For the revelation awaits an appointed time; it speaks of the end and will not prove false. Though it linger, wait for it; it will certainly come and will not delay."*

The word of God encourages us to write down revelation (which can be in form of a dream). The Bible says that wisdom is from God and from His mouth comes knowledge and understanding. Sometimes when you wake up from a dream, you might have understanding, which is why it is good to journal dreams. Sometimes, the answer can unfold in a series of dreams. God brings more understanding to particular dreams as time passes. If you struggle to find understanding with the dreams, pray for it, and God will be faithful.

In my life I realized reading and meditating on the word also helps in understanding. A lot of symbolism in dreams stems from the word of God. When seeking understanding for dreams, the word can provide good counsel. The Holy Spirit breathes life over the word that is implanted in your heart and you receive revelation of truth and understanding.

The scripture says in Proverbs, *"... And in all your getting, get understanding."* It is significant to seek understanding for your dreams. The One who gives revelation also gives understanding.

Look at the dream as a seed that God puts in you. This seed grows as the Holy Spirit pours out understanding, and the seed eventually becomes a fruit. This fruit becomes a full manifestation of the dream in reality, which could be in the form of a great work for the Kingdom, like becoming a great righteous leader for the nations. In the end God is glorified which is the most significant thing.

God is the end of every revelation. The revelation is a tool to experience an aspect of God like His love, peace, and power.

> *It is God's privilege to conceal things and the king's privilege to discover them.*
> PROV 25:2 NLT

I have come to understand that the more your relationship grows in God, the easier it becomes to understand His language. Therefore when God conceals a revelation (dream), He wants you to go on a journey of discovery by asking Him, so He may unfold the revelation at the perfect time. Enjoy this journey of discovery, because you shall get to know God in a deeper way which enhances your relationship with Him.

3. Visions

I encourage people to embrace their imagination. I call imaginations, "mental visions." The way I see imagination, is God is putting a canvas in your mind's eye and the Holy Spirit is painting a picture on that canvas. The picture reveals an aspect of God. What I discovered by using my imagination frequently, is that God expanded my realm of visions and they became even more vivid and real. This is in the form of open visions.

An open vision is when the painted picture becomes more real. You can see it with your natural eyes. This happens to me when I am half awake and half asleep, not fully aware of my natural surroundings, but aware of God's atmosphere, presence, and glorious images. Some refer to this as a trance.

Below is an example of an open vision I experienced:

On Thursday, January 9, 2014, I woke up and I saw this image right in front of my eyes, almost like watching a film. There was an old man with a white beard and he was putting on a white garment. To his right there was portal/gate that looked like a ring of fire. It was spinning around. Then I heard the man say, "This is a new heavenly realm." I sensed it was an open invitation to access the various realms of heaven.

After seeing this open vision, I saw three dice floating in front of my eyes. I focused to see the numbers on each face. It was like someone pressed the slow motion button, then my eyes zoomed in and I was able to see the numbers. The sum total of the numbers was eight. The prophetic meaning of eight is new beginning.

God wanted His children to experience new things with Him. It was a beginning of new realms with God and the gates/doors were open.

I remember after this encounter I agreed with what God was doing and expected to walk in new realms of glory, and indeed encounters like this increased.

When we agree with what God is showing us we experience the supernatural.

4. Voice

A couple of times in my life God has revealed Himself to me through an audible voice. This is where I hear His voice with my natural ears. As I mentioned before the first audible voice I heard from God was when He said, "My light is in your eyes." When He spoke this to me it created something in me. It gave me a grace to receive His revelations of truth and I remember after this voice the dream realm was really opened to me in a whole new and mesmeric way. When God speaks, He speaks with purpose and His voice harbors creative power.

Cultivating God's Communication

He also speaks to me through His precious still small voice, which I call a voice from within. His voice always communicates goodness like encouragement, love, hope, joy, and peace. You will know His voice because it always relays goodness and you shall see the fruit of His hand.

Here is an example of embracing the still small voice, and a powerful testimony of healing I witnessed:

On April 12, 2014, I received a message from a dear friend explaining that her aunt, Candace, had breast cancer and surgery was needed in a week. Her family and friends were praying for her and standing on the word. She also asked me to pray for her.

A couple of weeks before this request I had a conversation with the Lord Jesus in a vision and He gave me revelation on how to release healing. It involved releasing peace and joy with a heart that is aligned to His. Then calling forth heaven to invade a situation bringing complete wholeness. The Bible says that the Kingdom of God is righteousness, peace, and joy in the Holy Spirit. There is no sickness in heaven, but peace.

On April 13, I gathered with a fellowship of believers and the Holy Spirit took over the service. Then one of the leaders prophesied, "When you leave this place the first person you lay hands on, text, or email who needs healing will receive it in Jesus' name." Then I heard the still small voice, "Write a prayer for your friend's aunt and send it to her." By faith I responded and shared the prayer.

Prayer for Precious Aunt:

"My Lord You say healing is the bread of Your children and You overcame all sickness, transgressions, and iniquities on the cross through Your wounds and suffering. By Your stripes we are healed. We are seated in heavenly places with You, a place of triumph and authority. May Your perfect peace come upon the spirit, soul, and body of Candace and make her whole. Your name is above every name.

In the name of Jesus, cancer bow and flee out of the body of Your precious daughter. May Your joy fill her spirit, soul, and body and strengthen her. Holy Spirit overshadow her life and bring complete comfort and wholeness to Candace. Lord send Your ministering angels that will nurse, heal, and comfort Candace.

May the complete wholeness of Candace be a testimony of Your goodness and May Your Name be glorified. Jehovah Rapha (The Lord your healer) we thank You for Your mighty healing power and the invasion of heaven in Candace's life. Shalom!

Pray, meditate and declare this prayer. Jehova Rapha brings wholeness to our spirit, soul, and body."

My friend shared the prayer with her aunt and she declared it every day.

On April 19, my friend wrote to me and said, "My aunt does not feel the lump anymore. God is good. Thank you for your prayers and prayer."

I was elated and thanked Jehovah Rapha for His healing power. God loves His children!

Finally on April 23 my friend said, "They can't find the cancer!!! Praise Jesus!!! I just witnessed a miracle. Thanks for your prayers. Be blessed."

The miraculous power of God was confirmed and His joy and peace covered the whole situation.

In this testimony we see the fruit of God's hand which was healing and restoration. God is good and when we hear the still small voice and step out it in faith we see the fruit of God's hand. The more we step out in faith and we see evidence of God's hand with time we become so accustomed to the still small voice and we just know it is God speaking. With my life I have seen this process, the more I have stepped out in faith and see the fruit, the more I have become confident that what I hear from within is God.

Personally His voice has brought a lot of hope, purpose, and encouragement to me.

HOW TO POSITION YOURSELF TO HEAR GOD'S VOICE

Communicate Love

Desire to always communicate love. God is always ready to encourage and give hope. That is His nature. The Bible says that God is love. When you have this mindset, God will speak to you and give you a message of hope for the weary soul.

God has given me the opportunity to minister as part of the prophetic team in my local church. I realized during ministry when your mindset is to reveal the love of God, God communicates His words of love, and people are given hope and direction in life. Prophecy flows out of a heart of love.

Worship in Spirit and Truth

Worshiping God draws Him to you so that you can receive His voice and engage in dialogue. You can worship Him through dance, music, painting, and writing. One of the ways I love to worship God is through creative writing.

There was a period in my life when I was getting to know the personality of the Holy Spirit. I felt His presence one night and I asked Him, "What do you love?" And the Holy Spirit told me, "I love poetry." So the Holy Spirit asked me to get a pen and paper and He narrated a poem. I wrote it down. The poem was about revelation of the Holy Spirit.

In this instance we see important keys, like asking questions. The Holy Spirit loves it when we ask Him questions. He loves to teach and commune with us. Going beyond feeling the presence of the Holy Spirit and connecting with the personality is also an important key. We can do this by asking questions and indulging in dialogue.

To worship in spirit and truth is to engage with God and receive what He is saying to you. It is a union between Abba Father and child, communicating together in love.

Below is the poem I wrote with the Holy Spirit:

SWEET HOLY SPIRIT
Your breath full of life reviving my soul.
So pure, so gentle, my heart's delight
You wake me up and we soar together to a realm so glorious,
My soul overflows with joy
Your revelation a light to my path
Your presence, liberty to my soul
My mouth sings of praises, your goodness so vivid
Your creativity a wonder to behold, what a beautiful earth!
Creation sings, "The master craftsman makes all things beautiful."
Your love so tender and sweet, my soul find rests in You
Your flame all consuming, walls can't stand
Your power so amazing, there is no other like You
Your leadership so true, there is no other way
Sweet Holy Spirit, Your home is in me
Walk by Faith

Always believe God will communicate to you to reveal His nature. The Bible says that faith pleases God. This is what I call walking "in a heart of expectancy." Wherever you go, know and believe that God will speak to you. Jesus tore the veil to give us full access to our Heavenly Father and enhance our relationship with Him.

Bill Johnson, leader of Bethel Church, Redding, CA once said that faith is the currency of heaven. There is a divine exchange when we walk by faith and not sight. God sends His words of confirmation with love and power for our faith. May the author and perfecter of our faith, Jesus, give us a supernatural faith that is unwavering and may it take our relationship with God to new levels with demonstration of His power.

Prayer

> *"And the Holy Spirit helps us in our weakness. For example, we don't know what God wants us to pray for. But the Holy Spirit prays for us with groanings that cannot be expressed in words."*
> ROM 8:26 NLT

Prayer is a powerful tool to receive God's proceeding voice or word. Sometimes we don't know what to pray and the Holy Spirit helps us. When you pray in tongues, the Holy Spirit prays for you and He taps into the mind of God and brings fresh revelation to you. I realized when I pray in tongues, I receive revelation in form of visions which I decree and declare during prayer. I encourage you to pray in the tongues frequently.

Like all gifts which require faith, speaking in tongues is also an act of faith. At the beginning of 2013 I got into speaking in tongues and I believe it is one of the tools that accelerated my spiritual growth. There are tools God has freely given us to receive spiritual food and growth, like the word, praying in tongues, and fasting. We are spirit beings and we need spiritual tools to revive and empower us to do God's work. Speaking in tongues is a great spiritual tool. I have noticed when I pray in tongues my faith and confidence in God is built up when I am feeling down. I begin to have a boldness to declare the promises of God in faith and rest in His faithfulness. In Jude 1:20, it says that we build up our most holy faith by praying in the spirit (tongues).

Recently, a friend of mine had an impossible situation and did not know how to pray. So she decided to pray in the spirit (tongues) and there was a quick solution to the impossible situation. Sometimes we do not how to pray or even what to pray for, but when we pray in the spirit it is the Holy Spirit praying and not us, and He knows what we specifically need for breakthrough. One book which helped me to understand praying in tongues more and to embrace the good and perfect gift from the Father, was *The Walk of the Spirit – The Walk of Power* by Dave Roberson.

I always look at Paul and the impact He had for Jesus. He loved praying in tongues. One of Paul's quotes:

I thank God that I speak in tongues more than all of you.
1 COR 4:18 NIV

Perhaps Paul understood a mystery of God, speaking in tongues, and the way it could help in advancing the Kingdom. Till this day we read about Paul and the great contribution He had to the body of Christ.

A great portion of the New Testament was written by Paul through the inspiration of the Holy Spirit.

Thankfulness

Always thank God for His communication if you receive His voice through dreams and visions. Make those encouraging dreams and visions a memorial. Sometimes I relax before I sleep and reflect on the good dreams I had with God in the past, and thank Him for the wonderful and encouraging supernatural experiences. What I found out is that the more I did this the more I got wonderful dreams, visitations, and visions from Him.

The Bible says in Psalm 100 *"... enter His gates with thanksgiving."* I believe a "gate" could be a portal or door that leads into the dream realm. A heart of thanksgiving is like a key to this gate (door/portal) of dreams. This principle opened a whole new dimension of the supernatural to me. Visitations to heaven became more regular to me, and that brought so much joy.

One night I was giving God thanks for His goodness and the wonderful experiences I have had with Him, and He had a surprise for me.

Taken from my journal on February 14, 2014:

Last night before I slept, I said, "I would love to spend time with my first love, Jesus." It was interesting to know that it was about two a.m., February 14, 2014, Valentine's Day. Throughout the night I was thanking God for the different encounters I have had with Him in the past year. He has consumed my mind with good things and I am so honored to be a child of God.

Before I got up this morning, I was still full of gratitude for the great things God has shown me, and then something mesmerizing happened. I was relaxing on the side of my bed, partially awake and I saw this glory cloud enter my bedroom. I was calling my loved ones in the home to come and see it, but no one could hear my voice. It was an encounter that God prepared for me only. The cloud filled the whole bedroom and the room turned white with shining light. Then a gateway was opened in front of the room and my spirit was taken up rapidly. I felt like God sent me a glory taxi in cloud form to take me up to the heavenly. It was so amazing.

I found myself in this beautiful place surrounded by white crystals with a couple of doors on the sides. I was dazed and confused, wondering where I was. Then it dawned on me, this is another wonderful encounter I am having with God. I started to enjoy myself and I was flying all over the place with inexpressible joy. My peeled eyes were in awe at the creativity and brilliance of our Dear Father. The place was enchanting. After some time I heard a voice, "Are you finished?" and I said, "Yes." Immediately I was fully awake on my bed in complete amazement.

My first love, Jesus, had a wonderful gift for me on Valentine's Day. He allowed me to go to this glorious place to enjoy myself. God is really FUN. There is nothing boring about Him!

Word of God

> *"For the word of God is alive and active. Sharper than any double-edged sword, it penetrates even to dividing soul and spirit, joints and marrow; it judges the thoughts and attitudes of the heart."*
> HEB 4:12 NIV

The word of God is living and when you meditate on it, it opens your soul to receive His voice.

The Bible says that the Holy Spirit teaches us all things:

> *"But the Helper, the Holy Spirit, whom the Father will send in my name, he will teach you all things and bring to your remembrance all that I have said to you."*
> JN 14:26 ESV

When you acknowledge the Holy Spirit and ask Him to highlight scriptures and teach you about God, He will do so and they will come alive to you. These scriptures can only be revealed by the Holy Spirit and they are God's instructions to you and the body of Christ.

There are times I have read the word of God before I slept, and then during the night I have a dream related to the scripture I read. The word of God becomes an access point into the supernatural realm of revelation. I think of the scripture that says our life is hidden in Christ. Christ is the living word so when we read the word it activates a supernatural life hidden in Christ.

Yielding

> *Trust in the Lord with all your heart, And lean not on your own understanding; In all your ways acknowledge Him, And He shall direct your paths.*
> PROV 3:5-6 NKJV

Yielding your will to God and letting Him have His way opens the door to hear His voice. When we allow His thoughts to take precedence in our lives, and put our thoughts behind, He starts revealing His plans to us through dreams, vision, etc. When we agree with God's thoughts and co-labor with Him to advance His Kingdom that is when we see the Kingdom demonstrated with power and lives are changed. In relationships, there is always co-laboring in unity and love.

Our position is in and with Christ in heavenly places. These are some of the lessons I have learned on how to posture yourself in this seat and receive effectively from God.

Blessing for Hearing the Voice of God

Precious child, may the Spirit of God breathe life over your spiritual senses to receive the voice of God with clarity. May your spiritual senses be heightened and may you only know the Shepherd, Jesus' voice not the stranger's voice. May God awaken you morning by morning to receive His instruction and put His words in your mouth. May God open your eyes to see, like Elisha prayed to God and his servant's eyes were opened to see the glory of God, horses, and chariots of fire. May the eyes of your understanding be enlightened that you may know what is the hope of His calling, what are the glorious riches of His inheritance among the saints, May Sweet

Holy Spirit overshadow you every day and may His voice lead and guide you to all truth for the glory of God. In Jesus' name, amen.

Praise be to the God and Father of our Lord Jesus Christ, who has blessed us in the heavenly realms with every spiritual blessing in Christ.
EPH 1:3 NIV

God has given us every spiritual blessing to enhance our relationship with Him, therefore all the means of communication like dreams, visions and revealed words are free for all His children. All we have to do is choose to believe that we can freely access these spiritual blessings as children. This is our inheritance in Christ and God's Face is turned to us every day so that we can communicate with Him. Turn your face towards His and enjoy your loving relationship with Him.

Marlon Katsigazi is the author of *Factory Smiles.* Marlon's work is inspired by his personal experiences with God. Marlon believes that God has given each person an invitation to have a tailor-made relationship with Him. The journey of pursuing and discovering God (The Person of Love) is the most enjoyable and fulfilling thing. God is fun and loves His children.

Marlon's desire is to ignite hope and joy in people by revealing the love of God through creativity.

Discover some of Marlon's creative work about love and the romance of heaven on YouTube: http://bit.ly/Marlon-YouTube

Web: https://about.me/Marlon.Katsigazi
Email: casha43@gmail.com

The Comforter Speaks
Rob Coscia

I WOKE UP COUGHING again, that deep-chested wheeze that would never completely finish. A doctor had been treating me for bronchitis for months, but I wasn't getting any better. I was getting used to hacking up a lung like an eighty-year-old chain smoker in a gross sort of way, but this time was different. The pain shooting from my sternum to my back actually took my breath away. I went to my chiropractor to see if an adjustment would help relieve the feeling of being stabbed with a pipe. His reaction wasn't what I expected.

"Rob, I'm not touching you. Something else is going on here. I want you to get an MRI."

He called a friend to get me into a clinic for the scan, and then called me later that afternoon. "I'm so sorry. I don't know how else to say this. It looks like lymphoma. I've scheduled you to meet with an oncologist."

After poking, prodding, testing, and drilling me like they were fracking for natural gas, the diagnosis was a fist-sized non-Hodgkin's lymphoma mass in the center of my chest. I wasn't happy, but I wasn't panicking. In my life I've seen miracles. Good ones, not just the "every baby is a miracle" kind. I mean paralyzed-to-walking, blind-to-seeing kinds of miracles. I've prayed for many people that have been healed. So I prayed for one of those miracles now. My family and friends prayed. People from all over the country prayed. But nothing happened. The size and aggressiveness of the cancer made time an issue, as well as the treatment. Well-meaning people suggested that if I drank nine gallons of sea-salted lemon water a day, it would destroy any cancer. Well, sure it would, because it would drown me. I believe in good nutrition and hydration too, but it was a bit late for that. I did adjust my diet to help my body heal, but it would take about 625 hours of a chemotherapy cocktail to kill that thing.

In a matter of days there were more tests than I could count, surgery to remove fluid the tumor had forced around my heart, and my first chemo treatment, there in the hospital. The frenzy of it all kept the reality from sinking in, and I floated somewhere in the numbness between hopeful and terrified. The kind of chemo I was doing (dose-adjusted R-EPOCH) allowed me to do most of the rest of the treatments at home. My wife, daughter, and son were amazing, and there to help me with everything I needed. I lost most of my appetite, but they made a lot of milkshake runs for me. They set up our bedroom like a hospital room, making space for all the new medical things we had to become experts in, something that we never wanted to know. I felt fairly strong at first, but as I became weaker, my family was there to literally pick me up. I couldn't fully recline because of the pain and restricted breathing, so though it was difficult, the only way for both my wife and I to get some rest was for her to move into another room until the treatments were done.

A nurse showed us how to use the portable pump when she wasn't there, which would push six rounds of chemicals into me, a hundred hours at a time. We had all passed our medical crash-course, and everything was beginning to settle into a new routine. And that's when sometime at night in the middle of my second round, the enormity of what I was facing finally hit me. There in the quiet dark, the whine of the pump was reminding me every twelve seconds (I counted it over and over) that something was wrong with me. And what was wrong might not get fixed. I imagined the pump as a countdown clock, sounding off my last moments every twelve seconds.

"Why, God?" I couldn't keep from whispering the clichéd words. I had prayed countless times for others and helped people through major crises, but it didn't fully prepare me for my own. I had been a pastor for over twenty years, but my God-grid wasn't as up to the task as I thought. Though I was barely able to move around, I exhausted myself just trying to deal with all the thoughts racing through my mind hour after hour. I finally managed to find a resting spot, physically and emotionally, and fell deeply asleep for the first time in weeks.

I opened my eyes to a desert valley. The air was thick and hot, under a dark red sky. The ground was stone and sand, and there I sat, in a dream so real that I knew I was dreaming. The thoughts I had pushed down when I was awake began to invade my dreaming mind: "You've screwed up everything. Nothing you've done is good enough. You caused your own cancer. You're all alone, and you deserve it. Welcome to hell."

I heard footsteps. I knew it was Jesus. I began weeping quietly, believing He was about to tell me how badly I had failed Him. No pain could be worse to me. My head down, all I could see were His feet as He stopped in front of me. Then His hand reached down. I lifted my head slowly. And there was the smile that created the universe.

He lifted me up. I was in awe in the clearest sense of the word, but there was no fear of His disapproval like I had imagined. The love radiating from Him pushed my fear and self-pity away in waves. There was just no room for them in His presence. We walked, and we talked. He didn't explain why the cancer was happening, but every word from His mouth unscrambled my soul like He was solving a Rubik's cube.

Each step brought more intimacy, though that word isn't adequate. There was no point in trying to hide anything of myself from Him anyway. He was in my mind, affirming or correcting my thoughts as I had them. And the more I opened myself to Him, the more I could hear His thoughts. No, more than that, I could feel them. At first I was not sure I was allowed to do that. But then a kind of download surged into me. It was His joy. It radiated in both sides of my brain, in my heart, in every cell. The revelation that came with it still overwhelms me. He wasn't here because He was obligated. He wanted to be with me. I was His joy. He smiled again, and lifted His head to prompt me to turn around. Tall green grass, full trees, and a clear stream were behind us. Every place we had walked together had been transformed.

The whir-whine-click of the pump welcomed me back. I put my hand on my chest. I could feel the area that was still bulging with the cancer. But the dread was gone, and I could still feel Him. The voice He had in my dream was no different now in my heart. I let that voice soak into my waking mind. I knew Jesus called the Holy Spirit "the Comforter," but I hadn't understood that very well until now. For the first time in a long time, I quit trying to figure things out. I stopped obsessing over getting everything right so that He would approve of me. I just let Him love me. And every twelve seconds there was a reminder that He was with me, and that I was His joy.

Does God speak? Yes. Does God speak to *you*? Yes! Like anything worthwhile, hearing His voice is something you learn and grow in, one of the greatest pursuits of your life. But let that journey begin and be sustained by the thought that He wants to talk to you. He loves nothing more. He truly is your Comforter, and hearing Him as that is an essential part of your identity. Why? Because Jesus said so: "The Father will send the Holy Spirit to you in My name. He is the Comforter, Advocate, and Guide of your life. He will teach you everything you need, and help you remember all I have said to you, especially that I am leaving My peace to you. Not as some parting gift, but as an inheritance. In fact, I am commissioning your life with My peace. Live fully in it, so that you won't make room in your mind to be troubled, or your heart to be afraid." (John 14:26-27, my paraphrase.)

Why did Jesus first call the Holy Spirit the Comforter? Was it because His friends were about to become sad, and He wanted to encourage them? Partly, I suppose. But I think the core reason is that He wanted them, and you, to know Him in the kind of intimacy that comes from being completely open to Him. The Comforter is the most peaceful, kind, and encouraging Person in the universe, and He understands your pain, better than you do. He wants to heal you, strengthen you, train you to be amazing, and cause you to thrive. That's never going to happen if you won't listen for Him, or trust Him, as a Comforter. The Holy Spirit will help me correct things that I'm doing or seeing wrong, but if I only know Him as The Great Corrector, that's all I will be able to focus on. And it's all I'll be able to give away. God has so much more for you. When He says "How I think and see the world is not the way that you think and see the world, and My way of living and being and is not your way of living and being" (Isaiah 55:8-9), it's not a condemnation. It's an invitation. He is inviting you to do just what He has said; to see as He sees and to think as He thinks, by living in full awareness of who He is for you, and who you are becoming in Him. He wants you to see yourself and others as He does. He wants to talk to you, to guide you, to show you what's possible in Him, and how to go after it. He *wants* to talk with you. About everything. Nothing in your life is unimportant, because you are so important to Him.

Of course there are circumstances and relationships that need your attention. But what a difference there is between reacting to life and intentionally engaging it with the Creator of the universe. When you don't let God speak to you, to how He sees you and who He wants to be for you, you become progressively frustrated and drained. There are some days that seem as though everywhere you turn there is something else demanding your full attention. When you take on all the stress and anxiety that is being projected at you, you begin to think from that stress. As frustration grows, you start to lose your identity in Christ, and begin to agree with fears, insecurities, and lies, yours and everyone else's. But when you do make time for Him, you come away genuinely empowered to live in His love, joy, peace, patience, kindness, and goodness, in the fruit of the Spirit, in the fruit of the Comforter.

The apostle said this about Him:

> *The Spirit searches all things, even the deep things of God. For who knows a person's thoughts except their own spirit within them? In the same way no one knows the thoughts of God except the Spirit of God. What we have received is not the spirit of the world, but the Spirit who is from God, so that we may understand what God has freely given us. This is what we speak, not in words taught us*

> *by human wisdom but in words taught by the Spirit, explaining spiritual realities with Spirit-taught words. The person without the Spirit does not accept the things that come from the Spirit of God but considers them foolishness, and cannot understand them because they are discerned only through the Spirit. The person with the Spirit makes judgments about all things, but such a person is not subject to merely human judgments, for, 'Who has known the mind of the Lord so as to instruct Him?' But we have the mind of Christ.*
> 1 COR 2:10-16 NIV

To hear the Comforter's voice is to not be overwhelmed with performing a task, but to be overwhelmed by Him. Trust that Jesus Christ loves you. Truly, completely, outrageously loves you. I don't write that lightly. Life often teaches you to be guarded. You focus on all that might go wrong as a way of preparing yourself for the worst. Sometimes what we call spiritual armor is just the numbness we've developed that we hope will shield us from being hurt again. Instead of protecting, it just insulates us from truth and love. The armor of God is really a description of His presence, protecting you from the enemy's lies, empowering you to be all God sees you as, equipping you with all He has given you, and enveloping you in His love. When it says "put on the whole armor of God," (Ephesians 6.11), it literally means to sink into it like a blanket, to feel as one with it as your favorite, most comfortable clothes.

Trust is the heart's word for faith. It's in trust that you don't just hear God, you know Him. What He's really like, who He wants to be for you now, and who you are becoming in Him. Living overwhelmed by God's love, hope, and goodness toward you leaves no room to be overwhelmed by anything else. Even cancer.

Sometimes feeling helpless is a gift, because it's an opportunity to grow in the revelation that you never have to be hopeless, and a reminder that you don't have to work for His love. At those times, the enemy may come as an "angel of light," but he's only going to validate your pain, anger, and fears. He's only good at accusing. He's just awful at faking love, joy, peace, patience, kindness, and goodness, because He has none. They are the fruit of the Spirit of God. They are a description of what He is going to be for you. They are what you experience when He talks to you. The enemy wants you to focus on your last failure. God wants you to look for your next opportunity with Him. Stop trying to qualify for His love, and just be loved.

Christians spend a lot of time managing fear and anxiety, and very little time cultivating what God has provided to displace them. If His perfect, complete love really displaces all fear (1 John 4.18), then you should be focusing on His love, not the fear. God loves you as you are, but you won't hear Him fully as your Comforter if you aren't willing to trust His love to transform you. He is the King of Instead. Instead of grief, He gives you joy. Instead of mourning, He gives you gladness and dancing. Instead of worthlessness, He gives you beauty. Instead of oppressive heaviness, He gives you a song of thankfulness and praise. (Jn 16:20, Ps 30:11, Isa 61:1-3) The Comforter knows your pain, so deeply that He isn't willing to let you wallow in it. You don't rescue someone by giving them a thumbs up and a wink, and then leaving them in distress. You take them to a safe place, and then you heal them, restore them, and equip them to thrive beyond that experience. Psalm 18 speaks to that process so brilliantly: "He brought me out into a safe place. He rescued me, because He delighted in me. He made my feet like the feet of a deer, and set me secure on the heights. He trains my hands for war, so that my arms can bend a bow of bronze."

Life in Jesus Christ is a discipline. It's a completely empowering, joyful, life-transforming experience in Him, but it's still a discipline. It takes some intentionality to be conscious of the difference between stuffing down your negative emotions and actually giving them to God. Begin today to bring your thoughts to Him and let Him show you *why* you feel the way you do. Then let Him deal with the roots of it. As soon as you let Jesus bring light to dark, the dark loses power. Fear, frustration, anger, confusion, rejection, pain, and self-pity begin to lose their grip on your mind and heart. Make yourself vulnerable to His love as you listen for Him and read His word in the intimacy of knowing Him as Comforter. You really will begin to see yourself and all your circumstances as He does. You aren't the overwhelmed, stressed, misunderstood, bitter, hurt person you thought you were. You are confident, joyful, peaceful, and brilliant, because you are brilliantly loved. That love displaces negative thinking and fills your identity, releasing who you really are, regardless of what anyone says or does around you. Your new mindset is to live today as fully as His love for you.

Take a breath. The Comforter is with you right now. Take a walk with Him through all His blessings in your life. Let Him show you how surrounded by His presence you have been, regardless of what you have gone through. Allow Him to show you your circumstances and relationships as He sees them. With each step you take and every word He says, see that there is no reason to be anxious, and every reason to be grateful, hopeful, and fearless. His hand is out to you, and His smile is contagious.

> *Satisfy our souls each morning with Your unfailing love, so we may be truly glad and speak from joy each and every day. Give us happiness in proportion to our former misery. Replace the bad times with good. Let us, your servants, see Your great acts again, and let our children see Your glory.*
> PS 90:14-16

Rob Coscia has written a devotional book about his experiences overcoming cancer called *Forty Doors*, and contributed to another compilation book, *Hearing and Understanding the Voice of God*. He writes a daily devotional through social media. He and his wife Angi graduated together from North Central University. They've pastored for over 25 years, and have spoken around the globe. They have two (amazing) grown children and reside in Northern California. Rob is available for speaking engagements periodically, and for coffee anytime.

Devotional blog: https://robcoscia.wordpress.com
Facebook: www.facebook.com/rob.coscia
Twitter: @robcoscia

A First Encounter with Sound
Amy Axby

A FEW YEARS AGO, I woke early to a swirling grey, Kansas prairie thunderstorm. Trees bent over and thrashed in the wind. Rain and lightning and thunder rushed through the sky. I took my Bible and a blanket, and I sat near the window to watch creation kaleidoscope through the thousands of raindrops streaming down the glass. Immediately, an unearthly, rocking, crash of thunder shook the house. I jumped up, Bible in my hand. I thought something had exploded, it was that loud. I ran to the glass door, but saw only the storm, and I realized that the same thunder was still rolling. The sound was literally tangible. I had been through many storms, but I had never heard anything like this before. It was so sudden and loud, it hurt my ears. I could feel it in my chest.

There was no fire or smoke, but as I stood there I realized that this was a storm that would wake the kids, and if I wanted to read even a verse I was going to have to do it fast. I started away from the sliding glass door, but before I could turn, I was blinded for a moment by the brightest flash of lightning I have ever seen. It lit the whole house for an unusually long time, not a typical lightning bolt that flares and then dies, but like someone had turned on a light and left it.

Stunned by this sky-power and covered in chills, I started walking fast in the now pitch-dark; planning to hide in the bathroom with the light on before the kids came running. I was opening my Bible while I walked, trying to get a head start. I couldn't see where I was in the book; just hoping to find something quickly when I got to the light.

As I flipped blindly through the pages, I heard one word.

Stop.

I put a hand on the scripture to hold my place, rushed to the bathroom and closed the door.

When I flipped on the light and looked down to read, I was awestruck. When I lifted my hand to see where I held the page, it was Psalm 29:

The voice of the Lord is over the waters;

the God of glory thunders,

the Lord thunders over the mighty waters.

The voice of the Lord is powerful;

the voice of the Lord is majestic.

The voice of the Lord breaks the cedars...

The voice of the Lord strikes

with flashes of lightning.

The voice of the Lord shakes the desert;

A First Encounter with Sound

the Lord shakes the Desert of Kadesh.

The voice of the Lord twists the oaks

and strips the forests bare.

And in His temple all cry, "Glory!"

I read the passage three times, first out of disbelief, the second time, laughing, and the third time, for the first time in my life, I knew a holy fear.

In a daze, I walked out of the bathroom, into my bedroom, and fell on the floor, holding my face in my hands. Shaking all over, weeping, gasping for breath in the presence of a God I had known as a friend all my life. Now, I suddenly saw Him in a new light, as something more. The Wild Chief of All Things. King of Thunder. Master of the Universe.

And I saw my life, in His enormous, star-scattering hands.

I had heard His voice. Thundering, trumpeting, roaring. "What Lord, what are you telling me? You are mighty, You are mighty, You are mighty." I shook and cried; what to do next with this God that could strike the desert and strip the forests bare? But, the next thing I heard in my spirit was the chorus from an old song, "It's like thunder, lightning, The way you love me is frightening..."

I was laughing and crying now, standing to my feet and raising my hands as the dawn came streaming in. Worshipping the great I AM. Our Father, yes, and, yet, not so tame, not such a domesticated man that we can ever know exactly what to expect from Him. I felt He wanted me to know surprise and delight and awe that day, wanted to give me laughter, wanted to bring me to my knees in the knowledge of the sheer shocking glory of His strength, and then to raise me up again on the gracious song of His mercy, all through the power of the sound of His voice.

A few days ago, a video of children hearing for the first time came across my newsfeed. The doctors and nurses are kind. The modern miracles, so compelling, seem to say that hearing is for everyone. The fathers are so patient but also so eager, speaking in ways the child can understand, waiting for the moment the young one can hear His voice, asking out loud while also signing, "Can you hear me, honey? Can you hear me?" And every reaction from each child is almost exactly the same; a face full of surprise, then laughter, and, then, hands over face, weeping.

I wept with them too, tears of gratitude for a first encounter with sound.

Amy Axby currently lives in the Ozark Mountains with her husband and three children. You can find her blog, where she writes about love, fear, and courage, at *ladythefearless.com*. Follow and friend her on her personal page or the Lady the Fearless website page on Facebook.

Blog: http://ladythefearless.com

Healing for Hearing God
Toni Imsen

"Toni, are you getting something right now?" My group leader asked me right there in front of everyone in the group.

"I don't think so." I replied, feeling a little nervous.

In a gentle, yet challenging way he said, "I think you are. Can you share?"

"No, I really don't think I have anything to share." I said.

He let it go then. I felt hot and uncomfortable.

We took a short break and he spoke with me privately. He told me he believed that God was speaking to me and wanted to speak through me. He told me I had often said just the right thing at the right moment, and that I had something the group would benefit from hearing.

The truth is, I was experiencing God, and I had been for a while. I was a newly rededicated believer in Jesus at that time, but I was having God encounters on a regular basis. However, I had no clue whether it was God or not. All I knew was that I would see things, hear things, smell, taste, and feel things. Some of those things were just weird! I couldn't even describe with words what was going on, so how could I share these things with other people?

I shared my concerns with him during the break. "What if it's not God? How do I know if it is God or not? What if I'm wrong? What will people think of me? What if I hurt someone? What if it's the devil?"

There were plenty more insecurities where that came from. All my concerns, well, let's call them what they were; *lies*—birthed from *fears*, which were caused by *wounds*—were keeping me from receiving, giving, and working freely with Holy Spirit.

"Well," He said. "What if you are right about what you are getting and it is God, how will you know if it is Him if you don't take a risk? What matters more, what God thinks, or what people think of you? Sometimes you will hurt people, we all do, but that is not your heart's intent. I know you, that is not who you are. If you make a mistake or a mess, we can all clean it up together. That is how you grow in it all. Trial and error is the only way to mature in Christ. Trust Him and things will sort themselves out. Will you try sharing when we come back together?" I nodded my head in agreement, yet still feeling nervous about it.

When we all gathered back in that living room, we came together again in prayer and worship. I began to see what I saw earlier again. It was scrolling letters flowing by, as if on a screen in my mind's eye. They were fluorescent script letters and words, neon sign style. He asked the group again to share what they were experiencing. I was sitting there with my heart pounding in my chest. I felt like I would explode any second. I raised my hand up slightly. He nodded at me from across the room. I described what I was seeing, the scrolling letters.

"What does it say? Just read it for us." He urged. I was so scared, I just blurted out what I saw in my mind's eye. I can't even remember what it was now, only that some people began to cry, and some began to laugh. Some lay down on the floor and worshiped louder. I could feel the power of God flowing through me like a fiery earthquake. My voice was trembling and it felt like an electric blanket wrapped around me. There was a weighty Presence. I wondered if what I brought to the table was a good thing or not. I just didn't know. I was new at this whole thing. I had a lot to learn about God. After that night, I had an even more fierce desire to know Him. That's how it started.

IDENTIFYING WOUNDS AND HINDRANCES

What I know now, but didn't understand then, was just how wounded I was. I knew I was broken considering my childhood and what I was rescued from. What I didn't know was how those life wounds, the fears I developed and the lies I believed, all affected my ability to function in the spiritual realm. We, at least here in the USA, are mostly pretty well versed in our understanding of how dysfunctions, addictions, and general brokenness can affect our family lives, careers, and relationships. We've all been exposed to an overabundance of talk shows, news programs, online stories, and social media. We are taking in all this information daily. We have the scoop on every disorder there is out there. But, we don't know what we don't know, right?

There were a few things I didn't know.

I didn't know that my wounds were causing me to be suspicious. The things that have harmed me, scarred me, and changed me negatively were ruling me. Fear brought separation and disconnection from God and others. Fear is sneaky. It comes in all kinds of packages. I had the fear of God in an unhealthy sense coming from the models of authority I had. I was afraid of people based on my relational experiences. I didn't know that there were lies I believed that brought confusion, disillusionment, and despair. Lies looked like, thinking everyone would abandon me, people were not trustworthy and God was distant. Those false beliefs brought distorted interpretations, disappointment, and ultimately a mindset of hopelessness.

Could I still hear God? Yes, absolutely. Yet, I heard Him through what I will call *filters*. Some will call them *lenses*. Lenses color everything we see. If I put on a pair of ski goggles and the lenses are orange, everything has a shade of orange. I can still see what I am looking at, but everything will be interpreted through that tint. The filters cause us to see everything through a limited perspective.

As a young person, I had a message spoken loud and clear to me from my family of origin—that my opinion didn't matter. What I had to say wasn't important. Children were to be seen and not heard. So when I heard from God, it wasn't important that I speak it out because my voice didn't matter one way or the other. In my mind, I had no business saying anything. That wound introduced fears and lies. It affected the way I functioned in the spiritual gifts. I questioned the words I heard from God and I didn't trust myself to hear or interpret. The fears brought separation between others and me, because I didn't communicate. Those lies influenced my connection with the Godhead. The lies brought gaps of silence in my relationship with God. Those gaps brought distraction, anxiety, and sadness.

I was unable to trust what I heard God say or my ability to hear Him. Risk seemed to be the companion of hearing God. Risk was scary and so I withdrew from Him and other people in an effort to avoid having to step out and experience rejection.

How could I possibly hear, speak, and represent the heart of God to people with all this clutter?

I can see now how those fears and lies I believed were revealing themselves in questions I had for my leader. These questions are all too common. I hear them from believers of various levels of spiritual maturity. I know I was not alone in asking these questions. Looking back, I can see that when my healing increased, so did my revelation. My ability to use all of my five senses to "hear" God intensified. The ability to interpret those things also grew stronger with each healing encounter.

I believe that we are in a crucial stage of change in the world in which we live. I believe we are living in a time in history in which we cannot afford to let wounds shape us, fears lead us, and lies deceive us. We need clarity on what is happening in the present so we have the insight to create a brighter future. I believe God wants to give us foresight, so we have the ability to execute excellent oversight. Agents of progress and change are much needed all around the globe.

Governments, businesses, educators, communicators, families, the religious, and artists are all hungry to live in a greater condition. Our contributions to the world are vital to the well-being of humanity. We have the ability to be agents of hope and healing to a generation needing wisdom and nurturing.

He wants to heal our hearing. He wants to heal the wounds we carry, shatter the lies we believe, and remove our fears completely. I have a feeling there are some really strong prophetic voices yet to be uncovered, voices that can heal a wounded world. There is a world of hurting and lonely people, dangerously needing of our passion and compassion. Imagine a place where goodness accelerates.

NECESSARY HEALING

Healing came for me in many ways. There was no one method or formula for my healing. Some healing happened really fast and in unexpected packages. Other healing came over time through dreams, prophetic words, inner healing, physical healing, and every other way God comes in His faithfulness and steadfast love.

When God began to heal me, His voice became clearer and clearer. Not only were the messages getting clearer, but the content and detail emerged in full HD and surround sound. I began having vivid dreams with strategies for ministry and business. He would show me faces of people and their names. When I would minister to people, He would reveal the source of their issues. I would know when and where their wounds came, how, and by whom. I would hear names, ages, everything.

The Woman in Trouble

Ann was an old friend I had known since we were teenagers. We attended the same church, and were in a group that met in a home weekly for Bible study. One day I saw it on her. I saw something that looked heavy and guilty. It had a sense of desperation. Her eyes caught mine and I knew. I passed Ann a small note, "Do we need to talk?" We were in a group setting and I couldn't just blurt anything out. She looked at me from a few seats over in the circle we were sitting in with about 15 other people, and nodded yes.

During the break we went into another room. I looked deeply into her eyes and felt such sorrow. "You're in trouble aren't you?" I asked her.

"No, I just need prayer." Ann said, with a stiff expression. Her heart was suddenly harder than it had been in the living room.

As gently as I could, feeling great compassion, I stated, "No, it's more than that, and I think you know it. I think you are in the danger zone. I'm concerned. I have a sense that you are going down a slippery slope, and you know you are. You are choosing to do it."

I had known her for quite a long time and I thought I had enough relationship with her to know I could say things of that nature. She knew I was coming from a loving place, even though we had disagreed from time to time. I knew our relationship could handle this kind of conversation. This occasion had a different feel to it. Crossing her arms now, she said, "What do you think you know?" with an edge and rebellion I hadn't quite seen before.

Okay, here we go. I knew I had to tell her what I was hearing and it wasn't going to be easy. It wasn't comfortable for either one of us. "I think you are about to have a major affair with another man."

"No, you're crazy. And besides, if you think you know everything, who is it then?" I could tell she was feeling offended and testing me.

"Do you really want me to go there?" I wasn't sure where this all was going, it was happening so fast. Then all these details popped into my mind. I had no foreknowledge or any prior hints from anything in the natural realm.

Suddenly I knew who the person was, when the attraction started, all these details I honestly didn't want to know. They were all people I knew and loved.

I began to tell her details. I told her the name. I told her the approximate day and time and all the circumstances. I also told her how much God loved her and that He was compassionate toward her in this situation. I told her I believed that He revealed it all for the purpose of healing and redemption. I believed that God intervened before it was too late.

"Did you talk to him? What did he tell you? He swore he would never tell! How do you know?" Still trying to figure it out, a swirl of emotion and confusion came to the surface and she began to sob. Ann sobbed and trembled and fussed around for a good while. Grief ensued. I just listened and stayed with her. I comforted Ann as much as I could. We were in that room for what seemed like hours and it probably was hours. In some ways, she came to her senses. Ann seemed to snap out of deception and her eyes got really wide open. "Oh my God, what have I done?" She gasped. The truth began to come out about so many things. The marriage issues, the brokenness, so many things God wanted to heal. It seemed as though healing began for her that day.

Long term, the story of Ann didn't end so well. People don't always respond to these kinds of God interventions. Even when you hear God correctly, people don't always allow Him to move the way He intends at the time. Life is just messy sometimes. Life got messier for Ann and her family. Hearts got harder. Circumstances became more difficult as a result. Divorce followed several years later. There were layers of pain masked in Ann's life. I believe that someday, when the roots of pain are uncovered, healing will come.

LIFESTYLE REALITIES

The realities we face in our lifestyle of hearing and responding are as diverse as they are frequent. We don't always get it right. We misinterpret what we hear. We aren't sure of our application of what we hear. Whenever people are involved in anything, there is a potential for a mess. The only solutions are trial and error. The road to maturity is loaded with pitfalls and difficulties. Yet, we press on. We grow. We will see victory. There were plenty more of these stories over the next few years, stories of hearing God and being compelled to respond. I wish I could say things always went well for me, but they didn't. I made plenty of mistakes. Why am I telling you a story that didn't work out? Why am I telling you that things don't always come out well? I am telling you these things because this is our reality. We are not always going to understand everything that happens. We cannot reject the voice of God just because our expectations aren't met. We cannot avoid His call on our lives because it might be painful and difficult. I had plenty of good experiences. The sick were healed, demons were cast out, and God's goodness took over. I didn't give up, but I did do something I regretted.

Living this lifestyle of hearing God was extremely challenging at times. On one occasion, the revelation and details I was receiving felt like way too much information for me to handle. I honestly didn't want to know hidden things about people and situations anymore. It was just too overwhelming. I actually did a really stupid thing and told God I didn't want to hear anything anymore.

Well, guess what? It got really dark and really quiet for a while. I asked God why He was so quiet and why I hadn't heard anything. He told me that He was honoring my request. If I didn't want to hear anything, He wasn't going to speak unless I wanted Him to. I had that choice. When I told God I didn't want to hear anything anymore, I was thinking that I didn't want to hear anything difficult that would cause me to have to do something I didn't want to do. I didn't want to do things like have hard conversations or confront people. I didn't want to know personal information about people's lives and sin. It was painful to have those kinds of things in your reality all the time. What I really did was shut off my ability to hear good stuff too. Hearing God can be a two-edged sword. I apologized for my stubbornness. I told Him that I wanted to hear Him, but I wanted to know what to do with what I heard. I needed tools!

He was faithful to give me equipment and wisdom to go with the new experiences. My previous leaders and mentors could no longer keep up with what was happening with me. The only answer I was getting from them was to seek God and develop intimacy with Him, because they had not had those same encounters and really couldn't lead me there. They told me to stay as close to scripture as possible, to know it in and out. It was good counsel. Their encouragement was that I was going in the right direction and that I was on a fast track like they hadn't seen before.

There are times when you are called to be a forerunner. There is no map for the pioneer. It's not that I think I was the only one on the planet who was having these encounters, absolutely not. Those experiences could be found in scripture throughout history, and many men and women had gone before me having these kinds of encounters. Yet, in my sphere of influence, at that time, I felt alone.

It seemed as though people in my zone weren't talking about these things much, at least not in their everyday lives. Most people were just going to church a few times a week, studying the Bible, and spending time in prayer and worship. Those things are great, but there was a whole other dimension that seemed distant and disconnected from daily living. There had to be more than this. I knew there was.

Taking risks and listening to the still small voice produced fruit. Listening to my gut instinct became an important way to navigate this new world. However, in order to take risks, hear the still small voice, and listen to my gut, there were some things that had to be dealt with. There were some things I needed to know from the core of my being. There were some blockages that were keeping me from experimenting, exploring, and discovering the truths of the kingdom of God that Jesus preached.

LEARNING TO CLEAR, CULTIVATE, AND PROTECT YOUR SPACE

Growing in my relationship with God has taught me a few things, one of them being authority. I have been given all authority in Christ to remove any clutter that fills my personal space. My space includes my body (physical), my soul (mind, will, and emotions), and spirit (connects with God). It is my responsibility to keep those spaces clutter free. That clutter is often known as unbelief, and unbelief has a lot of faces.

It is important to clear some space up and function from a place of freedom. Sometimes there are many things to clear, (I have listed some below), but we have the tools. Jesus has already set us free.

Legalism – Legalism shows up as the "have-to's" and the "woulda, coulda, shoulda's" of life. The obligations of perfection and performance have a tendency to take over. I have to remind myself that my most fruitful life does not come from serving obligation, religious or otherwise. I cannot afford to hear only what God has said, but what He is saying now. I have to hear Him without the filter of legalism, which always points to our insufficiencies rather than our abilities.

Perfectionism – I struggled with perfectionism. I felt like I had to be perfect and have it all right to operate in gifts or serve God. I don't have to do everything perfectly all the time for Him to love me and work through me. I have to give myself space to learn, grow, and make messes sometimes. There has to be room to explore and experiment. Perfectionism must go. A lens of perfectionism will keep you on a never-ending treadmill of my next point.

Performance – The pressure to conform to the opinions of men, and fear of failure, stopped me from being me. Performance was a constant nagging presence, whispering in my ear about the importance of pleasing other people. I worried about what they thought of me. I was continually concerned about whether I was good enough and whether or not I could make everyone happy. My concerns were rooted in abandonment and rejection. Those things had to go.

Guilt – Guilt is one of those things that can be easily hyper-spiritualized. Healthy guilt can help us navigate the discerning of right and wrong. However, improper guilt, with a dark agenda can do a number on our ability to hear God. Obsessive concern about how we are perceived, or the potential damage we may cause will stop us from responding to the voice of Holy Spirit. If our sin radar is on high regarding our failings past or present, we need to deal with that issue. If you believe in Jesus and His finished work, your sin is paid for and so is mine. Ungodly guilt cannot flavor our God encounters. False guilt must be silenced.

Fear – Like guilt, there are healthy fears and unhealthy fears. Fear can warn us that something is wrong. Unhealthy fear can be paralyzing and deafening when it comes to hearing and responding to God. When we live from a fear base instead of a faith base, we will find ourselves living our lives from reaction and false securities instead of proactivity and identity. Unhealthy fear at its core is irrational and a bondage. We will live with the unrelenting threat of letting God down and having recurring disappointments. Unbelief is actually rooted in, and a manifestation of, fear. Apathy and hopelessness are the end results of fear. Unhealthy fears must be addressed and ultimately discarded.

Condemnation – A filter of condemnation looks like accusatory thoughts toward yourself or those around you. When we hear God through condemnation it often disguises itself as correction or discipline, giving the false sense of holiness. Condemnation is a trickster in that it disguises itself in the voice of a concerned father, but condemnation will spank you on a whim and send you down the road of lies and betrayals. If condemnation is allowed to run wild, it will result in a mindset of unforgiveness, anger, bitterness, criticism, and unhealthy guilt. Lenses of condemnation must be removed for a clearer vision for God's conversations with us.

There is no room for those things in your sacred space when you are practicing His presence. When I say practicing His presence, I am referring to the daily indwelling and conscious living with the Father, Son, and Holy Spirit. When you are living with judgments like those listed above, your ability to hear and believe God will be clouded, not only for yourself, but for those you encounter. Those filters keep you from loving and being loved.

We need to learn to clear those things away and cultivate a different atmosphere. Then, we definitely want to protect it from things that would come to clutter it again. Think of it as a garden that needs a space; it needs to be tilled, planted, watered, and maintained. Your spiritual life is the same way. It is a joy that will bear much fruit and flowers.

We can exchange the negatives and receive the positives. We can live our lives free and clear. We can remove old distorted goggles and receive 20/20 vision again. We have to know that we are chosen, good, holy, desired, and in full connection with Him regardless of time and space. You were planned for, foreknown, and loved.

The Collector

My husband and I received a call from some friends of ours to go pray for a woman and do a house cleansing. The woman, I will call her Sue, was experiencing some unusual supernatural activities in her home. Before we entered the home, one of the team members had mentioned that Sue had an item in her home, insisting it was part of the problem. It was an astrological diagram that someone made for Sue. One team member wanted us to make her get rid of it. We told the team member we didn't work that way. We didn't make people get rid of anything.

When we entered Sue's home, we noticed that it was filled with art from all over the world. We asked her about her art and she stated that she was a collector. She told us that the team member already informed her of the astrological piece being a problem and she asked us what we thought. We told her we didn't have an opinion one way or another and we would just begin with prayer and ask the team what they heard from the Lord.

While we were in prayer, my attention was being drawn to one part of the room where a Buddhist goddess idol was sitting. When I looked at the object, it winked at me. I had to rub my eyes, I thought I was just tired or something. She kept winking at me, as if to mock me. I didn't say anything or do anything about it. I just waited. When the time came for the team to share what they heard, another team member said the idol was drawing her attention also.

We asked Sue where it came from and she said she found it in a small shop in Asia in a back room, in a closet where the owner had it stored for years. It was old and dusty. The owner said she could take it with her if she wanted it. Sue said she was attracted to it from the moment she saw it. She didn't want to get rid of it. We told her she didn't have to do anything she didn't want to do. We told her we could break any curses the object carried, and that it had no power over her or her home. Sue said she would do anything the Lord prompted her to do as long as she felt safe in her home again. We asked her if we could pray through all the rooms in the house and see what happens. She agreed.

We made our way around the living and dining room and then we entered the kitchen/family room area. As soon as I stepped in that kitchen I got a horrible pain in my neck and shoulders, really excruciating pain, and a headache. It was so bad that I stopped her in mid-sentence of her story. "Excuse me," I said. "Do you have neck and shoulder issues?"

"Yes! How do you know that?" she asked.

"When and how did they start?" I asked her.

"My neck issues started around the time I discovered my husband was engaged in pornography and affairs which ultimately led to my divorce. I caught him in this very room right where I am standing!"

"Are you ready to see this pain leave you right now? In a few simple prayers we can get rid of this neck and shoulder pain."

Of course the answer was yes. We gathered around her and led her in a few prayers and her pain left. She shook her head back and forth and moved in ways she hadn't been able to move in some time. She was stunned and then suddenly she said, "Hold on a minute!" and ran into the dining room we previously walked through. Sue ran back in carrying a huge art piece that was hanging on the wall.

"I feel so free. I want to get freer and I have to get rid of this. It is an art piece painted for me by an old lover. It has to go!"

As we walked through the house we discussed a few of the things she brought to our attention. We prayed a little and talked a little. We told her she had all authority over all of those things. She had the authority to choose whether to give things away or destroy them. It was between her and Jesus. Sue was feeling empowered and no longer a victim.

There were some things Sue received that day in exchange for the lies she believed in, the lenses she was seeing through, and filters she was interpreting from.

Presence – Sue had a radical encounter with a good God. The Holy Spirit dwells inside of all of us twenty-four hours a day, and seven days a week. Sue got in touch with the Spirit inside of her.

Peace – We live in peace with God and peace is a fruit of the Holy Spirit's indwelling presence. Sue found peace that day.

Identity – Knowing who we are in Christ and all the benefits that go along with being in Him are ours. Sue found a new sense of identity and authority over herself and her space.

Inspiration – The ones who wrote what we know today as the Holy Bible were inspired. The Word is not only a written book that was inspired, according to the scripture, but the Word is a person, Jesus. He is our inspiration and our hope. Sue found a new hope that she could live pain-free and stay that way. Jesus made an appearance through revelation.

Acceptance – We need to know that we are fully accepted by God, cherished, valued, gifted, and wanted, and so are others. Sue discovered that she was a beloved daughter worthy of healing. She had already been cleansed and she knew it.

Authenticity – We are good enough just the way we are. Nothing can separate us from the love of God. We are free to be ourselves. We have the ability to operate through transparency, vulnerability, and openness. Sue discovered she didn't have to retreat into pain and isolation. People were not there to control and manipulate her, but love and validate her.

When we exchange lies for the truth, we will open up new avenues of communication with God and people. We can bring clarity and revelation in new ways. Our creativity is longing to be awakened and our sensitivities sharpened.

SOLUTIONS

The big question seems to be the "how" of healing. I don't want to create a formula as a broad-brushed solution to heal everyone. I believe the way we get there is very specific to each person and their need. However, the "Who" is consistent. We have a Healer and He is the greatest Counselor we will ever have. He has given us tools for our toolboxes to help us tear down strongholds and build foundations.

Jesus used different ways to heal individuals. Jesus encountered a man who was born blind. There was a question of who sinned, the blind man or his parents.

> *Jesus answered, "It was neither that this man sinned, nor his parents; but it was so that the works of God might be displayed in Him. We must work the works of Him who sent Me as long as it is day; night is coming when no one can work. While I am in the world, I am the Light of the world." When He had said this, He spat on the ground, and made clay of the spittle, and applied the clay to his eyes, and said to him, "Go, wash in the pool of Siloam" (which is translated, Sent). So he went away and washed, and came back seeing.*
> JN 9:3-7 NASB

Jesus used spit and mud, and then gave further instructions to see the healing made complete.

In another story a woman was healed by touching Jesus' clothing. He stated that her faith made her well. Here is the account:

> *And a woman who had a hemorrhage for twelve years, and could not be healed by anyone, came up behind Him and touched the fringe of His cloak, and immediately her hemorrhage stopped. And Jesus said, "Who is the one who touched Me?" And while they were all denying it, Peter said, "Master, the people are crowding and pressing in on You." But Jesus said, "Someone did touch Me, for I was aware that power had gone out of Me." When the woman saw that she had not escaped notice, she came trembling and fell down before Him, and declared in the presence of all the people the reason why she had touched Him, and how she had been immediately healed. And He said to her, "Daughter, your faith has made you well; go in peace."*
> LK 8:43-48 NASB

Jesus will meet everyone in the place they are and touch everyone in the way in which they need it. Also note, Jesus doesn't always have to be the one to initiate the healing. We can seek Him to heal our need and it will always look different.

THE GREAT EXCHANGE

One of the tools I have used to bring healing, for myself and for others, I call the Great Exchange. As human beings carry things that are not ours to carry. We walk around with lies, burdens, feelings or emotions, which, do not belong to us. Those things weighing us down can cause mental, emotional and physical torment. The Bible clearly instructs us to cast our cares on Him and to exchange yokes with Jesus so that our walk can be easy and light. (See 1 Pet 5:7-8, Mt 11:28-30.)

Asking for the guidance of the Holy Spirit, we can begin by speaking out and releasing all the falsehoods that have been weighing us down. We can—by a prophetic act of speaking—declare what is causing us pain and reject it. According to Isaiah 53, Jesus has already taken these things away permanently from us. The problem is, we either do not realize the depths of His work in reality for ourselves, or we have taken the burdens back upon ourselves to process and fix. It seems to have become a cliché these days to "just give it to God." Some do not understand just how available that transaction is. We can, through a prophetic act lay upon Him everything that burdens us whether we realize exactly what those burdens are or not. We can give back to Him everything we took back upon ourselves and exchange it for something else that is from Him. Good stuff! The form in which that transaction takes place can vary from person to person depending on specific instruction from Holy Spirit.

Mother with Cancer

A family came to see me one day and brought their beloved mother. Their mother had cancer. I'll call her Kim. Kim was not sleeping and having nightmares. She was elderly, frail, and quiet. Her son was doing most of the speaking for her, telling me her story of cancer and everything cancer includes. There was so much information it was hard to know where to begin in prayer with her. I began with asking, "Jesus, what do you want to do today?" I heard Him say, "I want her to make an exchange with me." I asked her, "Is there anything you want Jesus to have?" She quietly shook her head indicating no, in an effort to be humble and honor God. Then she said, "Wait." And then it came out loud and angry, cursing and wailing.

"I am angry, take my anger! I am tired. I am sick. Take it all, I hate everything..." Kim yelled and hurled herself around. The family looked stunned, she never did that before. It was completely out of character for her. She said there was more, but was stuck in communicating it all. I felt Holy Spirit nudge me and I heard a suggesting from Him.

"Write it down." He continued. "Kim is a list maker, have her make a list and write it down on that paper. Have her rip up her list and lay it at the feet of her son as if he were Me. I will give her something in exchange."

We did that. She wrote out a list of the things she wanted to be rid of: nightmares, nausea, fear, sickness, disease, weariness—all that came with having cancer. Kim was able to release relatives, doctors, and all who offended her. Her list was long. Jesus gave her a new list: truths, new words with precious promises on it. New identity, new dreams and scriptures were given to her in exchange that day. He gave her new sustenance to carry her through the next season. Peace was restored and prayers were answered.

The list was one form of how The Great Exchange tool works. My healing and Great Exchange looked different from hers, yet the principal is the same and the Healer is the same. Your healing may come through something other than making a list and laying it at the feet of Jesus by proxy. Your Great Exchange may mean writing your cares on a balloon and releasing it to the heavens. Your exchange may mean releasing a person and finding a new friend. The key is to give up something bad in exchange for something good. Whatever your journey looks like, you can be free. Your first step is asking Jesus what He wants to do. The answer may surprise you. The method may puzzle you, but the Healer will heal you.

Toni Imsen is an artist, published author, entrepreneur and corporate business owner. Happily married since 1990, she enjoys being a mother and a grandmother. Toni is an ordained minister and co-founder of multiple ministries in California. She continues to offer private ministry to individuals and groups. Continually creating works of art in various mediums, her passion is to cultivate creativity for the purpose of healing and transformation.

Web: www.toniimsen.com

Morning DJ
Seneca Schurbon

GOD SINGS TO ME sometimes. I'll bet He sings to you too. It comes disguised as that song that comes into your head for no apparent reason. Sometimes He can sound a lot like U2 or the Scorpions.

God is a prime suspect when you can't track it back to something you just heard on the radio or in a movie. For me it usually happens first thing in the morning, before my mind has been filled with other songs that I pick up here and there throughout the day that find residence in my brain. When you first wake up, you are fresh out of the spirit realm, whether you realize it or not, and you're still very receptive.

The first time I really noticed this and recognized it as God, I had just woken up and I was lying in bed praying. I got into a very worshipful state where I could feel Him hovering close and I could feel His heart melting for me. Then I heard the beginnings to "You Are the Sunshine of My Life."

I giggled and rolled up in a ball in the sheet. "Is that... Stevie Wonder? You mean God likes secular music?"

I sang back, "You are so beautiful to me." I threw in the bad high notes for the extra giggle factor. What a way to wake up.

The early morning wake up music continued, and I had an easy enough time accepting the love songs as being from God. Of course that jives with His character right? This part was fun. And I could even feel a relief as I left my boss's office for the millionth time in tears listening to "O-oh Child." But I was having a hard time with where it went next.

I started getting direction, strategy, and answers via the songs. Now those things are definitely my love language, so that was not the problem. I place a high value on this type of communication from God. But I felt that I was having to put a lot of trust into a way of hearing that I had previously not taken very seriously. I mean, it's just a song in my head.

One song was telling me something I needed to pass on to someone else. One of them was even telling me where someone was spending their afterlife. Beyond that, He was using rap and rock and even some German metal. It seemed nothing was off limits or too "unsacred" to use, and I'm as susceptible to fear of deception as the next person. I had hit my trust limit. I was questioning all this.

The morning after severe doubts, I woke up and heard the chorus of the Harry Chapin song "W.O.L.D." I would love to quote that for you, but I would hate to get Praying Medic into a copyright infringement suit. I'll just say it was incredible confirmation that left me roaring with laughter. You'll have to check it out if you don't know that one. God is so clever! Clever enough to make a believer out of me.

He also confirmed the heavy stuff by asking me to research an abstract phrase, and I've gotten much more comfortable with this form of communication.

Now that doesn't mean that I think every song in my head is from God. And it doesn't mean that I take the whole song as having His stamp of approval.

Generally the only part of the song that you're hearing is most likely the only part that you need to get. You can search the lyrics, and take what makes sense, but some of those songs have lyrics that aren't necessarily anointed. You might think of this in the way that certain parts of the Bible will resonate more strongly with you in certain instances. A song you've heard all your life and never particularly paid attention to might suddenly have new meaning in the right timing and context of your life.

This phenomenon has escalated to the point where the songs actually interpret my dreams. The most confusing thing about dreams for me is that the people are never who they seem to be. It's all so bewilderingly symbolic.

Last night I dreamt of a man on a platform speaking. I was there too: the innocent bystander. Then he disappeared and it was just me with a walrus who was making walrus noises in my ear. I woke up with the "what the heck?" question looming. Not even a second passed and I heard the opening line to The Beatles' song, "I Am the Walrus."

"Ok, I think I got it!" You know God was just having fun there. There would have been other ways to make that point. None as entertaining though. I've never liked The Beatles, but I searched Wikipedia over this lyric. Apparently John Lennon wanted to write the most confusing song possible, and this was the result. I bet he never dreamed it would be used by God to unconfuse me.

So why does He use secular music? Probably because Christian music has mostly been about us singing to Him. This is changing though. There is a sub-genre arising called "spontaneous prophetic worship" where the singer becomes a mouthpiece for what God wants to say. Lilyband, Reeni Mederos, and Joann McFatter are a few examples.

Still, I think secular music has done an excellent job filling the void, considering the sources. I mean Lindsay Buckingham singing about building you a kingdom because of a big love? Come on!

I know I'm referencing a lot of old songs. I think it's because those are the ones I can believe. I can hear "Just the Way You Are" by Bruno Mars and blow it off because I just heard it on the radio. And it's in that movie that my husband and all my friends like to watch over and over again. An old song that I didn't just hear seems more trustworthy to me. You might know differently and your belief system might give God more room to DJ than I do.

So if you get a song in your head and ask, "Where'd that come from?" Think about the lyrics. Does it sound like something God would say to you? Pay attention when you first wake up. Maybe a sticky note on the bathroom mirror to remind you to listen? And when in doubt, search the lyrics.

If you get a song with some derogatory or sexual content in the lyrics, don't freak out. It probably means that's not the part of the song you need to focus on. Usually it will just be the piece that runs through your head, but occasionally it will be the all-around intent of the song. I hope you enjoy the love songs, the encouragement, the strategy, and the revelation from your Morning DJ.

Seneca Schurbon fuses the natural with the supernatural in her company *Freedom Flowers*. She makes essences (not oils) for emotional healing and unblocking your spiritual gifts.

Additionally, Seneca teaches an online class that combines sound business strategy with prophetic insight to help Christian entrepreneurs launch and build their businesses. Pick up your free "Clues to Your Calling" worksheet at *www.yourdreamventure.com*.

Essense website: www.freedom-flowers.com
Business classes: www.yourdreamventure.com

Experiencing God's Voice
Ginny Wilcox

GOD'S GOODNESS IS THE SAME towards me today as it was yesterday; He doesn't change. What does change is my awareness of it. I don't live in a vacuum, I live in a Kingdom where the King speaks, and He speaks all the time. And, He's speaking to you and me right now.

It comes down to hearing God's voice for ourselves:

One thing we have been granted is the ability to hear His voice for ourselves. This may not happen immediately when we accept Christ as our Savior, but it can. Too often we begin by hearing His voice through others and never move beyond that. Or we've been taught that hearing the voice of God is only for the few elect among us. That simply is not true. So guess what? I'm here to tell you the Good News; you too can hear God for yourself! Actually, you need to hear God for yourself. And the reason is, we need to hear His voice in order to have any kind of relationship with Him. It's why He created us in the first place; He wants to interact with us.

If we want to hear God, the first thing we have to do is actually believe that we can hear Him. We have to believe and come to know that He is speaking to us all the time, and then tune in and actually interact with Him.

If we don't believe that hearing from God is possible, it won't be. If we think hearing from God is only for others, we will never develop the relationship we need, and He so desires. We will miss so much and maybe we won't hear anything at all because we're not expecting to or listening for Him. Our posture will not be leaning toward Him.

Some ways we can hear God's voice:

For me, hearing His voice starts with asking questions, leaning in as if to hear a whispered response. But I don't ask any ole questions; I ask specific questions, things I truly don't know the answer to. When we ask specific questions, we know when He answers them. How could we not? If I ask Him something I don't know the answer to and all of a sudden I know the answer, it follows that He is the one who obviously gave me the answer. And sometimes, it can be that simple.

Usually, a question that begins with "why" is not a great place to start. A better question might begin with "what" or "who." For instance: What are we going to be doing today? Or, who am I going to encounter today? Maybe an even better question would be something more specific. For example, "God, you know I'm having this issue at work. I'm asking for wisdom to know who I can turn for the answers I need to resolve these things." When a solution comes to a specific question that you had no answer for yourself, you know it was God speaking.

These types of questions invite a response and set our focus on what or who we may encounter that day. We will be looking for it, even expecting it.

How we hear His voice differs from person to person and from situation to situation. He's pretty creative and likes to demonstrate it.

Experiencing God's Voice

The actual hearing isn't always an audible voice as we may expect—although sometimes, it is. Most often it's an inward one, and even that can vary in tone. Our spiritual ears are not the same as our physical ears, just like seeing in the spirit isn't always the same as seeing with our natural eyes, even though it does happen. But both are ways in which God can speak to us. One time I heard God speak to me in such a loud voice I thought the people in the car behind me could hear Him too! His voice reverberated in my head so loudly that it only felt audible, although it actually wasn't.

Another way God speaks to us is through a picture or vision. Several years ago as I was ministering at the International Association of Healing Rooms ministry, I saw a picture over a woman I was praying for. As I closed my eyes I suddenly saw a broken cistern and knew it was a picture of her. It was a very brief image that only lasted a second or two but it was enough to for me to know how to pray. A word of knowledge can take on many forms, from hearing and seeing, to feeling physical pain. And these are only a few of the ways God speaks to us.

God also often uses my intuition to speak to me. For example, when He speaks to me via impressions, I suddenly know things that I didn't know prior to asking Him. Although it's not really discernible words, I know it's His voice because scripture tells us that His thoughts are not my thoughts, and what He just "said" or what I now intuitively know, is something I couldn't have known, but it's better than what I could have come up with. It often works like this: I'm seeking an answer for something or someone. I ask God the question, then the next thing you know, I have the answer.

When you work in the healing rooms, you do so as a team. As a team we would receive a form that the "patient" had filled out with their prayer needs and a little personal information. The form had things like, their name, marital status, religion, prayer need, doctor's care, etc. Once we got the form, we would pray over it to find out what the Lord had to say about the prayer need and to get His strategy. There were times when we didn't feel like we had received any strategy at all and that's when asking these questions became very important. Either way, after we had prayed, the "patient" would then come in the room.

In a place like this, God loves to pour out His love on those who have come seeking Him. It's a wonderful thing to be the vessel for this great love. When times came that I didn't know what to pray or even where to begin when standing in front of the person who came in for prayer, I would begin to ask God questions about them. I would ask God what He wanted to say to that person today, or how He wanted me to minister to them. I would ask Him to show me why they were in pain, or even what was the root of the pain, etc., all because I knew these people didn't come to see me. They came for an encounter with Him and for the healing that only He could do.

He demonstrated this to me many times. One Saturday, we were praying over a young man who had come in for prayer. We gathered around him and one by one, the members of the team began to speak encouragement and words of destiny over him. This went on for a while but the recipient wasn't acting like he was the least bit encouraged.

While waiting my turn to pray for him, I heard the Lord say, "Break the Eeyore spirit off of him." I said, "What, Lord?" He repeated it to me again and added something else. "Break the Eeyore spirit off, and impart the spirit of Tigger to him." That was very strange, but I knew I didn't imagine it.

When I stood before this young man, I didn't preface anything. I boldly did what the Lord told me to do. Everyone in the room laughed, except the person receiving prayer. I commanded the spirit of Eeyore to leave, and before I could even begin to talk about Tigger or anything else, he leaned in and wanted to hear more about what exactly an Eeyore spirit meant, because it resonated deeply with him, even if he didn't understand what it all meant. I actually didn't know what it meant when I first heard God say it either, so I asked Him. What He spoke was more in the form of impressions than actual words. Since I didn't know anything about this spirit before hearing God tell me to speak it, all I could do was open my mouth by faith and hope He would fill it! He did. As I opened my mouth, an explanation came forth. I told him it was a victim spirit, a self-pitying spirit, and it left him wide open to all the discouragements he'd been experiencing in his life. After telling him these things, I finished doing what the Lord asked; I imparted the spirit of Tigger to him. I spoke joy over him and freedom to dance and live with great expectation of what God was doing in his life. His whole countenance changed. He was open and happy and no longer sad and heavy-leaden. Joy was bubbling up and out of him. Of course everyone was still laughing in the room, but it was for a different reason now; joy had come down to stay. As a side note, every time I encountered this young man, I called him by his new name; Tigger, and I honestly can say, Tigger is who he is.

Another time we were praying over a woman, whom we all knew. This person told us she wanted prayer for addiction to be removed, but would give no details as to what the addiction was or any other specific needs. It was strange in that she seemed to not trust us with her "secret," so I assumed it was shame operating and keeping her from a place of trust.

Our prayers were going nowhere. No one seemed to be getting any revelation or specifics on how to pray for her. While I was doing my part by interceding, and seeking God for what He wanted me to say or pray over her when my turn came, I heard the Lord say, "Tell her your testimony; tell her about overcoming addiction yourself."

When my turn finally came, I stood in front of her and said, "I have no idea what your addiction is, nor does it matter, because God wants to heal you right now. And, God told me to tell you my testimony about quitting cigarettes; He felt you needed to hear it. "When I said that, her eyes got huge! She asked me how I knew, who told me her secret? "Well, God did, of course," I said. So I told her my testimony about quitting smoking and the changes I made in my life so that it would remain gone. I then prayed for her to have the same overcoming spirit. I declared that my testimony would become the spirit of prophesy in her life and the spirit of addiction would depart from her and she would gain freedom over it.

When God spoke to me about sharing my testimony, I knew it was Him. I wasn't even thinking about overcoming cigarettes, it hadn't even occurred to me. I was expecting to hear about some deep terrible sin or something. So much for my imagination, that wasn't on God's heart at all.

After asking/praying for these things I would usually get an answer, as indicated in the stories above. The answer never came in an audible voice, but instead it would come as a knowing in me. Once I started ministering and praying with this knowledge, other things or information would begin to flow out of me that I had had no knowledge of prior to asking. This is how a word of knowledge works.

Sometimes I would receive knowledge or information that was an answer to something someone needed, but to me it didn't make much sense. And because I was in a position of hearing God for them and depending on His revelation, I would by faith, begin to speak out the things I had heard. Soon after, the Holy Spirit would begin to flow through me and more and more revelation would pour forth.

These words were things only Holy Spirit and the person receiving prayer knew and there was no way I could have known them without God telling me first.

Hearing God for those around me is a wonderful thing, but often when He speaks, it's for me alone. He wants to be involved in every aspect of my life, and sometimes, He wants to have a conversation with no agenda or teaching. He wants to talk and spend time with me.

During these times, He speaks to me through teachings and things I read, like books, blogs, and scriptures. Most times, I wouldn't even be articulating a question, but was simply pondering something in my heart, and the answer would come up through whatever I was reading or listening to. At these times, I could almost physically hear Him smile. Don't ask me how that works because I don't have any idea, but hear that smile, I did.

I've learned that He is always speaking, but I may not always be listening. His voice is like a frequency on a radio station; it's always on whether we are tuned in (listening) or not. My desire is to be able to tune in and then rip the knob off so I never am in a place where I don't hear His voice. My joy is to interact with Him, and that involves hearing.

There was a time just a couple of years ago where I had been crying out for a spiritual mother or someone to mentor me. I had been teaching and equipping women through book studies for several years and was feeling inadequate to continue. I felt I needed someone to teach and equip me, one on one, so I could serve and teach others better. wanted someone to pour into me like I was pouring into them. There was no one to fulfill that role in my life at that time.

One day while driving home from work I was having a conversation with God, telling Him once again about my longing for someone to speak into my life. Actually, I was probably doing more whining than anything else, when suddenly, as clear as if He were sitting in the car beside me, I heard Him speak. He said, "What you are to them, I am to you. You teach, equip, and encourage more people than you realize. I am your teacher. I am your mentor and for this time, I'm all that you need." Wow, I heard Him so clearly it couldn't be mistaken for any thoughts of my own. He took my breaking heart in His hands and gently eased the pain. I was overwhelmed with His love. The fact that He would take the time to make sure that I knew He was there for me in my time of need changed me. Suddenly I knew it was true; He had been teaching me and sustaining me through it all. I guess we all need to hear encouraging words and be affirmed from time to time. And who better to hear it from than God Himself?

Hearing God literally has changed my life. Yes, I still hear Him speak through others, but there is nothing like a personal conversation with someone who knows you better than anyone else. He is my wisdom and my guide. If ever I'm lacking in either of these things, I know right away that it's me who has left the conversation, not Him.

He's speaking even now. Can you hear Him? What is He saying?

> **Ginny Wilcox** is a baker and a blogger living in Nashville, Tennessee. She worked several years as a healing technician in the Healing Room ministries where miracles happened every week. She blogs about those experiences and conversations she has with God while going about daily life. Ginny also blogs and is passionate about food and using it as a means to get people to gather back around the table for real face-to-face conversations again. She is a wife, a mother, a sister, a friend, a chef, a soapbox performer, an encourager, and a lover of Jesus. Her biggest desire is to see people free to know who they really are and be able to walk in that identity.
>
> Web: http://ginnywilcox.com

BIRTHING THE SUPERNATURAL THROUGH THE FIVE SENSES
J. D. King

I THOUGHT, *Is that you, God? If so, that's strange.*

While ministering with a team of leaders in a prayer service, I caught a glimpse of something unusual. A young woman came forward with what appeared to be a dangling, gold tube coming out of her nose. I had never encountered something like this in church before. Yet, as the hair stood up on the back of my neck, I recognized the unmistakable presence of God. As I tried to take in what was happening, the gold tube abruptly "vanished." Though not certain about what was transpiring, it was clear that I was having a "visionary" experience. What caught my imagination was confusing, but I knew the Lord was up to something.

Speaking to nearby ministry colleagues about the encounter, there was an uncertainty in the air. They didn't see anything and were generally uneasy with my report. While a lot of questions remained, there was still an underlying sense that God wanted to heal this woman.

As the service wrapped up, I approached the woman and asked if anything was wrong with her nose. She looked a little dazed and said, "As a matter of fact, my nose has been bleeding. I didn't even tell my husband about it."

So, with her permission, I began to pray in the name of Jesus, commanding her bleeding nose to come into alignment. The pain went away and her nose was completely restored.

I honestly wasn't ready for this strange encounter. At the time it felt like I was relying too much on a subjective experience. My Bible college training and sense of propriety were challenged like never before. Nevertheless, a visceral image that I only observed for a few moments cracked open the door to Kingdom advancement.

I am still trying to learn to apply this to my personal life and pastoral work. I desperately want to advance beyond the constraints of "religion" and have the Lord invade my imagination.

THE MIND IS THE DEVIL'S PLAYGROUND?

I understand that the idea of God speaking through the realm of the imagination doesn't sit well with everyone. I'm aware that a number of Christians are terribly uncomfortable with the realm of the senses.

I remember my childhood Sunday school teacher saying, "The mind is the devil's playground. You need to be careful with what you see and hear. If you're not diligent in all of this, it could send you to hell."

Later in the youth group, I was warned about the dangers of neon lights, popular music, and major motion pictures. More than once someone said, "Satan loves to use Hollywood and the arts to hijack the senses and turn the hearts of young people to the ways of darkness."

The way that leaders in my church counteracted this threat was to encourage the "dulling of the senses." One of the deacons said, "Why don't you get rid of television, dress more plainly, and learn to think more rationally?" The imagination, along with any deep-seated emotions, were deemed enemies of the gospel. According to this line of thought, what was needed was the neutralization of the senses.

Some of the concerns were justified. Satan has never been hesitant to malign things. In his attempts to distort God's purposes, He will stoop to any level. The devil enjoys highjacking the imagination in order to gain a foothold. In the context of all this, Paul warned believers about "vain imaginations" (Rom 1:21). So, we cannot afford to be ignorant of the devil's schemes in this area.

Yet, with that said, it's seldom considered why people have such vivid imaginations in the first place. Although churchgoers will often try to renounce their senses, the attempts are often to no avail. Humanity, whether redeemed or not, is inexplicably drawn to the visceral. While people are exhorted to pull away from the realm of the imagination, they are rarely able to do so.

I have always been captivated by a beautiful sunset or a haunting melody. Incredible beauty and wonder draw me like few other things.

I know some would consider this a tragic flaw, an example of great fallenness and sin. Yet, I see things differently. I believe that God intended for humanity to possess invigorated senses. He constructed men to truly feel and envision. From the time of conception, they were made to be cognizant of incredible realities.

BODY, SOUL, AND SPIRIT AT WAR?

As mankind was conceived in the Garden of Eden, God formed them as body, soul, and spirit. The characteristics of body and spirit are relatively understood, but the soul frequently requires more explanation.

This term is a way of describing the mind, will, and emotions. The soul encompasses more than just thinking and decision-making; it involves the broad spectrum of perception. Through it, man comes into greater awareness and understanding.

It needs to be acknowledged that the body, soul, and spirit aren't "warring components" as the Greeks envisioned,[1] but interdependent parts of the whole. Man wasn't designed to be carved up and compartmentalized. Theologians Walter Ewell and Phillip Comfort acknowledge:

> Man is a unity of body and soul—terms that describe not so much two separate entities in a person as much as one person from different standpoints.[2]

In a similar manner, N. T. Wright, the lauded New Testament scholar, fittingly describes the parts of humanity as simply a "differentiated unity." He confidently declares:

> My basic proposal is that we need to think in terms of a differentiated unity. Paul nowhere suggests that any of the key terms refers to a particular 'part' of the human being to be played off against any other. Each denotes the entire human being, while connoting some angle of vision on who that human is and what He or she is called to be.[3]

Despite reasoned assertions from scholars, a healthy understanding of humanity eludes many in the Christian community. Many churchgoers inadvertently misconstrue the New Testament. They insist that the soul is utterly decrepit and without value.

Rather than peering through a Hebraic lens, a Greco-Roman outlook is embraced. Gary Moon reluctantly acknowledges:

> Until recent decades the Christian theology of the soul has been more reflective of Greek (compartmentalized) than Hebrew (unitive) ideas.[4]

An example of the prevailing Greek outlook can be seen in the writings of Watchman Nee (1903-1972). He insists:

> All the works of the Holy Spirit are done through man's spirit; but the works of the enemy are done through man's soul. The Holy Spirit moves through the human spirit while the enemy spirit moves through the human soul. This is the basic point of difference between the operations of God and those of

the enemy. God's work is initiated by the Holy Spirit, but the enemy's work is commenced in man's soul.⁵

Sadly, this type of thinking pervades the Church. Numerous Evangelicals, along with those from the Pentecostal-Charismatic tradition, are unquestionably hesitant about the soul. While asserting the value of the Bible, its actual worldview and expressions are often dismissed.

THE SOUL RECONSIDERED

The Bible discloses that the body, soul, and spirit were designed to work together; facilitating relationships, creativity, and the purposes of God. The pieces of humanity, the "dust of the earth" and the "breath of life," were brought together to reflect the love and intent of the Heavenly Father.

After He finished, the loving Creator gazed upon His wonderful design and decreed, "It is very good" (Gen 1:31).

Sin ultimately distorted and marred humanity, affecting who we are at the deepest level (Gen 3:1-24). Yet, it must be acknowledged that the soul was no worse than any other component of humanity. All was equally damaged and all equally redeemable. The Apostle Paul confidently affirms:

> *The God of peace shall make all of you perfectly holy and shall keep your whole spirit, soul, and body without fault for the arrival of our Lord Jesus Christ.*
> 1 THES 5:23 ABPE

I don't believe that God intends for any aspect of humanity to be maligned or discarded. He is redeeming all of it and restoring it to its original purpose.

There are a myriad of reasons that the soul should not be rejected. First of all, beauty, wonder, and creativity are more than a youthful distraction. This is what provides motivation and inspiration. Can there really be any viable art or conversation without the seedbed of the imagination?

However, something greater is at stake. I'm convinced that the imagination is foundational to perceiving the mysteries of Heaven. This is rarely considered, but the soul of man was conceived by God to access visceral realities. The extraordinary way that our imagination gets caught up in color and sound are an aspect of its original design.

The imagination "sees" and "feels" what's hard to quantify. It's the place where the physical and spiritual intersect. Through what is envisioned and felt, heavenly purposes come into focus. I believe this reality was alluded to in the book of Job.

> *For God may speak in one way, or in another, yet man does not perceive it. In a dream, in a vision of the night, when deep sleep falls upon men, while slumbering on their beds, when He opens the ears of men, and seals their instruction.*
> JOB 33:14-16

This is more than mere poetry. It is depicting what happens to the imagination as the glory is refracted upon it. Just because much of humanity doesn't perceive it, doesn't mean that God isn't speaking.

BIBLICAL AND PERSONAL EXPERIENCE

After the encounter with the woman with a "golden tube," other visceral experiences took place. It was apparent that my perceptions had to change. The rationalistic impulse defining many of my previous experiences had to be discarded. It was time to peer beneath the surface and gain insight into what scripture says about imagination. My senses had to learn to distinguish between good and evil (Heb 5:14).

Many haven't taken time to consider how God communicated with individuals in scripture. Throughout the text, they were always listening, dreaming, and envisioning. They actually wanted God to communicate through the inexplicable realm of the imagination. Unlike believers today, they weren't afraid to engage their Creator through the agency of the soul. The ancients weighed out every encounter, considering what God might actually be communicating to them. Unlike us, there was never an inclination to renounce their senses. They believed in engaging the imagination and were content to wrestle with the mystery.

In the following, I would like to explore ways that God invades the soul and briefly reflect on a few of my experiences. I am learning that believers are called to live our lives like the ancients. God has so much more to say to those who have ears to hear (Rev 2:7).

SIGHT

Throughout scripture, visual realities erupted and revealed the mysteries of God's Kingdom. In one instance, God conveyed to Abraham the immensity of His covenant through the image of a smoking firepot and a blazing torch.

> *When the sun had set and darkness had fallen, a smoking fire pot with a blazing torch appeared and passed between the pieces. On that day the Lord made a covenant with Abram and said, "To your descendants I give this land."*
> GEN 15:17-18 NIV

It isn't just in the twilight hours that minds were invigorated. Visionary encounters also occurred in broad daylight. An example of this kind of exchange is observed in the life of Jeremiah.

> *The word of the Lord came to me: "What do you see, Jeremiah?" "I see the branch of an almond tree," I replied. The Lord said to me, "You have seen correctly, for I am watching to see that my word is fulfilled." The word of the Lord came to me again: "What do you see?" "I see a pot that is boiling," I answered. "It is tilting toward us from the north."*
> JER 1:11-13 NIV

The Prophet Amos saw a "plumb line" that confirmed God's intentions (Amos 7:7-8). He also witnessed a basket of ripe fruit (Amos 8:1-2) that revealed what was ahead for God's people. Seemingly normal images disclosed extraordinary realities as God communicated through them.

Peter would later catch a glimpse of a sheet filled with "unclean animals," signifying God's plan for redeeming non-Jewish people (Acts 10:9-16). In that same season, Agabus wrapped his hands and feet with Paul's belt, viscerally conveying the Apostle's grim future in Jerusalem (Acts 21:10-11). I first began to study these passages in response to my own visionary experiences. I wanted to comprehend what was transpiring around me. I knew that I needed to grow in the reality of the redeemed imagination and consulted the scriptures for guidance.

In one of my experiences, I saw an unusual shadow appear on the ear of a young man. I recognized that it wasn't in sync with the lighting and sensed that God was pointing it out. Immediately, I asked the young man if he had anything wrong with his left ear. He told me that he was experiencing infection that was particularly intense. As I prayed, the pressure left and he was totally healed.

In another situation there was a more dynamic encounter. During the closing prayer time in a revival service, a colleague grabbed my arm and I slipped into a deeper realm of the Spirit. Immediately I saw a blurred image of this man and then his mouth came into focus. I said, "Lord, I know this guy pretty well and don't think he's dealing with pain in his mouth." I sensed God saying, "Who mentioned anything about healing? I'm up to something completely different." All at once, I realized that this man was concerned about his ability to speak. He wanted to be better equipped to express his voice. As I prayed, he acknowledged a desire for greater confidence and strength. Through this visionary experience, I gained a window into the desires of a man's heart.

Like men and women in the Bible, I realized that exceptional things can be observed in the Spirit. Through pictures and graphic depictions, God will often clarify His purposes in the hearts of men.

SOUND

Hearing is another sensory dimension that I began to learn about. In one biblical passage, David was instructed to go into battle as soon as he "heard the sound of marching in the tops of the balsam trees"

(1 Chr 14:15). In another, the armies of Aram were defeated as they turned away from the nonexistent "sound of chariots and a sound of horses, even the sound of a great army" (2 Kgs 7:6).

When Ezekiel encountered God's glory, it sounded "like the roar of rushing waters" (Ezek 43:2). He also heard the clamor of an army coming together in the valley of dry bones (Ezek 37:7).

While being caught up in the Spirit, John the Revelator affirmed, "I heard behind me a loud voice like a trumpet" (Rev 1:10b). He went on to recount how he "heard a voice from heaven like the roar of many waters and like the sound of loud thunder. The voice heard was like the sound of harpists playing on their harps" (Rev 14:2).

These biblical accounts inspired me to listen with greater intent. In my own experience, sound has become an amazing catalyst for exploration. Much can happen in the Kingdom of God through the reverberance of a sound.

On one occasion, I was standing next to a pastor from the Netherlands and began to clearly hear in my inner consciousness, "knees." When I questioned him about it, he acknowledged that he had been experiencing severe pain on his cramped flight over to the United States. I prayed that the goodness and life of Jesus would begin to flow. Within a few moments all the pain left and he began to experience total breakthrough.

I had another encounter while ministering in a youth conference in Argentina. I began to go through the hall, praying for people. At one point I "heard" an unusual cacophonous noise. It was a conglomeration of voices, commotion, and the clambering of metal. It was actually quite disruptive.

At that moment I was advancing toward a particular group on the opposite side of the room and had to turn around to see what all this noise was. I witnessed a group of young people rapidly advancing toward me in fervent intercession. There was no yelling, no swords, or anything that would produce this imposing sound. I could only describe it as an astonishing commotion in the Spirit. You don't have to be too intelligent to sense that God was up to something in this situation. I began to pray and the fire of God began to fall. Through a fierce sound, I was picking up on what was going on in the Spirit.

I discovered that God can reveal His purposes through captivating sounds. This is a vital part of the redeemed imagination.

TASTE

I also began to see in the Bible that God communicates to us through taste. Job subtly reminds his readers that "The ear tests the words it hears just as the mouth distinguishes between foods" (Job 12:11). We see that the taste buds assist in drawing significant distinctions.

Throughout the Bible, there was an invitation to savor the wonderful things of the Lord (Ps 34:8; Heb 6:5; 1 Pet 2:3). The Psalmist exclaimed the following to God:

> *How sweet are your words to my taste, sweeter than honey to my mouth!*
> PS 119:103 NIV

This may sound strange, but there is an unrivaled "flavor" expressed in God's unfolding purposes. There's a natural tendency to turn this into a metaphor, but it's more than that. We find compelling accounts in scripture where God revealed strategies through the realm of taste. One of the better examples of this is found in the experience of Ezekiel.

> *I opened my mouth, and he gave me the scroll to eat. Then he said to me, "Son of man, eat this scroll I am giving you and fill your stomach with it." So I ate it, and it tasted as sweet as honey in my mouth.*
> EZEK 3:2-3 NIV

Centuries later, John the Revelator had a similar experience. As he encountered the Lord, he was also invited to "eat" a heavenly scroll.

> *I took the little scroll from the angel's hand and ate it. It tasted as sweet as honey in my mouth, but when I had eaten it, my stomach*

> *turned sour. Then I was told, "You must prophesy again about many peoples, nations, languages and kings."*
> REV 10:10-11 NIV

Prophetic destinies are sometimes revealed through the palate. Unexpected flavors can reveal the purpose and intent of God.

A few years ago I was ministering in a small Pentecostal church in Iowa. When it came time for prayer, I interacted with people in the altars. It was obvious they needed something from God.

When I came up to a middle-aged woman, I knew something was wrong. My throat began to get "dry" as I perceived some of the mounting problems she was experiencing. In fact, I began to get something like a "metallic flavor" in my mouth. I literally "tasted" what she was going through and was able to more dynamically pray for her. As more of God's presence came upon her, the bitter taste slowly began to leave my mouth.

I was astounded to observe in scripture the ability to know God's plan through taste. As one has oral sensations like this, it enables strategic insight and application. This is an unusual expression that I am learning more about.

SMELL

Perceptions through nasal passages are another aspect of the imagination that God utilizes. Throughout the Bible, the Lord actively employed fragrances to communicate His intent and purposes (Gen 8:21; Ex 30; 35:28; 37:29; Lev 1:9; 2:2; 3:5; 4:31; 6:15; 8:21; 23:13; Num 15:14; 18:17 28:2; 29:2).

In one instance, anointing oil, made with cinnamon, cassia, and other spices, was used to consecrate the furniture and utensils of the Tabernacle. This aroma would be an active part of what the people encountered as they entered into worship (Ex 30:22-29). Even the priests, who guided the intercession, possessed garments "fragrant with myrrh and aloes and cassia" (Ps 45:8).

In several places in scripture, man's rebellion became punctuated by putrid smells (Ex 16:20a, Isa 3:24, Amos 4:10). However, faithfulness and devotion was portrayed as releasing a fragrance "like the cedars of Lebanon" (Hos 14:6b).

In the New Testament, Paul speaks of Jesus presenting Himself before God as a "fragrant offering" (Eph 5:2). He also speaks of generosity as a "sweet aroma" (Phil 4:18). Beautiful scents were intended to permeate redeemed creation. The wafting of a sweet aroma was likened to the spreading of Jesus' great beauty and wonder.

> *Thanks be to God, who always leads us in triumphal procession in Christ and through us spreads everywhere the fragrance of the knowledge of Him. For we are to God the aroma of Christ among those who are being saved and those who are perishing. To the one we are the smell of death; to the other, the fragrance of life.*
> 2 COR 2:14-16 ESV

As I had unusual experiences with fragrances, I knew that I had to comprehend what the Bible was disclosing. Smell was not an expression that I had ever associated with ministry. So, these passages opened up the possibility of divergent encounters.

On one occasion an older woman approached me in a healing service in Canada. I had no idea what was going on with her, but I immediately caught an unpleasant odor. I was somehow aware that something was going on in her body. As I picked up on what smelled like "putrid flesh," I asked if she was being afflicted with cancer. She was quite surprised that I knew. I was already cognizant of her need before she even spoke because of what was triggered through smell.

On a different occasion I stumbled upon a strange odor in Oklahoma. I was praying for people at the end of a service when the atmosphere suddenly shifted. A group had just entered the sanctuary and caused a small disruption. As I approached them, I caught wind of a peculiar smell. One, in particular, looked rather unkempt. Because he smelled like "sulfur," I assumed he had been shooting fireworks. To be honest, I found the pungent smell a little disorienting.

As I engaged him, I quickly realized I was encountering darkness. I was unexpectedly picking up on the "odor" of the demonic. Diligent prayer ensued. As freedom came to this man, I realized that I did not pick up on his affliction the way I usually do. I perceived the underlying spiritual reality through the nasal passages.

I noticed that, in the Bible, God actively speaks to humanity through odor and the agency of scent. This is another way that He engages the imagination.

TOUCH

I also learned through scripture that physical sensation can be a means of guidance. Unusual tactile dimensions, as well as bodily impressions, can disclose realities that were previously unknown. Touch is another pathway of insight.

The stirrings of the Spirit often influence the physical realms of men. Job makes reference to this reality, disclosing the following:

> *A word was secretly brought to me; my ears caught a whisper of it. Amid disquieting dreams in the night, when deep sleep falls on people, fear and trembling seized me and made all my bones shake. A spirit glided past my face, and the hair on my body stood on end. It stopped, but I could not tell what it was.*
> JOB 4:12-16A NIV

Elsewhere Isaiah was commissioned for service after an angel touched his lips with a live burning coal.

One of the seraphs flew to me with a live coal in his hand, which he had taken with tongs from the altar. With it he touched my mouth and said:

> *'See, this has touched your lips; your guilt is taken away and your sin atoned for.' Then I heard the voice of the Lord saying, "Whom shall I send? And who will go for us?" And I said, 'Here am I. Send me!'*
> ISA 6:6-8 NIV

Jeremiah and Daniel were installed as prophets in a strikingly similar manner. (Jer 1:9, Dan 10:16). The mighty hand of God touches His servants, cleansing them and positioning them for impact.

In the New Testament, the reality of physical touch is on display through the laying on of hands and other bodily expressions (Mt 8:3, Mt 8:15, 9:29, Mk 16:16a, 18, Lk 4:40, 13:13, Acts 28:8). One of the more notable occurrences was when a woman who had been hemorrhaging with blood for twelve years touched Jesus. Scripture declares:

> *Jesus realized at once that healing power had gone out from Him, so He turned around in the crowd and asked, "Who touched my robe?"*
> MK 5:30 NLT

I've had to wrestle through some of these complicated issues of touch as I've tried to understand these passages. The Bible reveals to us that God uses bodily impressions, sensations, and other physical realities to release something of who He is.

Sometimes, when there's a deeper move of the Spirit, I feel what could be described as "electricity" in my left hand. When this is encountered I will often start moving my fingers back and forth as I feel intense strength moving through the fibers of my being. This often becomes a tangible trigger for me to advance in prayer or some other expression of ministry.

Once, while ministering in Colorado, I felt an unusual sensation pulsating through my right knee and upper leg. To my knowledge, I had never experienced prayer-direction through physical impressions before. Although I was about to start my sermon, I knew that God wanted to heal somebody in the room. I was drawn to a teenage boy on the second row. I asked if he was having a problem with his right knee. He reluctantly acknowledged he had pain in that part of his body. I began to fervently pray, and in a matter of seconds, he was whole.

Through scripture and experience I became aware that Kingdom realities are sometimes instituted through the agency of touch. It is another way that the intentions of God become realized in the lives of people.

EMBRACING THE IMAGINATION

God is touching hearts and capturing minds through the realms of the imagination. I'm convinced this is the reason the soul was created in the first place. Much like the first man and woman in the beginning of creation, our body, soul, and spirit have been brought to a place of knowledge and encounter. Like the patriarchs and prophets, believers today are being positioned to encounter incredible realities through the sensory realm. We're learning to love the Lord with our heart, mind, soul, and strength (Lk 10:27). Rather than forsaking our design, we're truly embracing it.

At long last, many are beginning to re-embrace the ancient patterns. Traditional Western assumptions, with its deep skepticism and anti-supernaturalism, will no longer constrain the righteous. These men and women are open to all that God says and does. They have souls invigorated with the beauty and wonder of the Kingdom.

> **J. D. King** has witnessed incredible works of the Spirit in his travels around the world. In addition to writing a weekly blog post at *www.authorjdking.com*, he also serves as a pastor at *World Revival Church* in Kansas City, Missouri.
>
> Email: jdking@wrckc.com

1. "Ancient Greek philosophy insisted upon a distinction between the physical and the spiritual. The physical world, they claimed, was inferior and the physical body was the prison of the soul. The spiritual realm was the reality, and the physical world was a shadow of that reality." (Gilbert Sanchez. "The Nature of Man." Vallecito, California: Chalcedon Foundation. 2015).
2. "Soul." Tyndale Bible Dictionary, edited by Walter Elwell and Phillip Comfort. (Carol Stream, Illinois: Tyndale House Publishers, 2001): 1216.
3. N.T. Wright. "Mind, Spirit, Soul and Body: All for One and One for All: Reflections on Paul's Anthropology in his Complex Contexts." Society of Christian Philosophers: Regional Meeting, Fordham University, March 2011.
4. Gary W. Moon. "Soul." Baker Encyclopedia Of Psychology And Counseling, 2nd edition, edited by David Benner and Peter Hill. Grand Rapids, Michigan: Baker, 1999): 1148.
5. Watchman Nee. The Latent Power Of The Soul. (New York: Christian Fellowship Publishers, 1972): 42.

Hearing God
Christina Klover Inman

I CAN REMEMBER MANY times when I had nothing more to go by than a feeling or an inner knowing on whether or not I was hearing the Lord.

God has a way of making us aware of things; where we would otherwise overlook something or not see the significance in it, He draws our attention to certain aspects and details. He does not always show us the full picture, but it is through seeking Him in prayer and allowing Him to develop our perception of discerning His voice, that He teaches us how to be aware and sensitive of His promptings.

As we learn how to have a relationship with the Lord through prayer, we begin to learn how He will speak to us. The Holy Spirit is key to hearing the voice of God, because He is the Spirit of the Lord, both revealing the heart of the Father and bringing all things to our remembrance.

John 14:26 says, "But the Comforter, which is the Holy Ghost, whom the Father will send in my name, He shall teach you all things, and bring all things to your remembrance, whatsoever I have said unto you."

When we understand God's character, who He is and what His intentions are toward us, we can better relate to how He thinks of us. Some people, due to life's circumstances, take on the perception that God is angry with them, or that He is seeking to punish them. But God is a loving Father, and He has good things for us, plans for our life and a purpose for us to fulfill.

We must come to know His intentions towards us, and that His thoughts toward us are not to punish and condemn us, but to love and encourage us. We begin to identify Him as gracious and merciful. We begin to recognize His desire to forgive us and restore us. As we mature in this knowing, we become secure in the Father's love for us.

God created us with the ability to hear His voice. He desires to speak to us even more than we desire to hear Him. Psalm 46:10 tells us to be still and know that He is God. When we are still, we are quieting our mind and finding a place where we can rest and focus on His presence. Sometimes that quiet place is a room set aside for prayer. A quiet, gentle worship song can help bring your mind into peace, and help you to focus on Jesus. God speaks to us through music, even making the lyrics and the words of the song quicken on the inside of us, as if someone were speaking right into us. Worship can lead you into the deep places of your heart, where the focus changes from our thoughts and emotions, to God's love and mercy.

I can remember a time when my oldest child was just a toddler. It was a fearful time in my life, filled with anxieties and uncertainties of how I was going to take care of my children. I had been diagnosed with a medical condition, and had suffered with it for almost four years. One day in particular, I was going through the house with my daily routine of cleaning and putting away laundry. I had been crying most of the day, feeling weak in my body and overwhelmed in my thoughts. I had one of my favorite Christian music artists playing on the stereo, and was singing with the music as I was doing my household chores. All of a sudden, something happened in the midst of that song playing, one that I had heard a hundred times before. In that moment, as I was singing to the words of the song, my whole body began to tingle. My eyes filled up with tears and my heart just overflowed with a weeping that seemed to come out of nowhere. I lifted up my hands and just started to thank God, not even sure what had happened. God spoke to my heart in that moment that He was in control of the entire situation. His peace flooded over my mind, and I could feel the anxiety that had me so bound just melt away. His voice came to me in what felt like waves of peace washing over my body, with a deep, inner knowing that I did not have to be afraid. I am sure that I could have pushed it out of my mind, that I was just being emotional, but His peace was so refreshing, so inviting. I just wanted to stay there in that moment.

I could feel inside of me, God had touched me. Even though I was afraid of the current state of my physical body, I could feel a strength coming up inside of me that I had not felt for quite some time. I did not receive a manifested miracle that I could see, because the condition I was struggling with was internal. But I knew that in that moment, God had met me in my living room that day. It was a simple act of loving God in worship, and He responded to me with a knowing on the inside that He was not going to leave me to fight my battle alone. He had strengthened me and given me new hope to walk out the faith for my physical healing and brought about an intervention that would save my life.

Several days later, I continued with the prescribed medications, but with no improvement or relief. I woke up one morning so frustrated. I stood in my kitchen and realized, I had never actually seen the doctor, only his assistant. I wondered, if I called and asked to see the doctor, would his diagnosis be different? I called up to the office and asked to be seen by the doctor and a day or so later, when that appointment day came, the real issue was detected right away. My treatment for almost four years was for a stomach condition. Upon seeing the doctor, I was sent right away to have an ultrasound and found that I had a severely diseased gallbladder. I was scheduled for surgery right away. I could not believe that after years of intense pain, one thought while standing in my kitchen turned the whole situation around. God had spoken to me again and given me instruction. It came to me as a thought, but it was His thought.

Two weeks after the surgery, all the symptoms came back, worse than before. More tests were done and it was discovered that some of the stones had been lodged, and were affecting my pancreas and liver. A second emergency surgery was needed, and I was rushed off to the hospital again.

Little did I know, that day in my living room, God had spoken to my heart that He had me in His safe keeping. I would have never known what was going on inside of my body, or how sick I really was, but God did. He gave me peace that day, speaking to my heart that He was in control and I could trust Him. It was experiences like these that taught me how to begin to trust I was hearing His voice. As He built that trust in my heart, I began to open my heart up even more to Him.

For me, trusting was a big heart issue. Not just trusting that God could speak to me, but also trusting that I could hear Him. I found it difficult to trust people, due to my many experiences of disappointments early on in life. I had shut my heart off from letting people in and had made it a lifestyle to live that way.

Disappointments come in many shapes and sizes. Mostly for me, it was people that I trusted making promises that were not kept, not feeling safe as a child, and not believing or feeling that I was truly loved. My struggles with my self-esteem and how I saw myself, and how I thought God saw me became a reflection of how I saw my heavenly Father. The issues of distrust I had developed toward people became a barrier between my heart and God's voice.

For those that have been hurt and wounded and find it difficult to trust, allowing God access to these places of our heart is a necessary part of our healing. I had to receive healing in my ability to trust and believe that God loved me, and to learn to see Him differently. This is why I believe it is so necessary for us to know God's character and His nature. He wants to speak to us. He desperately wants to interact with us in our daily lives. He desires good for us, and He knows things that we cannot possibly know.

Psalm 37:7 says, "Rest in the LORD, and wait patiently for Him." We rest, knowing that the Lord has promised He will hear us.

We can't always see what God is doing in our lives, or even make sense of it. But when we believe that He is with us and that He will hear our cry, as well as cause us to hear His voice, we have hope.

Hebrews 11:1 says, "Now faith is the substance of things hoped for, the evidence of things not seen."

God has created each one of us with a purpose, and it is holding fast to that hope that is sometimes our only anchor in life. If we will encourage ourselves to remember God's love toward us, we will walk in a mindset that what God has prepared for us is nothing short of good.

Once we receive Christ as our Savior, our spiritual ears open and we begin to hear the Holy Spirit. God wants to use everyday situations to show us how to hear Him. "Spiritual ears" refers to a hearing that is beyond our physical ability to hear, and more of a "knowing" on the inside of our hearts. God wants good things for us, and leads us into sharing His goodness with others. For instance, if you know that your neighbor is going through a difficult time, and you have a desire to prepare for them a meal ahead of time, you can discern that God gave you that desire. Satan is not going to prompt you to show kindness to your neighbor. Kindness and compassion are consistent with God's heart for us, and in showing that kindness to others, we are expressing His heart toward them as well. On a basic level, we can know we are hearing God by discerning the thought, and checking whether or not it lines up with His loving nature and character.

Christina Klover Inman is a speaker, teacher, and former associate pastor and armor bearer. Through social media and public speaking, she shares her personal testimony of God's amazing grace in her own life, and passionately encourages others to see the beauty that can come from our brokenness, through His faithful promises.

Email: pastorchristinaklover@gmail.com

I Hear the Voice of God
Faith Living

"Go pick up the cup," He said.

Was I literally hearing the voice of God? This voice was completely audible.

I'm aware that when most people hear God, they hear Him inside their head, but I was hoping to hear Him this way at least once. The prophets of old had heard His voice and though I didn't want to be presumptuous, I asked God if I could hear it, too. However, I wasn't expecting the strange message I received.

It was a sunny and breezy day as we drove across western Kansas to a friend's house. My Hunny and I were riding in silence enjoying the rhythm of the waves across the golden wheat fields when I heard a soft, male voice speaking directly into my right ear. I flinched and looked over my shoulder knowing no one could be there since we were in a small pickup with no backseat. Immediately I turned to my Hunny and almost said, "Did you hear that?" but quickly changed my mind because his pleasant, dreamy expression was unchanged. He hadn't heard anything.

Was it God? Was it an angel? Was it my imagination? Why would God tell me to pick up a cup? What cup? Where should I pick it up? Was there anything in my mind remotely connected to a cup? What was I thinking before the voice spoke? I wracked my mind for explanations and came up empty. In frustration, I set the whole experience on the "not-for-sharing" mental shelf because it sounded wacky. It wasn't a wise message, or a warning, or even a direction. It was baffling and I didn't understand it.

We arrived at our friend's house and were enjoying our "catch-up" time together when my Hunny mentioned how much he liked the coffee cup she'd put his coffee in. Immediately she said, "You do? It's yours!" At which he laughed, "I didn't mean to take it!" But she explained that it was a gift from a boyfriend and when the relationship ended she asked God to bring a resolution regarding the cup. It saddened her to look at it, but she couldn't throw it out since it was special and attractive. "Please take it. I want someone to appreciate it." She explained.

I jumped out of my chair prickling with excitement. My message was an important answer to her prayer! We had to pick up the cup!

For years afterward, I was in awe that I'd heard an audible voice from God and that He'd given me an important message. The experience was a cherished treasure.

Years went by and I hadn't heard an audible voice again. I wasn't pursuing audible anymore. Now I simply wanted to hear from God without any doubts that it was Him. Somewhere I got the idea to start talking to Him. So I began doing this as I drove around Denver doing my part-time, semi-retired job as a courier. I chatted to Him about every thought and masked my conversation publicly with the Bluetooth I wore. If someone looked at me weirdly, I'd point to the Bluetooth and they'd assume I was in a conversation over my phone. I'd chatter to

Him like I would a friend. Should I have lunch here or there? Should I turn into this driveway or that? What should I wear tomorrow for work? After a few days of doing this, I began to hear answers. The voice was so soft I nearly ignored it. It was inside my head, and sounded similar to my own thoughts, yet I hadn't created this answer. I hadn't imagined what my answer would be. I was simply babbling and this answer simply came—immediately.

Being accustomed to "head chatter," I had almost blown it off as part of the noise. But something caught my attention. This was different. It was a direct reply to my question and not the kind of reply I would have made. I hadn't created it and it wasn't constructed in my imagination.

Imagination usually feels familiar. I recognize it as mine. I do the drawing and creating. Usually.

This was pointedly and obviously coming from another mind. The answers weren't my thoughts. I pulled over to the side of the road and stopped to breathe deeply for a minute because it freaked me out a bit.

Was God finally answering my request to communicate?

After a few moments of calming breaths, I asked another question and immediately another answer popped into my head. I continued talking and more responses came to my mind freely as though I had dialed into a working frequency.

Continuing on my route, I tested this new thing. I stopped asking questions for an hour to see if it was a fluke and would go away. But as soon as I asked another question, another answer responded.

Then suddenly I began to worry. Could I be talking to some other spirit, good or bad? Maybe I was speaking to the whole spiritual realm. I struggled with the concept of hearing God's voice, even though I desired it. Being a properly raised preacher's kid, I worried about going into dangerous territory and hearing deceitful voices that meant to lead me astray. I told my voice about this problem and He said, "Test Me." So I tried, but without conclusion because no matter what question I devised, I knew that evil had the correct answers, too. How would

I know who was speaking to me? Unresolved, I said to my voice, "If you are God, then You know what I need to believe. Help me."

This time the comment wasn't words. It was an impression. It reminded me of two friends having many heart-to-heart talks over the course of years. They begin to know and trust each other so deeply that there is nothing that can't be said.

I focused on the impression enough to ask, "Are you asking me to get to know you like I would anyone?" Immediately the impression was of someone nodding their head in agreement.

This voice was asking me to trust it before I was sure of its origin and that scared me. This was like jumping off a cliff. Then I realized this is how any relationship works. We have to take a risk and jump into it before we find out. It was logical, so I pulled my courage together and continued the conversations.

The voice answered questions simply. It didn't preach and it wasn't pretentious. No matter where the conversation began, it ended with an answer that was loving, wise, or peaceful.

Then there were the days I'd ask questions like, "God, what should I do about this? Am I making the right decision?" And He answered with "What do you want to do?" It was frustrating, like talking to a psychiatrist who answers a question with a question. Comically, I'd rephrase the question in a feeble attempt to pin Him down to a direct answer. That was hilarious. Could I outsmart God? Of course it never worked and I'd stand empty-handed pitifully sobbing, begging Him to tell me what to do.

Finally I'd consider what I wanted to do which lead to another series of validating questions. "Okay, I'm choosing this. Is that a good choice?" That didn't work either. Again, I'd sob and stomp my emotional feet like a child saying, "Why won't you tell me what to do?!"

"I am with you. Make your choice," He'd say. Eventually I understood that He refused to be my dictator. He'd given me free will and that fact was forcing me to be brave, trusting Him to be with me, always.

Even now, I forget sometimes and ask Him "What choice should I make?" but His silence is deafening and then I remember with a smile. I'm seated in Heavenly places beside Him where I can choose and then expect Him to always love my choice because it comes from the heart He placed inside me.

Then sometimes our conversations were simply about the menial details of life.

One day I had a delivery address with no suite number. The building was large, old, and unlettered. I stood looking at it baffled and asked Him to help me. I didn't want to waste an hour walking to each entrance and hallway only to turn around and try another. He said, "Go in this door. Now go up those stairs." I did, and at the top of the stairs was the door bearing the company name. Wow. I hadn't backtracked or taken one wrong turn. I was impressed!

In other cool moments He'd provide parking spaces in difficult places. Downtown is a challenge to a courier who wants to stop in front, dash in and be gone. But in the twenty-some days I ran that route, I only had to pay for a parking space once because I'd look ahead at my itinerary and tell God what I was going to need at the next stop. Often I would arrive just as the previous delivery vehicle was vacating the only "Loading Zone" space.

It makes me feel uniquely special to get these favors from the God of the Universe. But, the single most undeniable proof of His identity is the love He has for people whose actions are pure evil.

At that time, my challenge was Aunt Marge, who had drained my father-in-law's estate without disbursing funds to the inheritors. I had bound and rebuked this thieving spirit many times. It didn't work. She stole half the estate.

Afterward, I prayed all the correct prayers of forgiveness but my heart felt the deepest betrayal and victimization. God pieced together the family history, painting the picture of their various means of surviving the Great Depression. Aunt Marge had learned to become a trusted confidant to those who had money. With patience and attention she had become an Executor more than once and many inheritors never received their inheritances.

The moment God told me that He loves her as much as He loves me, my heart screamed. I pouted and couldn't speak to Him for days. How could He?

Then He reminded me of how frail humanity is all over the world and showed me the fear at the beginning of every evil human action. He said fear had driven her to this survival method as a young girl and she had come to believe this course of action was God's gift to her.

Even though I was appalled at the scenario, an incomprehensible measure of compassion grew inside me for the fearful torment she'd carried with her every day of her life. I knew this compassion that was growing inside me was His heart healing mine. He adored her right where she was, in the middle of the most erroneous conclusions and hurtful actions. His heart adored her with a tenderness only a Father could have.

No devil in hell or earth can fake that kind of transcending love and I finally stopped questioning the identity of the voice. This was truly the Creator of the Universe, and He was becoming my best friend.

One day His Spirit Presence gave me a magnificent impression. I will try to put it into words. "Just go with everything you receive from Me. Go with it and trust Me to be the one giving it to you. I am big enough to make Myself known to you. I am big enough to cover it if you understand it the wrong way. If it's your thought, I can make it My thought because we are One. Trust Me unconditionally and expect Me to be part and parcel with you always working in tandem. Besides, even if it somehow were your biggest error, I am big enough to make it straight."

Scripture says He makes our paths straight. We don't make them straight ourselves.

A few times I put Him on hold to check His words against scripture when they appeared to be contradictory, but research unveiled His truth hidden behind slanted translations and doctrines. He was patient while I did this, but my heart felt unexpected sadness in the end. I was disrespecting Him. Checking on Him wasn't unconditional trust. It was fear. And that revelation caused me deep remorse.

In tears, I told Him about my regret and He sweetly answered, "Take all the time you need. I love you and I'm not going anywhere. I will be right here when you have chased your insecurity to its end. As you do this, you will chase fear from your heart and finally be free."

He asked me to be brave and told me that in my research I would find meat to eat and bones to spit out. He came along each time showing me truth and each time setting me free of some unknown fear I'd been carrying. Oh, how I was humbled to walk into the unknown with only Him beside me.

Everything He said was true. Everywhere He led was right. He wasn't unreliable. Not once did His words result in error. God is capable of everything. We aren't required to check His validity and He isn't afraid to prove Himself.

So, I took the reins off and let Him be God. In whatever way He chooses to communicate with me, I will listen. It can be anything from spiritual to physical to unknown. In "awe and trembling" I give Him unconditional permission to share Himself with me. Laughingly, I asked, "Just please don't scare me, God. Please."

He agreed and that's when His messages became wildly interesting. Once I got a message through blackbirds and another time through an atheist. Sometimes a flash of inspiration or a picture would pop into my head. Sometimes a song came out of nowhere and played continuously behind my thoughts. Each message bore intensely personal meaning. It was a bit like having a Psychiatrist living inside my head, digging out the stuff I didn't know was there and then leading me so gentlemanly to its resolution.

An audible voice saying "Go pick up the cup" is no more heart-pounding than birds saying it's time to sell my house and move out of the city. He's a BIG God and He doesn't live within our boundaries. He speaks through everything He's created. It's point blank personal and nothing matches knowing the God of the Universe orchestrated a message only to me. Tears of humble reception overtake me. He's like a Lover coaxing us into submitting to His Love. "Come! Be My Love!" He says.

As our conversations continued, my "head chatter" grew quiet. My mind became peaceful and when fear spoke to me, I recognized it. In clenched hands or tight muscles I recognized it. It wasn't normal for me anymore. It wasn't home.

"I will live in the House of the Lord forever," David said. So I quickly run from fear and return home. It's the place some call "open heaven" or "His presence." It's a "sweet spot" where everything becomes heavenly, where I have favor and joy, and where I began calling Him, Father.

It's probably correct to say that I was hearing God's voice inside my "head chatter" all my life, but I was hearing other voices I couldn't identify and as a group they comprised "head chatter." Free floating, unidentifiable fear followed them. We take it for granted and assume it's normal, but it's not. We were made to hear our Creator. He inspires us. Other voices bring fear.

He defined my head chatter by identifying the voices. I heard them in the night, and yes, they were frightening for a while. I commanded them to leave and that worked, but sometimes it took hours to finish. Then I'd be tired the next day. As I was wondering if this would go on forever, Father said that simply turning my head to face Him was the greatest weapon I possessed. His voice is all-encompassing compared to others. I can go inside it and be safe. They may be speaking, but what is that to me? They are hollow, emptiness, and will leave for lack of attention. I give my ear only to the voice of my Beloved.

Nowadays when someone says they can't hear God's voice, I suggest my exercise. Start talking to Him about everything throughout the day. He hears all thoughts and is a participant in every action. He WANTS us to know Him. He's big enough to make it happen and teach us how it works.

I could have lived my life with head chatter, and never found the source of my fears. I could have continued getting my guidance from other

I Hear the Voice of God

people who hear God. No one said I had to find the courage to rock my status quo. God would love me just the same. But, I was never sure if those people were really hearing God. How would I know unless I heard Him myself? And as for status quo? Well, it resembled the definition of insanity—doing things the same way but expecting a different outcome.

Ironically, we all seem to hear His voice at the time of death and that's accepted in our society. Hospice nurses see it all the time. Our spirit knows the voices around us. They may be angels, or may be God, Himself. I made the unnerving observation of recognizing God's voice in some words from a bipolar schizophrenic. She also heard other voices and sometimes thought they were God too. The identities were wildly mixed up like soup, but her hearing was completely uninhibited. I asked her if she knew God and she immediately got excited, "Yes, I do! We speak all the time!"

I agree this could prompt one to shut down this conversation and run for the hills, choosing never to identify any voice. But when His voice took precedence inside her mix, it was the only time her words were profoundly, even wisely sane. I was glad that He was still speaking, even in her soup. It comforted me on her behalf. She was not shut out from His presence. No one is.

We villainize hearing voices in our modern day because so many voice-hearers have demonstrated murderous, chaotic results by shooting children in schools or people in restaurants. But there are many voices, and if we close the door to all of them, we also close the door to God and leave ourselves without His guidance and companionship. It's ironic to me that sometimes other cultures and religions don't have this fear and accept God's voice as normal for everyone.

It's a journey, a process. Some would call it either an adventure or pure insanity. Regardless, I'm grateful He gave me the courage to face my internal struggle and simply say, "I want to hear You, God!" It's ironic that I didn't know He was like a lover eagerly awaiting an invitation to converse with the love of His heart. He was more than ready.

The biggest challenge for me now, is explaining this to other people. Hearing from God sounds wacko, yet ironically we consider ourselves normal by living with head chatter. There is a difference and the courage to unwrap the gift is warranted.

Recently I watched a show about hearing-impaired people and it was the perfect example of how hearing God changes things. Hearing anyone changes things. Our quiet chuckles and silent snickers mean something in a conversation. We understand a sigh or a moan. It generates empathy and we suddenly connect.

The Cochlear implant device can create hearing and when the device is turned on for the first time, the reactions of patients demonstrate how sound connects our emotions.

While a written sentence can be read with understanding, the inflections of a voice can change the meaning. This is the problem we face in basing our faith on a written word, even when it is the Bible.

We, as authors, search for ways to assimilate emotion through descriptive words, but we can never touch the depth of a sob or a sigh.

So ironically, some 150 years ago, we created an icon of the Bible and labeled it the "Word." But, Jesus is the Word. His voice carried faith since the beginning of time before Bibles existed. Only in modern times did we think that hearing God's voice was mystical, and unreliable. We feared that our imagination or other voices might lead us astray, so we leaned exclusively on the Bible, thinking it would solve our problem. But it only exacerbated the problem by isolating our minds to head chatter.

It has always been the voice of God that changes us, even when we read the Bible. We forget He is not ink word on a paper page. He is real Spirit speaking to our hearts as we read and He continues talking when we lay the Bible down to go about our day.

I love the Bible as I love many books written from revelation and inspiration from Him. I also love God's voice in whatever venue He chooses. I recognize it now. It's personal and it's familiar to me. The most secure identity and completeness lives inside the voice of our Lover.

Hearing God's voice changes everything.

Faith Living was a preacher's kid who went searching for Truth and found that it required a heavy price even as it bestowed its glorious rewards. Her experiences became miraculous testimonies of victory and overcoming.

Faith's passion is to continue learning more about the practical aspects of victorious life in The Kingdom and how to live FROM that place daily. She explains the revelations and insights she receives simply so that anyone can share in the joy of overcoming that Father God has provided for us all inside The Kingdom.

Faith shares her journey on her blog and in her books available on Amazon and Kindle. She can also be found on Facebook under the name Faith Rockrimmon.

She lives with her family in the southern Colorado foothills.

Blog: www.faithlivingnow.com
Email: faithlivingnow@gmail.com
Amazon Author page: amazon.com/author/faithliving

You Can Hear God's Voice Clearly
Kevin E. Winters

FOR YEARS there has been a standard teaching in the church regarding the experience of hearing God's voice. It is what most would call a landmark teaching. It is a teaching that at one time in my life I wholeheartedly embraced. It was also all I expected to experience regarding the voice of God. That was until I had a dream many years ago. It was a dream that would shift my paradigm regarding the idea of hearing the voice of God. This dream would challenge my mindset and push my faith. It was a life changing moment that would lead to an incredible experience with God.

In this landmark dream I was on the phone conversing with a woman. As the dream progressed and our conversation continued, I decided to minister prophetically to her. At that point I started to feel impressions in my spirit. All of a sudden words of knowledge began to flow to my mind. As the words of knowledge flowed, I started to notice something strange. I noticed that the deeper I tuned into God, the more audible His voice became. I remember thinking to myself, "How is this possible?" It left a strong impression in my mind upon waking.

At that particular time in my life I was learning how to minister prophetically by faith. So I did not immediately make the connection with what God was really showing me in the dream. I was more excited by God challenging me to step out to minister prophetically by faith. If I am to be completely honest, the idea of hearing God clearer than a still small voice just seemed too surreal to take seriously.

However, that would not be the last time that God addressed me about the voice of God and hearing clearly. It would be later that year as I sat down to write my book, *God is that You, Me, or the Devil*, that God would really begin to open me up to this truth.

I remember that day so vividly. I was sitting at my computer working on the chapter that defines the ways God speaks. I had already written about dreams and visions and I was just starting to write about the "still small voice." As I sat writing about this subject, God suddenly started talking to me about what really happened with Elijah and the still small voice. He started challenging me that we could hear a clearer more discernible voice. Initially I reacted with a sense of wonder. It was the same feeling that I first felt when God presented this idea to me in the dream. I had always been taught that God speaks in a still small voice. Now He was telling me something different. It was very challenging to believe and I struggled to let go of my old way of thinking. This inner wrangling really hindered my ability to write about the subject. People had taught me an age-old truth, and God was telling me something different. At first, I tried to mesh God's idea with the old idea, but that did not work. So I moved on to writing other parts of the book. I know that it seems obvious who I should have believed, but I didn't believe God.

I held on to this truth for years, never sharing it with anyone. I believed it, I could explain it, but I just didn't yield to it. God however, did not give up on me regarding this issue. This time God presented it to me in a unique way. One morning as I awoke from sleeping, I heard a song in my heart. There was nothing strange about this experience.

I usually wake up with the sound of faint worship in my heart. This time however, I heard a familiar song. Even though I was familiar with the melody I did not know but a few of the lyrics. So I searched online for the lyrics, found the song, and downloaded it to my phone. Then I sang along as the day continued. Later in the day I started to notice that the song in my heart was becoming progressively louder. I felt like Moses when He saw the burning bush. The Bible says that Moses turned aside to see why a bush on fire did not burn. I too was turning aside to see what was happening inside of me. As I gave my attention to the song I noticed that the song was loud, distinct, and clear—it was audible. This lasted for two weeks. During that time my days and nights were filled with audible worship. Then it all came to an end and the music I heard in my heart had a new quality. Once it returned to a normal volume level it appeared to be more distant than low in volume. This was all very fascinating to me. This however, was not the end, because something else had occurred during the time of audible worship—God started talking and it was just as He had shown me in the dream. The more I tuned in to hear, the clearer His voice became. It seemed audible.

MY SHEEP HEAR MY VOICE

Even though my main idea for what I am going to share moving forward comes from 1 Kings 19, I think it is plausible to make the case for hearing the clear voice of God. Jesus says in John 10:27, "My sheep hear My Voice." He clearly lays out for us that it is not only possible but also a right of the believer to hear the voice of God. Not only is it a possibility and a right, it is one of the most common experiences in all of scripture. When reading the Bible you are going to see the phrase "and I heard a voice" or "in a dream a voice said." Each time it is a clearly discernible voice. In Acts chapter 10, the Apostle Peter fell into a trance and heard a voice speaking to him.

WE HAVE SENSES

Most people do not consider the reality that we have spiritual senses. Hebrews 5:14 tells us that strong food belongs to the mature who have had their "senses," not "sense," exercised to discern good and evil. Jesus likewise in Matthew 13:15, points out to us issues with our "eyes" and "ears." Most of us only focus on developing the sense that God opens up to us first. When I first started hearing the voice of God I experienced Him in three ways. I felt the voice speaking to me. I heard a clear voice speaking, and I saw in dreams and visions the voice of God. While these are all the valid ways that we hear, they are all distinct ways that we experience God through our various senses.

Most of us understand what it is to "feel" the voice of God. It is probably the most common experience of all. It is perception at work. The Bible says Jesus perceived in His spirit (see Mk 2:8). The Apostle Paul said, "Men I perceive..." (see Acts 27:10). This is our sense of feeling in our spirit.

Some of us "see" in the spirit. Again this is a common experience. Most of the Bible is full of dreams and visions. These images from God come through our spiritual eyes.

Last there is our sense of "hearing." This is also seen in multiple places in the Bible, but is rarely seen today. In fact it is considered to be an awe-inspiring experience when it happens, because it rarely does. Most of us have become accustomed to "feeling" and "seeing" and we have neglected to develop our last sense—our spiritual ears.

There are two distinct ways that the audible voice of God is heard in the Bible. First, we may hear an external voice, such as that heard by Moses. Second, we may hear an internal audible voice, such as what was heard by Peter in his vision on the rooftop, or like Ananias when Jesus spoke to him regarding the Apostle Paul. When I say we can hear the clear voice of God, I am referring to an internal audible voice.

Some of you no doubt, think I am referring to what we hear with our natural ears. But, I am referring to what we hear with our spiritual ears. This is an important distinction to make. The way we hear with our physical ears does not equate to how our spiritual ears perceive sound. For instance, Daniel says in his experience with an angel, "and I heard the sound of his words..." (see Dan. 10:9). He did not say the sound of his voice, but the sound of his words. The same is true of the voice of God. You are not necessarily going to hear a voice with pitch and tone, though it may appear that way. You will hear the sound of His words. It is really not that different from hearing a song in your head. Even though you may hear what you think are notes, you are not really hearing in the natural sense of the word. You are perceiving the sounds as they appear as impressions in your mind. The same is true with the voice of God. You will feel the sound of His voice and it may even appear to have pitch and tone. I have heard it as a gentle man's voice. In fact, I have heard it so clearly at times preaching to me, that when I go to speak for Him I merely repeat what I heard. It can be that clear!

WHAT REALLY HAPPENED

If we are going to progress into a new understanding of hearing the voice of God, we need to start from the beginning. So let's start by looking at what actually happened to Elijah when He heard the still small voice in the cave.

In 1 Kings 19:9-13 you will find that there are three distinct terms used to describe Elijah's experience with the voice of God. They are "the word of the Lord," "a still small voice," and "a voice."

In the passage, we are presented with a scared and tired Elijah who has just received a threat against his life from Queen Jezebel. The threat takes place on the heels of one of the greatest demonstrations of God's power mentioned in the scriptures. Elijah fears for his life and seeks refuge in a cave. While he is in hiding he suddenly comes into an awareness of God speaking to him. This can be described as perception. He felt the word of God in His heart. During this initial encounter, God questions him regarding why he is in the cave. At this time God also instructed him to go to the entrance of the cave (1 Kings 19:11). Elijah however, remains where he is. Everything else that follows happens on the heels of this information.

While Elijah is still in the cave, the Lord passes by and Elijah sees various experiences at the entrance. One of these experiences was described as "a still small voice." It was at this moment that Elijah obeyed God's initial instructions and went to the front of the cave. Upon arriving at the place he was initially commanded to be, he heard a clear voice. That voice repeated the exact same question as the "word of the Lord" which came to him in the cave.

What I am hoping is evident is the progression within the story. One, Elijah perceives that he needs to go to the front of the cave. Two, God is saying something that can only be described as a whisper. And three, as Elijah gets closer to where he is supposed to be, he realizes that it is God speaking to him. While this passage has been a base teaching for years regarding hearing the voice of God, you will notice that the still small voice in an attribute of a condition. You will also notice that the whisper has no clarity, but the voice does.

WHY ELIJAH HEARD GOD WHISPERING

So why did Elijah hear a whispering voice? There are four things that led to the whisper: disobedience; a lack of focus; spiritual warfare; and pain. I am going to discuss two of them in this essay. If you are interested in reading a more detailed summation, pick up my e-book on Amazon, titled, *You Can Hear God's Voice Clearly: How to go from the still small voice to the clear voice of God.*

Disobedience

One of the most evident things that we see in the passage is Elijah's disobedience. God had instructed him to go to the entrance of the cave. Then God Himself went to the entrance of the cave. Guess who was not there when God started speaking. Elijah's disobedience led to distance between himself and God and likewise, the voice of God appeared as a faint whisper.

Many times we underestimate the damage that disobedience has on our relationship with God. This happens to all of us. We all go through seasons or situations when the voice of God seems unclear to us. I used to say, God why are you so quiet? I would ask this question when His voice would seem faint and hard to detect. Then He taught me this truth in Elijah's experience. Now I can identify what is happening. Whenever the voice of God is unclear in your life, you may be in place of disobedience. Just like in Elijah's experience, when we are is a place of disobedience we are akin to being distant from where God wants us to be and likewise, His voice seems distant.

Lack of Focus

This is something that we sometimes don't consider. The voice of God is clear to those who learn the value of focus. Elijah's experience with the still small voice is symptomatic of his depression. His mind was on himself and his situation. He became self-centered.

The good attribute of the still small voice is that it calls us to a deeper focus. It was the still small voice that made Elijah explore and look deeper into what the whisper was actually saying.

So many times we miss God because we are not willing to take the necessary steps to get closer to His voice. The whisper is a call to keep looking deeper. You will find that this truth also applies to our spiritual eyes. Many prophetic people can attest to the reality of God using a faint image that became clearer and more focused as they kept looking. You will likewise see this in many visionary experiences in the Bible. Many of the prophets say such things as "as I was looking" or "I kept looking." What they are saying is that as they gave more attention to what they were seeing they were able to see more revelation. This truth likewise applies to hearing God's voice.

Elijah recognized the prompting of God, got up from his place, and dared to walk closer to God's voice. Moses does the same. He saw a bush burning with fire, but it did not burn. Then it says as he turned aside to see why the bush was not burning. As he got closer to what God used to get his attention. He heard a clear voice speak to him.

IT'S A PROCESS

As you can see; God spoke to Elijah in a voice. I understand that this is going to be hard for many people to embrace. However, you should know that learning to use your spiritual ears to hear is a process.

I said to God as He spoke to me about this issue, "Lord, how do we get there?" I asked Him this question because I was not hearing this way consistently. This was His response, "Elijah had to get up, and take the necessary steps towards the entrance." In other words, it's a process. Again Hebrews says our senses must be exercised "by reason of use." You will find this to be true with all of the spiritual senses.

CLARITY

Another thing I want to write about is the benefit of hearing the voice of God. In our study of Elijah's experience we see something interesting. When the word of the Lord comes to him the author is able to articulate what God said. When Elijah heard the voice at the entrance of the cave the author is again able to articulate what is said. But when the author writes about the still small voice, there is no clarity as to what was said. This happens more than enough times to a lot of people. They have a sense of uncertainty as it pertains to the voice of God.

One reason God wants to encourage us to push into the voice of God is so that we will not be so overwhelmed with uncertainty. The still small voice often times leaves people in the place of saying to themselves, "I think God is saying something to me." God wants us to know that we can hear clearly what He is saying. Again Jesus said, "My sheep hear my voice and I call them by name" (see John 10:3). That means we can expect to hear clearly.

CONCLUSION

In conclusion, I pray that I was able to inspire in you a deeper yearning for God's voice. The Church has been great at developing feelers and seers. Now it is time for the Church to realize that it is also possible to hear God's voice clearly.

You may obtain a far more extensive version of this teaching in my e-book, by the same title. I also have a book titled, *God is that You, Me, or the Devil?* In this book, I deal extensively with issues of discernment. It covers such topics as how Satan speaks; how to recognize deception; the role of the mind in the hearing process; what God talks about; how we feel when He speaks; how to position ourselves for an encounter; and so much more. It is 20 years' worth of insights that will change your spiritual life for the better!

Kevin E. Winters is a prophetic minister that has been walking with God for over 20 years. His passion is that you know God intimately, find His purpose for your life, walk in power, and that you be victorious in spiritual warfare. God has gifted him to teach and preach prophetically. His ministry is marked by the wisdom and insight that God has given him. To most that hear him he is considered a balanced source of revelation. He is also an author, a poet, an artist, and a visionary.

Currently, Kevin shares God's word through his online ministry. He can be heard weekly on YouTube, Facebook, and Periscope sharing with the world what God is saying and doing in this hour. By trade he a graphic designer and illustrator for the Federal Government. His hobbies include making music, creating art, and enjoying his family.

He resides with Tanya and their four children in Maryland. They are also long-time members of the *First Baptist Church of Glenarden* where they serve under the leadership of Pastor John K. Jenkins, Sr.

Web: www.doinglifeonfire.org
Email: doinglifeonfire@yahoo.com

SENSITIVE PEOPLE
Lori Orlando

I CONSIDER MYSELF to be highly sensitive, having a heightened sense of smell, touch, sight, hearing, and also emotions. I view it not only as my identity, but also as a gift, and God is revealing to me His purpose for such a gift. Although, for many years I didn't appreciate being sensitive and suffered a great deal for it.

God is Love and I am the daughter of Love. Everything ever created was created by Him and He has given His children authority to represent Him on this earth. To bring His healing love, His saving love, His redeeming love, His providing love, His resurrecting love to all of creation.

Over the years I have made some observations of the different ways God communicates His heart to me. This isn't to say that having these heightened senses and being aware that God is using them to communicate with me makes me any more special than any of His other kids.

He's our Dad, and He knows how to get our attention. He has given us eyes to see and ears to hear Him, so to me it's only natural that our senses would be supernatural.

These are just some ways He has communicated with me.

HEIGHTENED SENSE OF EMOTIONS

One evening a couple years ago, I became overwhelmed with a great sadness, and I just couldn't shake it. In my flesh, I wanted to leave Winnemucca and had zeroed in on a new place to live—Elko, Nevada. There are people I love there. I even began looking for jobs for my husband. It came on suddenly, and my response was of the flesh instead of the Spirit.

The Holy Spirit had given me the area to pray about, but instead of hearing that I was supposed to be interceding for someone else, I was trying to sooth my own sorrow, sorrow that in fact was NOT my own.

I received a call the next morning that a friend of our family had been in a car accident that same evening and died while being trapped in her car that had caught fire. This accident happened in Elko, Nevada. I missed this and a beloved mother died. I can't tell you how it feels to fail so badly. If not for God's grace, I am not sure I would even be here to tell you this story.

Sensitive people may have the ability to feel the emotions in a crowded room and be able to zero in on a specific person in that room. Or they can become so overwhelmed by feeling everyone's emotions that they are unable to focus on God's peace to see who He wants them to see. There's grace for that, and it takes practice to do the doable, but it absolutely can be done.

Recently I was experiencing a hectic day at the hair salon where I work. The phone was ringing off the hook and there were so many conversations happening all at once, I started to become a wee bit frustrated. Then one client in particular came in during all the chaos, but what came in with her was chaos multiplied. I couldn't ignore what was happening anymore. I focused on God to be my peace and then I began releasing His peace into the atmosphere. To do this, I had to intentionally ignore all the voices and noise and speak directly to Papa. I spoke under my breath and said, "Father, thank you that you are my peace." When I did that, peace took over me and quieted my nerves, then in my imagination I started to let that peace flow from me to everything and everyone in that room. Instantly, all the drama that had been carrying on all day stopped, and everything became calm. Even the woman who had come in, being hysterical with fear and anxiety began to breathe easier and calmed down, and I hadn't even spoken a word to her directly.

It is truly amazing how easy it can be to allow God's peace to take you over and calm you down, and then to let that flow through you to others. And that is His desire, to bring heaven to earth. I don't imagine heaven being full of chaos, do you?

HEIGHTENED SENSE OF SIGHT

Sensitive people with a heightened sense of sight are able to see the smallest details that others may simply overlook.

Another recent thing happened at work was when I spotted a prescription pill on the floor in a corner. This could have been a danger to a small child who may have picked it up and popped it in their mouth. My response was so effortless, yet it was a response to my Daddy to take care of what He wanted to take care of. He cares and we care because of who we are. Easy peasy.

A friend's experience:

I was talking with a friend recently and he shared a story with me about his own heightened sense of sight. He and his son were driving past a field and he spotted a very little boy wandering in that field. The field is next to the railroad tracks.

He and his son went to the little boy, who was far too young to be out there alone.

Although the little boy was afraid of my friend, who was a stranger to him, the friend was able to keep the boy from going closer to the tracks, where by this time a train was approaching.

He was able to keep him safe until the boy's parents who had been frantically looking for him were spotted.

We simply see and respond, either with action or prayer, which is also technically an action.

HEIGHTENED SENSE OF SMELL

Sensitive people with a heightened sense of smell are able to sniff out trouble, so to speak.

Once when my husband and I lived in Phoenix, I smelled a strong chemical smell around the area where we would park our car at the back of our apartment complex. Every time we would leave or come home, it was there. And when I asked my husband if he could smell it, he said that he couldn't.

I didn't understand how something could be so invasive to my smeller and yet it didn't even faze my husband. Was I losing my mind?

Then one day when I was at work, my husband called to tell me that two cops had been rushed to the hospital when they were overtaken by fumes from a meth lab nearby that had been raided, and they were evacuating our complex due to those dangerous fumes.

In this situation, had I known God was speaking to me and known that I had the ability to pray into this thing, those cops may not have been injured. I'm not beating myself up over it. I am merely recognizing the situation for what it was and the possibility of what could have been, had I done what I believe God was trying to show me to do. Hindsight can be 20/20 if one is able to look at the failure to act as having a purpose. It shows us that we are learning and growing. It gets us to pay attention the next time something similar happens, and it will. At that point, we will have seen this before, and can actually do something.

We have access to better than 20/20 foresight when we see with God's eyes and trust that we are indeed seeing accurately.

A few years ago, I once again began smelling a chemical odor near where we currently live, and this time I blessed the area. I didn't even suspect another meth lab, but I did feel an evil presence as I would walk by this area where a lot of activity was happening. I blessed the man who owned the property, and I thanked God for the ability to see, hear, and smell every offensive thing that was coming from this place. And then soon after, at that same property, another meth lab was discovered and raided. No evacuations this time. No injuries to anyone! Amazing!

HEIGHTENED SENSE OF TOUCH

As a child of God you may begin to allow yourself to feel what God feels in any situation where God means to then touch that person through you.

Sensitive people with a heightened sense of touch can also feel sensations like heat or vibrations when touch is involved.

You know how you're able to touch someone's forehead and feel if they have a fever? It's like that, but with a number of different things.

I do hair for a living, and I am able to sense with my fingers when someone needs a firmer or gentler touch and respond to their needs accordingly.

I believe that because it comes so natural to us to be able to touch and feel other's needs, we may take for granted that this is God communicating with us and responding through us.

I remember an occasion where I could feel the rolling of the earth beneath my feet during an earthquake that was happening nearly 200 miles away. It was another instance where I wasn't sure what was happening until later. But being made aware that He is speaking in such things and that I can trust I am feeling accurately can take away my need to figure out what is happening and hear what God is telling me at that moment.

HEIGHTENED SENSE OF HEARING

For me my favorite thing to be sensitive to is hearing.

A couple different times I have been able to hear little baby frogs trying to find their way out of my screened in porch where they have become trapped, trying to get outside to water. And because I have heard them, I have been able to help them out.

I have been able to hear insects trapped beneath objects too big for them to move in order to remove the barrier for them. (Something I admit I don't always do, because I don't always allow God to show me His love for insects.)

One time when I was at my sister's house, we were sitting on her backyard deck, and she heard a noise and asked me what it was. I stood up and really put my ear to the wind and then I said that it sounded like a bird in distress. I said a quick little prayer and we went on with the rest of our visit.

She called me a day or two later so excited to tell me what happened. She admitted that at first when I told her that the noise sounded like a bird in distress she thought I was nuts, until my brother-in-law came in from their expansive backyard and told her what he had found. A bird's nest had fallen on the ground and inside the nest was a baby hawk. The mother bird was standing nearby. My sister asked, "How could you possibly know there was a bird in distress?"

I told her it was Jesus.

I believe that because it comes so natural to us to be able to touch and feel other's needs, we may not even be aware that this is God communicating with us and responding through us. My intention here is to try to help people be more aware that this communication is happening, and how amazing God and you are.

I trust Holy Spirit will lead you into all truth, and my hope is that this little piece helped you to see that you probably have already been hearing and responding to your Papa but just didn't realize that's what was happening.

You and He make an awesome team. May you experience your supernatural senses; eyes to see, ears to hear, hands and feet to touch, nose to smell, and tongue to speak of and taste the goodness of God.

> **Lori Orlando** describes herself simply as "a wife, a mom, and a grammy." She is a salon owner, does hair for a living, and is the "beloved daughter of our wonderful loving Papa."
>
> Email: orlandopanda33@yahoo.com

HEARING GOD'S VOICE
Glen Hartline

It was 1987 and I was sitting in my maroon Oldsmobile Cutlass Supreme, stopped at a pedestrian crosswalk on the Louisiana Tech campus. It was a hot and humid summer day and being a freshman student new to the campus, my mind was consumed with the worries of all new students to a large campus. I was preoccupied with reviewing my schedule for the day, going over it in my mind and trying not to forget the location of my next class and where I was designated to park. As I sat, seemingly unconcerned with the people walking in front of me, my mind was awakened from its wandering and my attention was drawn to an unusual shimmering from the rays of the sun. Walking in front of me was a girl. The edges of her person seemed to glow, enhancing the brilliance of the sun. I had never seen her before and she wasn't just any girl, to me she was the most beautiful person I'd ever set my eyes upon. My heart leapt inside my chest and my eyes followed her as she walked across the road and then out of sight, but not out of mind. Who was she? I wondered. I couldn't stop thinking about her. I wanted to talk to her, get to know her, but then fear and inadequacy crept into my thoughts. What if I never saw her again? Even if I did see her again, what would I say to her? Would she even want to talk to me?

Fast forward to 2015. It is once again a hot summer day in Louisiana, only instead of sitting in my car, I'm sitting on my back porch staring across the yard and into the pasture. Again my heart leaps inside my chest as that same vision of beauty I saw 28 years ago is once again walking in front of me. I did meet her again at Louisiana Tech and yes, she did want to talk to me. She has been my wife for the past 24 years and we have talked every day since. The conversations were awkward and brief at first but now our communication flows naturally back and forth, to the extent that many times we don't even need words to communicate, knowing what the other is thinking before words come out of the other's mouth. It's a level of communication that doesn't just happen; it is the result of years of relationship developed in intimacy.

HE CRAVES COMMUNION

Some of you reading this are wondering if you'll ever be able to consistently hear God. Maybe you're questioning God's desire to speak with you because of things you're struggling with, thinking that as long as you're struggling or have sin in your life you won't be able to hear from God. Maybe you think that consistently hearing from God is for those who have "gotten it all together" or have reached that "special" level of spiritual maturity. Let me assure you that none of those reasons or questions have any basis in reality. Not only does God desire to speak to you, He is speaking to you; the problem is that you just haven't learned how to discern His voice. As a matter of fact, He not only longs for you to be able to hear Him, He desires to have communion with you, establishing a personal rapport with you that is nurtured in intimacy over time. That has always been His desire. John 1 says that Jesus was with God in the beginning. The Greek word for with is "pros" and it speaks of being side by side and face-to-face in an intimate relationship. It is in that environment that God said, "let us make man," and it is in that environment that you were created. You were created in communion for relationship and God has never stopped speaking. He initiated this intimacy with you and He has never stopped the conversation, you just haven't recognized His voice. Many times when you hear His voice, you think it's just your own thoughts. Every time this happens, you are missing an opportunity to engage in conversation with Him. He is always talking and engaging you. Hopefully I can shed a light, helping you discover the unique way you hear His voice.

HE SPEAKS YOUR LANGUAGE

Audible Voice

In December of 1998, I was at home alone, sitting at the computer surfing NFL sites on the Internet. Up until that time I had lived a nominal life as a Christian. I had been born again and baptized at the age of eight, but had not really given God much of a place in my life. I didn't believe that God spoke to people today, much less desired to engage you in a conversation, and believed that those who proclaimed to be able to hear God's voice were either liars or mentally ill. So there I was reading posts about the current NFL season when suddenly an audible voice entered my room, knocking me to the floor. (By audible I mean that I heard it with my natural ears just as if I was listening to another person speaking to me, but with a much greater intensity.) "This is your last chance, will you serve me?" The voice shook me to the core. Instantly my beliefs that God no longer spoke to people were utterly destroyed, as every cell in my body acknowledged who had just spoken to me. I knew I had just heard audibly from God! After some time I replied, "Yes, I will serve you," and instantly I became aware of my relationship with a God whom I would eventually know as Father. I was propelled into a conversation with Him that has continued on until today.

Initially, for approximately eight months, most of our conversation consisted of me praying in tongues and Him speaking to me in either an internal audible voice or a vision. This went on for eight to ten hours a day and it was during this time that I was learning who God was and that He really did want to engage with us and speak to us about every aspect of our life. We are God's children; He is the one who created each and every one of us. Like any good and loving father, He desires to spend time with us as individuals. It's all about Him desiring to have a close intimate relationship with each of us. That's what He began declaring to me from the beginning and that is what He is declaring to you right now. He is engaging you in a conversation that is unique to you and Him, it is unlike anyone else's; He will speak to you in a way you can understand. So if you weren't knocked to the floor by a booming voice, don't worry. He has another way for you.

Images

My son Riley was very young when this all began. During this time, as I mentioned before, I was spending eight to ten hours a day with God. I was also working 40 to 50 hours a week at my job; so much of the time which was devoted to spending only with God was in the evenings and early hours of the morning. Because of that Riley would often ask me if I would pray by his bed when he went to sleep. Now during this time I would routinely have angelic encounters as well as hear from God. To Riley this was all normal, so at the age of four when he received the baptism of the Holy Spirit and began speaking in tongues, I didn't question it. He also began telling me about hearing God's voice and seeing in the spirit on an almost constant basis. Keep in mind that he was only around five years old at the time.

Now there are many ways we hear God's voice; one of them is seeing. This is when God gives you an image in your mind and then the interpretation comes afterwards. This is how Riley would see or hear God. Riley would come to me and describe what he was seeing when he looked at a person or was praying for an individual with me, and most times it would be in a cartoon format. Because what Riley would describe was cartoonish, I at first discounted it as childish imagination, but as time went on, I realized more and more that what he was seeing was accurate. The Lord then began teaching me that He speaks to each one of us on a level and in a language we can understand. Since Riley was so young and watched cartoons on television, God knew he would understand and be able to receive that type of image. God was speaking to him in a language he would understand.

It is easy to discount what we see as our own imagination. It was mid-December around 2004 and I was ministering with a friend of mine in Branson Missouri. This was a small congregation of believers who were mostly Messianic Jews, and didn't believe in celebrating the normal Christian holidays like Christmas and Easter, believing them to be pagan in origin and totally detestable to God. My friend had spoken that night and I was asked to stay and minister prophetically to those who wanted a word. The pastor of the congregation was praying for a middle-aged man when she asked me if I could give him a word from God because he was at a crossroads in his life and needed to make a decision. Immediately when I turned to look at him I saw in my mind an image of Santa Claus flying over cities in his sleigh throwing gifts down the chimneys of each house. Now remember this is December, it's Christmas time, and these people don't believe in celebrating the holiday. My immediate thought was that the image was of my own imagination and so I tried to blow it off. I continued to seek the Lord for a word but all I saw was Santa Clause. At that time I decided to just go ahead and step out there with it. I told the man what I was seeing, Santa Clause flying over houses and dropping a gift down the chimney of each house. The man had a funny look on his face then proceeded to explain his situation. He had been a minister in a local church for many years. He loved the people but was feeling like God was telling him it was time for a change. He had just received an invitation to start traveling around and ministering to various home groups and was wondering if that was God's will. God answered him in a way that both of us would understand. God told him that He was calling him to travel, ministering to home groups and that he would bring a gift for each home group he came across. To the man the word was very specific, but to me it seemed like a vague image created by my own mind. Don't automatically discount the seemingly strange or vague images that pop in your mind, many times if not most of the time they are from God.

Visions

Visions are another way you can hear God speak, and although they are similar to images there are some differences. Unlike images that tend to be single static pictures, visions tend to contain motion, much like watching a movie, or have multiple images fit together like a slideshow. The neat thing about visions is that the interpretation tends to be more literal than dreams. Most of the times I've had visions they tended to represent events or people, instead of the event or person having some spiritual "meaning."

At the end of May in 2001, I began having a particular vision and would have it three to four times a week throughout the summer. Accompanying the vision was this overwhelming feeling of dread. In this vision I would see a very large tidal wave coming across the Atlantic crashing into and over large skyscrapers. The vision would then switch to a man getting out of a car and walking up stairs to enter one of these skyscrapers that appeared to me to be a bank. The man was carrying a briefcase, and at the moment I noticed the briefcase, it would open and a large black circular bomb with a fuse, like you would see in cartoons, would come rolling out of the briefcase. At that moment the vision would end. The visions stopped after the attacks of 9/11. I never did understand the meaning of the vision until after the attacks and I wasn't sure I could have done anything even if I had known.

Why would God give me the vision and not the meaning? Simple, He probably was giving me the meaning, I just didn't understand and was so new to all this that I didn't even understand to ask. Sure I probably should have prayed about it and for it, but we don't always do the right thing with what God gives us and that's okay. He will continue to speak to you and show you things to come; knowing that over time reacting correctly will come.

Also, you need to understand that God doesn't just show you things because you have to do something with it. Many times you just see things because you have the mind of Christ and the heart of God. You see them because it's one of the things on His heart and He shares it with you.

Another time, it was early one morning and I was in my car driving to my office. I was worshipping God as I drove when suddenly I went into an open vision. An open vision, to me, is when you can see it as if you were watching a movie. In the vision, I watched myself preaching in this old church with beautiful wooden pews and bright red carpet. As I preached I would see a person with their head bowed. I would stop preaching and when I did they would raise their head so I could see who they were. At that moment I would begin prophesying to them. This went on for a while until I had prophesied to at least five people and then the vision was over. As I came out of the vision I found myself parked in the parking lot at my office, not really sure how I had gotten there. I knew each person I had prophesied to in the dream, so throughout the day I either spoke to them personally or called them and told them what the Lord had said.

Dreams

Throughout history, scripture is laden with people whom God has spoken to through a dream. I have had numerous dreams from God, however this is not a way I hear Him often. This is a way my wife Kate and son Riley commonly hear God. That being said, God does talk to us in dreams and I believe He does so more often than we realize. Dreams tend to be much more figurative than visions, so it is very important that you develop a habit of writing your dreams down and asking God for the interpretation. You will learn the dream language that He uses with you.

Like I said in the beginning, He deals with us as individuals and speaks to us in our own language, a language we will understand. That is why when interpreting dreams it is important not to just go by what symbols or objects are thought to commonly mean.

Let me give you an example:

As I mentioned before, my wife Kate commonly has dreams from God. Many times she has had dreams about cats. Usually, these cats are coming to her and she protects them. The cats in her dreams that did not seek protection were killed. Now according to traditional dream interpretation cats are not good things. They either represent an independent spirit, in a bad way, curses, or something evil. Now understand that if you interpret her dream using common "dream language" you would interpret her dreams as Kate nurturing an independent spirit or ungodly problems in her life. The problem with that interpretation is that Kate loves cats and God knows it. Cats are good things to Kate, precious creatures to love and nurture. What God was telling Kate in her dreams is that there would be those who are precious to God that He would be sending to her to help and protect. Not long after those dreams, we had a series of women who had found themselves in bad situations come to us, and Kate took them in to live with us for a while until they were ready to move on. We must always be conscious of what things mean to us or who people represent to us when interpreting a dream. There is no "one definition fits all" when dealing with God speaking to us. He always speaks to us in a language that is unique to our personal relationship with Him.

Impressions

Probably one of the most common ways I hear God, especially when ministering healing, is through impressions. Impressions to me are when I just seem to "know" something about someone, or I'll look at a person and feel something in my body. Many times these feelings or senses are very subtle. Most believers experience them to some extent, but many do not pay them much attention. Neglecting these subtle manifestations of God's voice cause us to miss many opportunities to not only hear what God is saying, but prevent us from being a tremendous blessing to someone else.

A few months ago, while ministering in a church and teaching on our unity in Christ, I noticed a man sitting on the back row with a woman whom I assumed was his wife. As I looked at him I seemed to know that he really didn't want to be there, but the Lord wanted to minister something to him. I also kept getting the impression that someone was there, probably that man, who had a back and knee problem and that the knee was due to an injury. I interrupted my teaching to pronounce that there was someone there who had a knee and back problem and that God was going to heal them. I stood there and watched as everyone sat there silently. I looked in the direction of the man and noticed the woman nudging him and talking to him, then eventually he stood and starting walking toward me. He told me that he had injured his knee that week, and that he routinely had back problems. I spoke some things over him concerning his relationship with the Lord and then prayed for him and watched the look of astonishment come across his face as he was hit with the reality that God just healed him.

Impressions are a very subtle way God speaks to us; subtle however does not mean it's less significant. When that seemingly minor impression is communicated by you to the intended person, the effects can be life-changing. That's the way it is anytime God speaks. No matter how you hear it, it is still God speaking. No one way is greater than the other. It's all God communicating with His children, inviting us into a greater communion.

PRACTICAL APPLICATION

Now for the million dollar question that I get asked almost every time I go minister. It never fails, whenever I speak about my times with God and our conversations, I'm always asked, "how can I hear God for myself?" Unfortunately, there is no one answer that fits every person. Remember in the beginning when I talked about how God speaks to us as individuals and in a language that is specific to us? Well, He really does, so you just have to discover what His conversations with you sounds, feels, looks, or smells like. You must discover it for yourself.

There is a spiritual principle that says you go in the direction you stare at. Another way of saying it is that you become the thing you gaze at, which is why I've noticed that one of the easiest ways to facilitate hearing God's voice is to start focusing on Him in every aspect of your life. No matter what I'm doing or what situation I find myself in, I try to find Jesus in it.

One of the biggest struggles I have always had in my relationship with God is believing that He would actually provide for me financially. Because of that, I have made it a point to acknowledge Him in every aspect of my financial situation. Even when I'm walking around and find a penny on the ground, I acknowledge God in it by picking the penny up and thanking God for providing all my need. I realize it may seem to be "just a penny" but to me it is still provision. If I start acknowledging Him in the small things then I open myself up to being able to receive the larger provisions. When I acknowledge Him in the small things, I also find that I can hear what He is speaking to me in those small instances.

I used this very principle, even gave the penny example, when teaching on identity one evening. The next day a friend, Patrick, who had not been in the meeting, called me and during the course of our conversation mentioned that he kept finding pennies. He said that it was interesting to him because they were always laying heads up. Immediately I heard the Lord speak to my heart, "Heads up! My provision for him is at hand!" I was able to relay that to him, and since that time I too have been finding pennies and they are always laying heads up. When you start acknowledging God in the small, seemingly coincidental occurrences in your life, you will find that He will begin to make it obvious to you that it's not a coincidence—it's Him! I would continue to find pennies laying heads up, but never really mentioned it to anyone other than my wife Kate and my friend Patrick. Then one day another acquaintance came into my office and started telling me that she had found three pennies that day. I then said, "This may seem like a strange question, but were they heads up, heads down, or both?" She looked at me with a bit of a puzzled look on her face and replied, "You know what? The strange thing is that they were all heads up"! At the moment she said that they were all heads up, another lady in the office immediately announced, "That means money is coming soon!" God will do whatever it takes to prove to you that He is speaking to you and that you are hearing His voice, you just need to discern it.

Another practical way to enhance or even activate your ability to hear God's voice is by practicing it with like-minded friends or family. When my kids were younger, I would invent games to get them to listen to Holy Spirit's voice. Now I realize some people have a hard time believing God would participate in your games, thinking He only speaks to us for specific, holy, or important Godly reasons, but He doesn't. He enjoys joining in our games and even enhances them. Whenever we were traveling in a car or out to eat I would ask someone to pick a number between one and 100, or think of a color, flower, or animal. Then the rest of us would ask Holy Spirit what the number, color, or animal was. Now we weren't guessing or trying to read the person's mind so you can relax, we were asking Holy Spirit who leads us into all truth. Many times one of my kids would get it right, especially my son. Like I said, Holy Spirit would even make it more interesting. My daughter would often have trouble sticking with what she was thinking about, especially when it came to colors. On numerous occasions my son would get frustrated with her because Holy Spirit would show him one color and then another. My son Riley would then turn to my daughter Sarah and say, "you're changing your mind again!" He would then tell her the color she was originally thinking of and then the one she changed to. He was almost always right when he did that. Sure

Holy Spirit could have just given my son the final color, but He was taking the opportunity to teach my son to trust what he saw. Riley could have easily just questioned himself, thinking that his mind was just imagining things and he was indecisive, but instead, he trusted what he was seeing was from God and sought the reason why. You don't need to make this harder than what it is. You are hearing from God, trust that you do and then ask Holy Spirit to teach you to understand what you are hearing.

Lastly, I want to describe an exercise I routinely use in my classes when teaching others to discern God's voice. I will break the class up into groups of four to six. I instruct them to stand in a circle with one member standing in the center of the circle. You can also have that one member sit in a seat. The one in the center then closes their eyes while the others start walking around them, maintaining the circle, so as to prevent the one in the center from being able to distinguish who is who. Then as the members of the group walk one will reach over and tap the one in the center on the shoulder and they all stop walking. At that moment the person that was tapped listens to what God is saying about the one who tapped them. This can be a word, impression, vision, feeling, or just about anything. I tell them to say what they receive it's a safe environment and okay to be wrong. We can learn from our mistakes just as well as from our successes.

I remember a time I was using this exercise, helping a group in New Zealand hear from God. I broke them up into groups of about six and in one of the groups was a lady who claimed she had never heard from God; we will call her June to help make the example easier to understand. Now when it came time for June to be in the center, she nervously sat in the chair and closed her eyes. At that time Sandy, (not her real name) who had not been in the meeting or in any group, walked into the room. Upon seeing her I quietly directed her to stand directly behind June. I also directed Sandy to be the one to touch June, knowing there was no way June could know it was Sandy. She hadn't been in the room previously. After Sandy touched June on the shoulder there was a long silence. I gave June plenty of time to listen, but discerned that she was questioning what she was getting so I told her to just say whatever it was she was hearing or feeling. She then declared, "I don't think this is God, I think it's just me because all I feel is expectancy.

I can't explain it I just feel an expectancy." At that moment everyone broke out in laughter. You see, that feeling of expectancy was from God. Sandy was early on in her pregnancy and that was God's way of proving to June that she was hearing His voice!

Hearing from God is not some magical ability or mystical experience. It is as natural as the everyday communication you have with your spouse, parent, or child. You are hearing from God, you just now need to hone your discernment of His voice by practicing listening to Him and expecting to hear. Don't limit the ways He can speak, but allow Him to teach you how he specifically communes with you, His unique, precious child.

Dr. Glen Hartline is a veterinarian, minister, author, radio show host, husband, and father. Healing and the prophetic are constant aspects of his life and ministry but he is more known for his intimate relationship with God. That intimacy began in 1998 after hearing the audible voice of God and has been nurtured through years of supernatural encounters. He currently travels both nationally and internationally preaching and teaching schools of Intimacy, identity, and healing where he not only prays for the sick but imparts the reality of living a supernatural life through the intimate union we share with our Heavenly Father. His *Heart to Heart* radio program can be heard every Tuesday and Thursday on the Fourteen 12 radio network. He can be contacted through his website and on Facebook:

Web: www.h2hministry.com
Facebook: www.facebook.com/wghart

Hearing the Voice of God
Melody Paasch

To hear is something we do naturally. It's biologically involuntary. It's built into us, but hearing the voice of God is not really about our ears. It is more about a sense of perceiving thoughts belonging to Him, with an innate capacity to connect with Him. He is the one who created us, and He is the one who sets and calibrates our ability to hear Him. He has given each of us spiritual ears to "sense" and "see" what He is saying. "See" in the sense that we perceive, and "see" in the sense that He sometimes speaks in imagery.

LISTENING

Hearing is key and what we all strive for, but listening is different. To listen, takes a cognizant and deliberate action on our part. To listen and understand (as the word of God says) is a very intentional matter. It's a selection made by accepting the authority of God as our greater source, while acknowledging that He is all wisdom. To choose to listen is to make the decision to gain the passage that He offers in communication with Him. As in everything, all that God offers is freely given. Listening with our spirit connection to Him gives us the ability to absorb and have access to what He says or even thinks. He loves sharing secrets with His people.

RELATIONSHIP

Hearing the voice of God for me, has been a matter of time and experiences shared. It's been about relationship. You may learn to perceive a new friend's voice by hearing it regularly. You converse often. Your memory begins to note the tone of their terminology and expressions. Over time you become familiar with the inflection of their voice. They don't have to introduce themselves every time they pick up the phone to call you, because you are conditioned to recognize who is speaking (without caller ID). You become intimate in your exchanges and you can easily identify their unique sound. It's about becoming familiar with His voice and language.

PARTNERSHIP

God's desire to speak to us is a form of partnering with us in His purposes. This is His great pleasure, to interface with us for many of His plans. He directs, He enlightens, and He clarifies by speaking to our senses. His mind (we are promised the mind of Christ if we are in relationship with Him) is like a network or shared computer system, which syncs His thoughts with our own. He simply integrates His thoughts through our mind and we receive it by His connection to our spirit.

If He has made us in His image, then a part of His DNA resides in us, and He therefore can speak directly into that fundamental composition of shared DNA. I believe that He has reserved in each human being, a compartment that holds a deposit that belongs to Him. This is the place He has situated the network He has equipped us with.

RECOGNIZING GOD'S THOUGHTS

Recognizing God's thoughts or messages may at times feel as though something has randomly dropped into us, and floated up to arrive in our mind or thoughts. It can often seem quite arbitrary, like something we could never have come up with in our own limited reasoning. It might seem like a rare epiphany. This of course, is the practical side of hearing or sensing His voice, but there is nothing magic about it. It is learning to stay plugged into the source, the shared network, which is God's heart. This quite simply, is conversing with God, and then waiting for Him to respond. He is always talking; we just need to accept that He is interested in speaking to us. That is when it becomes natural like flowing in intimate conversation with a close friend.

SEEING WHAT HE SAYS

In the context of the first chapter of Jeremiah, we are instructed by example that we can "see" what God says.

> *The word of the LORD came to me saying, "What do you see, Jeremiah?" And I said, "I see a rod of an almond tree." Then the LORD said to me, "You have seen well, for I am **watching over My word to perform it**."*
> JER 1:11-12 NASB

God is speaking of His word as though it is so tangible that it can be seen, but with the spiritual eyes and not the physical. To see, is just one of the many ways we sense God's interaction and communication. Some of us "see" the message before we receive the understanding of it.

DEVELOPMENT OF THE EAR

When God ponders a thought that is related to His desired collaboration with us, He sends the idea to us through our shared network with Him; which we receive based upon our faith in Him. When we hunger to hear His voice and we ask Him to speak, we must also expect Him to answer. He waits to see how we receive what He says. Faith comes by hearing and faith built upon sensing God's "Rhema" or revelation becomes action. The revelatory word of God releases energy in the spirit realm to develop greater levels of the gifts He gives. God's revelation comes to you by direct conversation between His Spirit and your own. The more you trust Him to honor your request to hear Him, the more He will speak to you. The more your hearing is developed, the better you will hear.

AUDIBLE OR UNIQUE MESSAGES

In my personal experience, He seldom speaks audibly, but it has definitely happened. I was in Colorado Springs at a conference several years ago, after seeking Papa for months about my next stop from Dallas, Texas. I think I had pestered Him enough that He finally audibly answered, and without any question that He was addressing me. Unfortunately, I still did not believe with my whole heart that it was His voice, and I vehemently rebuked the devil for any deception. To my surprise, the confirmation came later, when three Washington State pastors and a Dallas prophet, asked when I would be moving to Washington State.

HE ENJOYS HIMSELF

He *is* God after all. And can do whatever He chooses. By the way, in case you haven't experienced it yet, God has an incredible sense of humor and sometimes loves to goof around! There are random times when He will wake me with a literal knock on the bedroom door or by calling my name. Other times, He has been known to send wafts of fresh brewed coffee or bacon frying on the stove, to wake me when there was no one else in the house. Like I said, a real sense of humor! These tangible times are some of my most favorite moments with Him. The adventure of hearing Him becomes more and more fantastic as you grow in it!

If you ask and take the time to listen, you *will* learn to hear Him speak. Then you'll want to begin to ask what He would like you to do with the information He has chosen to give you. Keep your spiritual ears and eyes open. Don't miss the adventure!

Melody Paasch is the founder of the *"Now, Interpret This!"* online school of dream and prophetic studies. She travels nationally and internationally, speaking about learning to hear God in relationship, whether that be in your sleep or waking hours. Her heart is to lead individuals to their God-given destiny, and to see them fulfill their creative purposes. You can learn more about her school and about her personal services at the web addresses listed below. And Melody's books, *"Now, Interpret This!" Dream Journal* and *The Ivory Ferret* can be located easily at this web address: *bit.ly/melody-paasch*

School: www.nowinterpretthis.org
Personal Services: www.melodypaasch.com

Hearing God for the Basics but Not Much More
Cheryl Fritz

INTERESTINGLY ENOUGH, though I had been a believer for several years, I still had no confidence in my ability to hear God. I was able to discern the convicting power of the Holy Spirit, but that's where my confidence both started and finished. I could sense His gentle nudging and perceive when He was steering me to make a better choice. I realized when He was challenging me to take a thought captive or to set aside a behavior that was less than His personal best for my life. Like most believers, I could sense His still, small voice summoning me to forgive those who had wronged me. It seemed like I could hear Him for the basics. For instance, I was usually able to pick up on His leading as it pertained to the do's and don'ts of my behavior, but honestly, that didn't make for much of a relationship.

Hear me when I say that it is not my intent to undermine the value of such leading and direction. It is transformational and absolutely necessary in order to effectively grow and mature as believers. Hearing God as He teaches us to renew our mind is essential. We can't live the Christian life apart from it. My frustration, however, was birthed out of a desire for wanting to hear Him with more confidence in other areas. I wanted to be attentive to more of a conversational dialogue with Him, and honestly, I was beginning to wonder whether that type of experience was even accessible or available.

TRAINING AND ACTIVATION

Little did I know that God was about to start me out on a journey that would forever change the course of my life. He cleared a path for me to begin to connect with a small group of believers who were teaching people how to hear from Him prophetically. Being quite the skeptic, I found myself pushing back from this. I didn't have a grid for it. While intrigued, the whole notion also made me quite uncomfortable, even to the extent that I was nervous that I was positioning myself to be led astray into false teaching or false doctrine.

A friend had invited me to participate in some basic prophetic training, and though I was cautiously curious, I politely declined. She explained that in the training they would do activation exercises (something that was totally foreign to me.) They would seek the Holy Spirit and ask Him to share an encouraging word for the others in the class. They would then give prophetic words for each other in order to get some practical experience as well as to bring edification, exhortation, and comfort.

Well, shall I just say that the whole notion made me cringe! Dare I step out and take such a leap of faith? Was such a thing even appropriate? Was this truly a move of God or were these believers just deceiving themselves or even worse, leading others astray? Those were all thoughts that I marinated in as I sidestepped the opportunity and retreated back into my neatly packaged, unchallenging Christian life. Nowhere did such practices have a place in my comfort zone, and so I dismissed this and went about my daily life.

It soon would become clear that Holy Spirit was about to stir the pot. My first experience came quite unexpectedly. While leisurely driving down the road I happened to pass by a young lady who was walking down the sidewalk. Clear out of thin air an image came to my mind. I wasn't seeking it. I didn't ask for it, and neither did I see it with my natural eyes, but in my thoughts I perceived a bag of money. It was wrapped in burlap and had a dollar sign on it. The very next moment another image popped up. In my thoughts I clearly saw a stack of books. Then again, without anticipating any of this to happen, thoughts started to come to me about what those two images meant. The young lady was a student, and she needed money for books. Now clearly, the thing that I should have done would have been to stop and bless her with some money for books, but being someone who had never heard God in this way before, I barely flinched. I continued to drive down the street and go on about my business.

Nevertheless, He persisted in calling all of this back to my remembrance. On and off throughout the next few days my attention would turn back to what had happened and what I had seen. In addition to that, I was approached again by the person who had invited me to take the basic prophetic training. This time, in light of recent circumstances, I was beginning to warm up to the idea.

Admittedly, I was terrified by the prospect of corralling up with a bunch of strangers for the purpose of learning how to hear God in order to speak a prophetic word over each other. I hadn't made peace with the idea of getting "activated" in the prophetic. The whole thing seemed too mechanical and totally contrived and fleshly. It didn't seem spiritual at all. I was of the mindset that if God didn't "zap" you with that ability, then it just wasn't going to happen.

Even still, my friend continued to intermittently extend the invitation. Over time her persistence finally wore me down, and I conceded to doing a private class with just her and one or two other people, and only through online chat. I didn't want to meet any of these people, or even see them, because I found that prospect to be totally intimidating.

Much to my surprise, I found the whole experience to be unlike anything I would have ever anticipated. It was exhilarating. I felt like a deaf person whose hearing had been restored. I felt like my spiritual eyes and ears had popped open, and for the first time in my life, I began to understand how to hear my heavenly Father in new and exciting ways. I learned how to access the screen of my mind (the same place that we imagine or daydream.) God taught me how to use it like a chalkboard. I would go to the chalkboard, and He would write something on it. He would bring pictures, words, and thoughts. He would communicate freely and openly with me, and I didn't have to beg Him to do so or jump through hoops hoping that in response He might show up. I didn't have to twist His arm in order to get some dialogue going.

Expectation was the catalyst for communication. I learned to sit at the feet of my Heavenly father with a childlike expectation that if I began to communicate, He would meet me on that same line. This was perhaps the most valuable thing that I had ever learned in my Christian experience apart from the gospel itself. In response to that I have dedicated my life to training and equipping others. Holy Spirit is talking. He has a lot to say, and He would like to communicate both *to* you and *through* you. If you're someone who has wrestled with some of these same things that I have mentioned, I would encourage you to step out and surround yourselves with other like-minded believers who can partner with you on your journey. Allow God to train and equip you, and don't be surprised if He does it in cooperation with those whom He has already prepared for this type of assignment.

Cheryl Fritz is the founder of the wildly popular 12,000-member *Inside Out Training and Equipping School.* She is ordained through *Royal Family International.* In addition to that, she also travels both nationally and internationally equipping the saints for the supernatural work of the ministry. She and the 48-member training team at *Inside Out* host over 30 free online classes that reach a global audience.

Facebook Group: facebook.com/groups/insideouttrainingandequippingschool/
Web: insideouttrainingandequippingschool.org

God Speaks One Way and Then Another
Cyndi Millett

IS THERE MUCH ELSE that is at once so profound, yet so simple as hearing the voice of God? This has, at times, been a touchy area for me, containing both joy and perplexity. Hearing His voice has often been different than I've expected and this has been one of the most difficult struggles people have confided to me.

For me it seemed, at first, more like I *felt* Him than heard Him. In nature I would sense His tangible presence on the back of my Arabian whose hooves beat in my ears, or the gentle zephyr manifesting that carried a slight weightiness. He was there.

Other times, His "voice" came in dreams as: foreknowledge, direction, warnings, seeing enemy plots or reactions, or words of knowledge about peoples' struggles that I might pray and intervene. I had recognized Him in a dream as a preadolescent, so much like the famous painting by

Danny Hahlbohm of Jesus pointing over the boy's shoulder at the helm of a ship. Both as watcher of the unfolding scene, and as a participant in a smaller boat floating down a winding river littered with garbage, the trees along the bank stripped bare like winter, I saw Jesus pointing over my shoulder showing me the way. That vision of the night became a beacon for my life; it was an assurance that no matter what comes, He is here guiding me through.

At times His voice is more like a sense or impression, an ethereal awareness of something vague or specific, a repeating thought/theme, a name/face, a feeling/mood, a body sensation, a prophetic sentiment, etc. Sometimes I will zone out like in a daydream, watching something unfold, whether it be about someone else or me doing something, and suddenly I "come to" my present surroundings. Over time and through experience, I've realized these moments are "instructions" or "truths" I can act on and see His will be affected. I've learned, and am learning still, to stop and think about what I'm thinking about (metacognition) as therein is often a clue, His thoughts becoming mine. On occasion it's more like seeing into something, a situation becomes clearer as I "look."

One might object that these descriptions don't fit "hearing" the voice of God, but hearing is often different than we expect, so, it seems when people talk of hearing God, realistically, what is meant is *recognizing that God is communicating,* rather than hearing only by one's ears.

Sometimes while visiting with friends, certain words of others will come alive as if He quickened them with a life of their own, or in the movie theatre when a character such as Gandalf speaks an eternal truth that resonates in my soul as if He had spoken it on the inside of me. Similarly, I will feel His presence move through my whole being in waves and tingles when I am focused on, or newly understand something, like He is saying "pay attention, I want you to know and remember this."

Sometimes when I read scripture it suddenly opens up to me, and I "comprehend" what I didn't previously; I have the Knowledge of Him, His own knowledge. It's like He drops bread crumbs or clues for me to follow, a treasure hunt of sorts, that leads to a deeper understanding of something that only started as a niggling thought, or as an irritable sliver working its way out because it doesn't belong.

I've had some rather unusual hearing experiences where my spirit interacts with God while my body rests. Once I awakened in the night by my own voice agreeing with Jesus for my husband; my hand was on his chest as I exclaimed, "Yes Jesus, Yes JESUS, YES JESUS!"

For a while I had a season of *deep sleep*. I would go to bed and wake exhausted, remembering nothing. I started to get a bit anxious and sought an answer, which came in part as I dreamt I was crying out, encased in blue flames; then shortly after, I received a prophecy of Him making me His Signet. Through the prophetic word, He indicated it was not because of my stature or maturity (something I had been contemplating as explanation for the strange occurrences, e.g. both a refining process and growing pains seemed plausible), but because He had chosen me for His purposes. A signet is an official seal or an insignia bearing the authority and will of its owner, and representing authentication of the item or message it is attached to. For example, in past times hot wax could be poured onto an official document and a metal engraved stamp bearing the King's personal insignia was pressed into it. The unique crafting of the image in the stamp would be recognizable as the King's to anyone in the realms who saw it, and as long as the seal was in place, it was treated as his authentic signature, bearing his and his kingdom's power. My point is that sometimes we hear God in *imperceptible ways* our mind or ears don't first perceive, Spirit to spirit.

Following the prophecy, what started out as a dream changed to an encounter, waking me to present time because of the burning heat I felt, literally, which continued for some time after I was awake. The important thing was, I knew it was *Him*. I had been watching and listening to Jesus teach me on powers, principalities, deliverance, and using His name.

On other occasions His voice had seemed quite audible too, like the time the elders gathered around a man experiencing a crisis. I was startled out of my reverie by, "Give him the poem you wrote last night: The Rock on Which I Stand." My whole inner being jumped at the sudden "loudness" of His voice. I did as I was told, and gave him the poem. I saw the fellow again at a time when I needed some kindness myself; he thanked me and confessed he still had the poem, and what it had meant to him. I was so glad I had listened and acted.

Now and then He has someone send a text or share something He wants me to know, like, "Cyndi, you hear me very clearly, you don't always need confirmation." Part of growing up in hearing His voice is trusting we've heard correctly, without proof. This was sometimes quite disconcerting for someone who wanted to do everything perfectly and avoid conflict or other uncomfortable moments—it's risky to act in faith, but it's a primary way we may grow.

There was a time I experienced something akin to the psalmist's reference in Psalm 139, "Though I make my bed in hell..." I was seeking the Lord tenaciously, and had ordered a book online written by a Christian man. So much of it resonated and yet, soon I again heard His voice loud and clear tell me to "Get rid of that book. It's witchcraft!" I was befuddled. The only thing in it that seemed less churchy than usual was the brief section on seeing auras, and I had reasoned away caution regarding certain wording on the website as "trying to reach everyone." As I headed to the trash, I flipped through it wondering what had prompted Him to speak in such a way and again heard His gentle admonishment clear and loud, "Why are you still reading it? I told you to get rid of it." Pretty clear instruction right? Sometimes the issue isn't *whether* we heard. It's *trusting* what we hear regardless of the evidence, or lack thereof. Some lessons are learned the hard way as I later rescued the book from the trash, "just in case I'd been wrong." (I've since decided that self-deception is quite possibly the worst kind of deception; we should at least be our own friend.)

Later on a group Skype conference with the author, his wife, and others it became clear not only that some form of Gnosticism (e.g. an esoteric or secret mystical type of knowledge only a select few can understand or gain access to; often at odds with accepted teaching) was in the *mix*, but clearly occult practice. This was the "witchcraft" He'd warned me about. At that point I was out. I had no doubt I had heard God speak on the particular matter of the book and how He also felt about my online participation with the Skype conference teaching. However, during that season extending about a year's time I had become quite confused at particular moments, as to *who* I was "hearing," or which experience was from which source. Was some devil trying to ward me off from some good God stuff, like a scarecrow in a field? I wouldn't be deterred! Or was I really ignoring His message?

During that season, at one point I began to feel a liquid, anointing oil I presumed, running from the top of my head, and then down my forehead, yet nothing was there in the natural; this would repeat periodically, yet seemed positive. I also experienced new sensations in my body in ways that were definitely spiritual, not physical; I wasn't absolutely certain of the source of these, but it didn't seem bad or frightening. That may have been the oddest part of all—*nothing* that occurred seemed "frightening." This was odd because in the early years of my walk with God, fear was a huge problem for me in regard to both natural and spiritual things for a lot of reasons. But eventually I began to feel increasingly uncertain and unsettled, having several dreams with the repeat theme of a tipping point. I would be driving and then reverse and end up tipping backwards, falling over a ledge of some sort. I knew to pay attention to these dreams; they were a warning. I also knew more than one spiritual source was communicating to me. One time there was a *presence* that arrived by my bedside in the dark; it traced a barely perceptible trail down my forearm which made me tense and catch and hold my breath. This was different than the visible angels I encountered. It was unseen but felt, and behaved differently. And another time I felt an insistent poking in my upper shoulder joint at my prayer group, accompanied by a voice saying, "Speak up, tell them…" Was this a holy angel, or malevolent imposter?

During this season, I'd even humbled myself and asked on two separate occasions for my prayer group to pray for me, because I needed to understand what was happening. The answer I received both occasions was that I was learning discernment. My senses were being trained to perceive. Eventually in our journey, we will likely encounter the counterfeit of God's ways, and those who walk in it. Ultimately, it's what we do at the tipping point that counts.

In hindsight, the mixture of the genuine and the counterfeit was what created confusion for me to begin with, yet, He patiently allowed me to learn about discerning spirits, and ultimately, to not lean on my own understanding, but recognize and unquestioningly trust and obey His voice. No is no for just as good a reason as yes is yes. There have been times of absolute clarity in learning to distinguish and hear His voice and other times of feeling uncertain or confused. Knowing the written word well has helped me discern between many things correctly, so if you're not that familiar with the Bible, I highly suggest reading it and learning to understand it. If you become familiar with God's character and ways, it becomes easier to distinguish and decide the source of what you may hear or feel experientially.

Overall, it's felt as though once I was comfortable hearing Him one way, He would then *seem* silent for a time in that particular manner, and switch to another. For example, after I got familiar with understanding how He was speaking to me in dreams, I seemed to have fewer dreams and began having more sense impressions while awake. At another point, it seemed He spoke audibly less often, as He began to train me further by introducing various other ways of hearing—which meant I had to pay more attention and exercise senses besides my ears. We have several "spiritual senses" that mirror our natural ones. At first I felt He had stopped speaking to me, which felt really disconcerting, but then I began to realize He was still speaking, not hiding or withdrawn, but simply speaking a different way. Although it was uncomfortable, I've learned and am learning His language and to hear and distinguish "His voice" from my own soul, and other spirits. Hearing God's voice is more about recognizing the various ways He speaks, and being certain that if at first we don't perceive Him, eventually we will, one way or another. He is simply that loving and that good.

Cyndi Millett is a lover of people and passionate seeker of Truth. She ministers prophetically, assisting others in deepening their understanding and relationship with God, and in healing of the soul and body. Union with God, identity, transformation, and mental health are common themes in her open, transparent writing.

Cyndi is currently working to obtain her Bachelor of Arts in Psychology. She is joyfully married to John, mother to five adventurous young men, and resides in Canada.

Email: liifetree12@gmail.com
Blog: http://liifetree.wordpress.com

Table for Three Please
Holly Cusato

I ONCE HEARD IT SAID that if you want to see your spiritual gifts work, go where you are a stranger—an unknown who isn't thinking about what other people will think. I got to put this to the test during a business trip to Atlanta, Georgia.

Several other Atlanta-based team members had planned for us to enjoy a "girls' night out." On the appointed night, Jenny, Dina, and I headed to a popular restaurant abuzz with professionals enjoying drinks after work, and groups eating dinner. At our table-for-three, we enjoyed each other's company, fine wine, and shrimp nachos. A handsome young man delivered our drinks, smiling from ear-to-ear. Jenny was the only single gal at our table, so of course she got kidded about the handsome waiter.

I was drawn to this young man without knowing why, and couldn't let the evening come to a close without engaging him in a conversation.

Over the anxious protest of bachelorette Jenny, I beckoned the young man to our table one last time.

Since I had no official reason to call him over, we made small talk until the young man began to share his story. Out poured the fact that he was 34 years old and had recently wrapped up a successful career as a Computer Programmer to pursue his passion in acting. He educated us on Atlanta's blossoming movie industry, including some movie stars who recently passed through town.

"What might we have seen you in?" I asked, "A movie? Or a commercial perhaps?"

"Nothing major yet," the young man smiled with hope, "but I won't give up; I audition as much as I can."

I don't remember exactly how one statement led to the next, but in sharing his tale it came up that he was a successful athlete who played basketball through college. Years later, he still enjoyed playing basketball with friends.

The young waiter said he had hurt his Achilles tendon playing basketball over a year ago. The doctors warned him it would take up to three months to heal, if he stayed off of it. But alas, he admitted he couldn't sit still and never slowed down. A year later, he is still in pain, to the extent that it is now hurting his acting career. And this is where everything changed, for him and me. His next words were my cue.

"But I pray to God every day that He will heal me," he said with hope. I didn't have to await further instruction; I knew exactly what God wanted me to do. I was equipped for this.

"Well you are doing it wrong," I replied.

"What do you mean 'doing it wrong?'" he said, surprised.

"You aren't supposed to ask God to heal you. You are supposed to command it away!" I was already in motion as I spoke, moving from one side of the table around to the other. Before he knew what hit him, I was standing directly in front of him. I looked him in the eye and said, "God loves you very much, and wants you to be well, to be pain-free. I would like to pray for you, but I am also going to put my hands on your ankle. It's your right one, correct?"

"How did you know it was my right one?"

"So it is, then? God told me that!"

"No way! How did you know that?" he says again.

"God told me! Because He wants you well!" I exclaimed with excitement.

"That is amazing! How did she know that?" He asks Jenny and Dina, who are still in their seats just as confused and amazed as our young waiter.

I lean down and put both hands on his right ankle and say one of the shortest prayers I have ever spoken. I realize through the noise of the restaurant, the young man can't hear me. No one else around can hear me. I have only the spirit-realm to talk to.

I start with the bad spirit first and command, "Spirit of pain, I command you to leave this young man's ankle right now in the name of Jesus Christ! Achilles tendon, in the name of Jesus Christ I command you to be healed!" And then I add, "Spirit of God, I thank you for blessing this young man with a perfect ankle."

Seconds pass, and I don't want to prolong what might be an embarrassment for this young waiter in his place of employment. I stand up, smile and proclaim, "You are healed!" When I stand, I realize he had continued talking with my two teammates, so I turn and head toward my chair on the other side of the table.

Before I reach my seat, the young man says, "Whoa! What did you do? My ankle feels... different... it feels heavy... something is happening!"

Such excitement bubbles up inside me and I exclaim, "God is healing you! He is healing you! What do you feel now?"

"It feels better! It's amazing! The pain is completely gone!" He starts bouncing up and down, like an athlete getting ready for the big game. He cannot contain his grin as he gives me a great big hug and then continues bouncing around the aisle of the crowded restaurant.

Within seconds, a second waiter approaches and asks what all the excitement is about. The healed young man points to me and says, "I'm healed! She said God healed my ankle and it doesn't hurt anymore!"

The second man responded, "I wish she could do something like that for me; I'm in pain all the time."

With a short step, I am in front of the second young man and I say, "Of course God will heal you!"

To which he sadly replies, "God won't heal me. He doesn't even know me."

"Oh but He does know you! And He wants you to be healed. What is causing you pain?"

"My knee."

"Your left one, correct?"

"How did you know that?"

"I told you God wants you well, so He told me which knee was in pain." After preparing the second young man the same way I prepared the first, I bent down in the middle of the restaurant and put both of my hands on his knee.

This prayer was different than the first—it had to be. The first young man was a believer; he had already been praying to God to heal him. But this young man was so lost he thought God didn't even know who he was.

Knowing once again no one but the spirit realm could hear my prayer in the loud restaurant, the words fell softly from my lips, "God, you promised us signs and wonders, and this young man needs exactly that! Pain, I command you to leave; knee, I command you to be healed!" I felt my palms heat up, a sure sign that God had heard my prayer. I left my hands in place a few more seconds, knowing the love of God was pouring into the young man.

This time when I stood, I assumed the best possible outcome and asked the young man what he felt.

"It's gone! The pain is gone already! I can't believe it!"

"Oh but believe it! God loves you that much!" Before I could say any more the second young man began hopping away shouting to his fellow co-workers, "I'm healed! I'm healed!" The first young man, still just as excited, trotted off behind the second to confirm their stories were true.

At this point, I realized I had caught the attention of most of the tables around us. The next few moments were a blur as I headed back to my seat, alive with excitement for how mighty my God is.

Since I was over 800 miles from home, I'm guessing I may never see those two young men again, but perhaps that is what gave me the courage to jump out of my seat and come to their aid.

> *"And these signs will follow those who believe: In My name they will cast out demons; they will speak with new tongues; they will take up serpents; and if they drink any deadly thing, it will by no means hurt them; they will lay hands on the sick, and they will recover."*
> MK 16:17-18

DURANT

I just heard from my friend Gail that her daughter's doctor proclaimed her as healed! A five-millimeter cyst that threatened removal of her ovaries is completely gone. What does that have to do with me? About two months earlier, I had run into Gail in the middle of Durant, Oklahoma, after not seeing her for 20 years.

Driving back to Texas after a healing conference in Missouri took me and my parents through Oklahoma for several hours of this 400-mile journey. Knowing we would need dinner, we decided on Durant as a good stopping point. After my handy iPhone produced the list of 40 or 50 restaurants in Durant, we decided we were in the mood for Tex-Mex. It was a random pick, but we navigate to Salitas.

I certainly didn't expect to see a friendly face greet us at the door, but there was Gail, a friend from high school and fellow dance team member, working at the hostess stand. It was instant recognition, followed by instant connection.

After a few moments of catching up, Gail guided us to our table-for-three. She stopped by our table toward the end of our meal and eventually shared how worried she was about her 18-year-old daughter. The doctors had found a cyst on her daughter's ovary, and it was not a good sign; they were considering removing her ovary. I didn't jump out of my seat right away, but moments later I couldn't contain the words, the prayer bubbling up in my mind—it had to come out.

At the front of the restaurant, I approached Gail and asked if I could prayer for her daughter. I asked Gail to stand in place of her daughter for the prayer. I had Gail place her hands on her own lower abdomen in the approximate location of the ovaries, and I placed my hands on hers. We both agreed to focus on her daughter as I prayed.

I began my prayer just like I was taught: first command the spirit of infirmity to go, and then order her ovaries to be healed and whole. Without a thought, the next words that spilled out of my mouth surprised me. My prayer reclaimed her future according to God's will for her life, that Satan could not steal her daughter's future children. It is obvious looking back, of course, that was the prayer God needed to be spoken over her life, as the dark one is a thief.

Gail and I parted ways as re-found friends and agreed to stay in touch. And since I started with the end, you know the rest. We don't always know the outcome of our healing prayers. God asks us to be obedient, to offer prayers to those in need, but we don't always get to feel the amazing joy of celebrating when they are so beautifully answered.

The thief does not come except to steal, and to kill, and to destroy. I have come that they may have life, and that they may have it more abundantly.
JN 10:10

DALLAS

I praise God that my Lord can land me in the exact restaurant over 80 miles, or even 800 miles from home, to answer someone's desperate prayer. It is exciting and amazing to be used by God, to see the power He has entrusted us with, come to life.

But my final story is much closer to home. One day, I noticed a woman at work was no longer being her bubbly, happy self. As I thought about her, the small, still voice shared that a female in her family was recently diagnosed with cancer. I will be perfectly honest with you— I did not want to act on this information. In fact, I sat on it for a week. To approach someone far from home—easy. To approach a co-worker could have ramifications.

But one quiet afternoon in the office I spotted my co-worker, who I'll call Emma, and knew it was time. The grief she wore on her face pained me. I couldn't continue being so selfish. I approached her and shared that God put it on my heart that something was wrong.

More specifically, "Perhaps a female in your family might have been diagnosed recently?" I asked questioningly.

"That's amazing," she said, "How did you know that?"

"God told me!" I said with excitement as her response told me it was accurate.

She went on to share that her sister had just been diagnosed with a form of aggressive skin cancer that had the potential to spread rapidly. The doctors were operating that day to remove the majority of it, and then run additional tests to confirm whether it had spread. The more Emma shared, it was clear she was worried as she waited for the news.

To offer Emma an explanation of where I was going next, I shared the story of my friend Gail and how she was able to stand in for her daughter when I prayed that night in Oklahoma. Emma was more than willing to do the same and stand in for her sister. I asked Emma to place her hands on herself, but at the site of her sister's surgery and I placed my hands on hers.

"Cancer, I command you to leave Emma's sister right now in Jesus' name! I command full restoration of her body back to God's perfect design."

After finishing the prayer for Emma and her sister, I asked that Emma be so bold as to tell her sister that she is healed—that we have to stand on the promises of God. I was blessed to hear a week later that the cancer had not spread, and the doctors were very pleased with the outcome of the surgery. I even got an email from Emma's sister the next week, thanking me for being open to being used by God.

> *"For I know the plans I have for you," declares the Lord, "plans to prosper you and not to harm you, plans to give you hope and a future."*
> JER 29:11 NIV

STANDING ON THE PROMISES OF GOD

Why do I share these stories? Because that is how I learned—hearing other healing stories and agreeing that I could do the same. We are blessed to live during a time that on-line videos are plentiful, TV is available 24-hours a day, and books can be downloaded in mere seconds. Healing ministries are taking advantage of all of these mediums to spread the good news that divine healing is still for today. From the early greats like Oral Roberts, Jack Coe, Kenneth Hagin, and Lester Sumerall to the modern day teachers like Andrew Wommack, Bill Johnson, Randy Clark, and Curry Blake to name a few—all are available to witness their faith for healing. And you and I were granted the exact same measure of faith they were!

But all of the modern day teachers point back to a single source of truth—the Bible. The Apostle Paul wrote a beautiful letter to the church in Ephesus (the book of Ephesians) that speaks to God's plan for the Saints—both in Paul's time and in every age to come. I was once encouraged to read this book of the Bible over-and-over again, until I believed it applied to me. I would encourage you to do the same. Paul's prayer was that our Heavenly Father would give us "the spirit of wisdom and revelation in the knowledge of Him" and that the "eyes of our understanding be enlightened" (see Eph 1: 15-23). Paul's desire was that we may know the love of Christ, and understand our role in sharing that with the world.

After learning of these available resources I absorbed everything I could watch or read until I started to believe it. I learned about my identity in Christ, what it means to be a righteous daughter of the most-high God, and how to tap into the power of the Spirit within me. I learned that God's will for us is perfect as the Bible promises, and that any sickness and disease comes from Satan. God has mighty plans for each of us that Satan tries to steal at every turn.

I learned that all of the healing stories in the Bible were not Jesus showing off His own power or relationship with God—rather each story was meant as an example, a guide for us to follow so we would do the same and more. I now understand that what Christ accomplished on the cross gave me authority over Satan and his demons, and it is my responsibility to bring the perfection of heaven into the realities of earth. Healing physical pain and ailments is just a step, a course correction on the journey back into God's perfect will for our lives.

My favorite lesson was that the Bible contains God's promises to us, and we only have to stand on the promises of His Word. I stand on the promise that if I lay hands on the sick, they will recover. I stand on the promise we all have a prosperous future ahead. I stand on the promise that our words, when spoken in Jesus' name, carry power, that we only have to "say to the mountain, 'Move from here to there,' and it will move; and nothing will be impossible for you." (See Mt 17:20.)

And finally, I stand on the promise of 1 Corinthians 2:16—that I have the mind of Christ. Hearing the voice of God is only as far away as my own thoughts. The tug that made me call the young man over to our table one more time. The tug that had us pick one particular Tex-Mex restaurant in the middle of Durant, Oklahoma. The tug that made me notice when a co-worker was down and simply ask God why. The tug is Christ in you.

Once you start believing that God wants to use you to bring the kingdom of heaven into earth—understanding the "tug" is easy. There is no sickness or disease in heaven—so it is never God's will for sickness or disease to exist in our lives on earth. It is God's will that we all die of old age. It is never God's will that we see our loved ones die young, or suffer from ailments. So it is safe to say, if you see someone suffering—it is not God's will for their lives. Rather, it is Satan stealing our God-ordained futures.

I hope my stories inspire you to act, to see suffering, and know it is not God's will. To know that if you speak to the problem in Jesus' name it has to submit to your authority in Christ. Go about your daily life and simply be open to being used by Him, to respond next time you feel the "tug."

> *For we are His workmanship, created in Christ Jesus for good works, which God prepared beforehand that we should walk in them.*
> EPH 2:10

Holly Cusato lives in Dallas, Texas and spends her days in the corporate world. After living most of her life as a Christian, it was only in the past few years she learned to serve as a minister of healing through the love and power of Jesus Christ. She shares her stories so that you might realize you have it in you as well. Normal people are making miracles happen.

Blog: https://supernaturallifeblog.wordpress.com

How the Lord Talks to Us
Tanya Vezza

THE OTHER NIGHT, MY husband and I enjoyed a rare night out. Our finances were tight, but we felt strongly led by the Lord to make reservations at a fairly expensive restaurant that we'd never eaten at before. The restaurant, Harvest Seasonal Kitchen, is located in the heart of a quaint and romantic historic downtown square. It is a farm-to-table concept with an interior design of upscale, rustic farm ambiance, with soft ethereal lighting. The hostess led us to table twenty-two; a cozy, two-person mahogany-colored table nestled deep in the restaurant. My eyes were immediately drawn to the regal looking, high-backed chairs covered in soft blue velour. As I sat down, I glanced up at the painting that decorated our seating area, a farm-themed, charcoal drawing of a fruit basket, titled "Fruit of Labors." We feasted on the most scrumptious locally sourced produce, meats, and wines. Of course, being that it was a rare splurge, we overindulged and extended our dinner into dessert and coffee.

Deliriously over-stuffed, we decided to stroll around the downtown square after dinner. Most of the buildings on the square were built in the late eighteen hundreds to early nineteen hundreds. As we were turning the first corner of our walk, I noticed the fading name "Hope & Sons" on an old brick building. We next walked by a waitress on her break sitting by the back door of the restaurant where she worked; her t-shirt said, "There's Lovin Over There." As we passed her, a co-worker of hers came out and struck up a conversation. His shirt had a large, edgy eagle graphic in the center. We continued walking until our stomachs were comfortable enough to return to our car, and wanted to end our night out with a drive through the country. As we were nearing our car, I glimpsed at the silhouette of a near-to-term pregnant woman in the distance. We reached our car and began driving out of the square, passing a beautiful black Range Rover.

All of these details may seem random, haphazard, or even insignificant to the average person, but the Lord orchestrated our entire evening and was speaking to me throughout the course of our date night. For several years, our family has been in a very challenging wilderness season that seemed to have no end in sight. Recently, the Lord has been communicating to us that we are in transition to a better season. It didn't strike me until we pulled up in front of the restaurant and I saw the sleek modern "Harvest" sign, the Lord reminded me that we are moving into a time of harvest in our own lives. The small downtown square was buzzing with people, and we were running late, so my husband dropped me off to check in while he found a parking spot. The hostess looked up our reservation, turned to her assistant, and said, "They'll be dining at table twenty-two." My heart immediately leapt for joy because the spiritual significance of the number two is a double-blessing; twenty-two conveyed a double-double blessing to me. The Lord was communicating the same theme again, through slightly different means. While I was sitting at our table waiting for my husband to join me, my attention was constantly drawn to the beautiful vacant blue chair across from me. In the midst of gazing at the chair, a gentle thought came to my mind that blue is the color of royalty, and we are His children, which makes us royal. My husband joined me and we were able to begin our date. During dinner, my eyes kept being drawn to the painting at our table. Finally, things connected with me when I read the title "Fruit of Labor." Amidst many years of trying difficulties, my husband and I have faithfully sown into the lives of anyone the Lord has put on our hearts, without ever seeing any change in our own circumstances. I nearly cried in the restaurant as I felt the Lord impress upon me that we were going to see the fruits of our labors and reap the benefits of the seeds that we had sown. The fancy restaurant and change of scene, as well as the ways the Lord directed our dinner, all pointed towards the themes He has been speaking to us recently of a coming harvest and transition into a time of prosperity.

After dinner, as we walked, the Lord continued to speak to and encourage me. He conveyed a message of hope to me through the name "Hope & Sons" on the historic building. The t-shirt the waitress wore reminded me of the Lord's love and that there is even more of His love waiting for us "over there" in the new place He has prepared for us. I have always liked eagles and hawks. They seem majestic to me in their sweeping movements of flight, soaring high above the Earth. For some reason, I always feel better when I see hawks, and am filled with the thought that something good is about to happen. The co-worker's t-shirt, depicting an eagle in flight, was a reinforcement of the message of hope the Lord had given me mere seconds earlier. We then turned to go back to our car, and I glimpsed at the pregnant woman who was nearly full term. Seeing her brought to my mind the Lord's recent messages to us that we are entering a new season and the impression He has given us recently that He is birthing something new in us. It also gave me hope that the advanced stage of her pregnancy might mean that we are closer than we know to the new thing the Lord has for us. Range Rovers are my dream cars and my favorite color for them is black. Whether I ever own one or not, they are beautiful and just looking at one makes me smile. Everything that is important to us is also important to the Lord. Seeing that Range Rover at the end of our evening was the culmination of everything the Lord had been speaking to me all night; hold onto hope, because I am transitioning you to a new place that is good.

The examples shown throughout the course of our evening illustrate how the Lord uses many ways to communicate. They also demonstrate how subtle and personally tailored His intentions are toward us. I believe people often miss the numerous ways the Lord speaks to us because His methods are so subtle. He is always right beside us so there is no need to speak loudly. He is also a gentleman, so He tailors His approach in a manner that is personal without infringing on us in a forceful way. Because of the manner in which the Lord speaks to us, as well as being constantly around us, most people mistake His overtures as chance or coincidence.

Over the course of my life, I have become attuned to ways the Lord speaks. The initial challenge is recognizing how He interacts with us. Luckily, as soon as you are able to connect with any form of communication, hearing Him becomes easier with each interaction. The main methods of communication the Lord uses with me are: speaking directly, speaking through others, speaking through circumstances, and alternative means of communication.

SPEAKING DIRECTLY

Examples of how the Lord speaks to us directly include:

- Putting impressions on our heart
- Gently but consistently bringing things to mind
- Dreams
- Visions
- On rare occasions, hearing His voice

Oftentimes, what people consider "sixth sense" or "intuition" is really the Lord speaking to us. A few years ago, the Lord put a former high school friend on my husband's heart. He hadn't seen or talked to this friend in years. Over the course of several months, my husband would mention that this man was in his thoughts, and that he needed to give him a call. My husband had every good intention of calling his friend but life always got in the way and he never ended up speaking to him. As it turned out, his friend was in an extremely dark place, and sadly, the man ended up taking his own life. My husband was devastated by his friend's death because he realized the Lord had been reaching out to him because his friend was in need of help. After this experience, he vowed that if the Lord ever put anyone on his heart, he would reach out to them because the Lord had some purpose in bringing them to mind.

SPEAKING THROUGH OTHER PEOPLE

Examples of how the Lord speaks to us through others include:

- "Divine appointments"
- People directly speaking to us
- Prophetic words
- Impressions or things on their heart they feel they need to share

I use the term "divine appointments" for interactions I have with other people that I have not planned, but are clearly orchestrated by the Lord. For example, a couple of weeks ago, I was having a rough day. In the midst of my chaos, a dear friend called me up and invited me to go shopping with her at a new store. It would have been easier for me to stay home and deal with some issues that needed my attention, but for some reason, I really felt that I needed to go out with my friend. While we were shopping, she turned to me and said, "Did you know that your housing development is one of the most sought after locations?" She continued, mentioning that people were getting into bidding wars in my neighborhood and that our house would likely sell quickly, if not even before going on the market. Then, she turned and looked at me and said, "Have you considered that selling your house and getting the equity from it might be the way for you to get a clean start and position yourself for a better financial future?"

Her simple statement brought to my recollection that I also had two other people casually mention selling our house within the past week or so. It became clear that the Lord was trying to speak to me about letting go of our house.

When my husband and I spoke that evening and looked over our financial situation, it became clear that desperately clinging to a house we could no longer afford was ridiculous. The Lord was speaking through my friend; and He was correct. The equity from our house will allow us to get out of debt, move forward, and make investments that will position us for a better future, things that we would not be able to do had we not "heard" the Lord speaking to us through my friend that day.

SPEAKING THROUGH CIRCUMSTANCES

One example of how the Lord speaks to us through circumstances:

- Seeing meaning or correlations between things happening in our life or those around us

OBJECT LESSONS

I use the term "object lessons" for experiences in life that teach me a spiritual, as well as a temporal lesson. When I was younger, I was much more carefree and willing to take risks without fearing possible mistakes. In fact, I never viewed mistakes negatively, but rather as learning opportunities. Somehow, over the years, I developed a fear of making mistakes and what it would cost me and those I loved. One afternoon, while driving home with my children, I was so deep in conversation with them that I made a wrong turn. Almost immediately, I realized my mistake and was able to quickly and easily get back on track. As I headed out in the correct direction, it dawned on me that if I happened to get off course in other areas of my life, the Lord would just as quickly and easily be able to get me going in the direction He intended for me. He was always gently leading me and I had nothing to fear.

ALTERNATIVE MEANS OF COMMUNICATION

Examples of how the Lord speaks to us through alternative means of communication include:

- Music/Songs
- Media
- Social media
- Movies
- TV
- Articles of clothing (such as shirts with words on them)
- Printed materials
- Books

- Bible
- Magazines
- Pamphlets
- Flyers
- Billboards
- Fortune cookies
- Paintings and other art (in various mediums)
- Photographs
- Secular and non-Christian means

The list of alternative ways the Lord uses to speak to us is as large and varied as each individual person. This list is by no means exhaustive, but includes some of the most common ways I encounter the Lord speaking to me through methods that may not always be obvious or expected.

It is not uncommon for me to see or hear multiple things from the Lord during the course of my day. My family is in a period of transition and breakthrough. Given the season we are in, things are in flux all around us, and in many ways we have lost not only a sense of comfort, but our bearings. I have been praying to the Lord and asking Him for encouragement and wisdom. Recently, I met a friend for coffee during the evening. I started my car and as I drove away from my house, the song "Two Tickets to Paradise" by Eddie Money came on the radio. It is an older song that isn't usually played, which made it stick out in my mind. This song is encouraging to me. The lyrics include:

> *"Got a surprise especially for you*
> *Something that both of us*
> *Have always wanted to do*
> *We've waited so long*
> *Waited so long*
> *We've waited so long*
> *Waited so long"*

Given our current circumstances, I could sense the Lord's delight that He has a special surprise He is just as excited to give us, as we are to receive. The lyrics also spoke to how long we've yearned for the things the Lord has promised us.

The next morning, I was woken by my radio alarm to the ending lyrics of American Authors, "Best Day of My Life,"

> *"This is gonna be, this is gonna be, this is gonna be*
> *The best day of my life*
> *Everything is looking up, everybody up now*
> *This is gonna be the best day of my life*
> *My li-i-i-i-i-ife"*

After waking up, I ran errands. While I was out, I drove past a church with a sign saying "MOVE" and the letters had arrows coming from them pointing "up." I took that to mean the Lord was saying it is time for my family to "move up."

I returned home and spent some time relaxing and catching up on Facebook. A particular post caught my attention. It was a quote that said, "You must be brave enough to release something good to make the space for something great." The Lord has been speaking to us lately that there are certain things we need to let go of in order to move forward. This Facebook post was another reinforcement of things the Lord has been speaking to us.

There is another way the Lord speaks with us that many people don't even consider, and many would find controversial. The Lord can use anything or anyone to communicate, which means He also uses secular culture and non-Christians. Because everything and everyone on earth is made from God's hands, He can use anything as His mouthpiece; oftentimes, non-believers don't even realize the Lord is speaking through them or using them as His instrument.

As I'm sure you are aware by now, music is a common way the Lord speaks to me. I'm sure some of my more traditional Christian friends would be very surprised to know that the Lord has used songs by rap artists such as Eminem and Ace Hood to encourage me. Eminem's songs "Not Afraid" and "One Shot" are my favorites because each song speaks of overcoming fears and obstacles head on, while taking the risk to live out your dreams and realize your full potential. God led me to the song "Lord Knows" by Ace Hood during the darkest and most challenging financial experience my family has ever faced. My husband

and I had both lost our jobs, we had exhausted our entire savings, we had a mountain of overdue bills, and we were running out of food and didn't have the money to buy groceries. "Lord Knows" just appeared on the opening page of my favorite free music streaming website one day. I felt the Lord saying, "Listen to that song." I clicked on it, and the lyrics instantly spoke to me.

> *"Dear Lord,*
> *I understand all the problems that I'm about to express to you*
> *Are things you already know*
> *Well here goes nothing...*
> *Dear Lord I'm on my knees and I'm begging please*
> *Just guide me father this is a time I'm really in need...*
> *Man only Lord knows what the hell I done really been through*
> *All the nights I hadn't no food*
> *Dear God tell me what I'm gon do...*
> *I was down and out remember that like yesterday been out that struggle break it this year I'm blessed to say...*
> *And I thank you Jesus for guidin me, for keeping me*
> *In your name I pray*
> *And only Lord knows"*

This man had been through the very same struggles I was facing and had found his way out. It gave me a sense of hope that if he had gotten through it, so could I. In his own way, this rapper reached out to the Lord. He was brutally honest with the Lord about his feelings. But, in the end, he was still going to the Lord. God is big enough that He can handle our feelings. In the end, what He ultimately wants from us is a genuine, honest, and transparent relationship.

The more extreme or overt the manner in which the Lord reaches out to us signifies how important it is to Him that we recognize He is the one speaking to us. The loudest I have heard the Lord communicate is when He had an agnostic speak to my husband. My husband had a dream in his heart. It was a very big dream and it was very personal and specific. I am the only person he ever shared his dream with. As the years passed and the dream wasn't realized, it appeared unrealistic that it would ever be fulfilled. The dream was starting to fade from my husband's thoughts. One day while we were having dinner with family, an agnostic family member excitedly pulled my husband aside to tell him about a dream he recently had. My husband was in his dream. With acute precision, he described down to the minutest detail, every part of the dream the Lord had placed on my husband's heart. The Lord orchestrated things so it was unmistakable that He was speaking. By speaking this way, God strongly captured my husband's attention and helped bring his dream back to life.

The Lord is constantly reaching out to us. The only real obstacle to unfettered communication with Him is attuning our hearts, minds, and senses to the myriad of ways that He is endlessly reaching out to us. Once you make that initial connection, it opens up an entire world of uninhibited and unstoppable communication. So, how is the Lord trying to speak to you?

Tanya Vezza is a stay-at-home mom, who has been married since 1998, and has two teenage children. She loves to cook and travel. In her spare time, she likes to write. Tanya has a unique relationship with the Lord and enjoys writing about the adventurous life He has called her to experience in Him.

Blog: www.tanyavezza.com
Email: tanya@tanyavezza.com

Hearing from God
Katie Regan

GROWING UP, I BELIEVED that the only way to regularly "hear from God" was to read your Bible. I was raised on a quiet farm in the rural prairies of North Dakota, and worshipped at the same Norwegian Lutheran church that three generations of my family had faithfully attended since immigrating to America over a century ago. Here my mother was the organist, and my dad was a Sunday school teacher. Although our church didn't have any teachings about the manifestations of the Spirit, my father believed in speaking in tongues, and miracles. He wanted them, so naturally I wanted them as well. I wanted to be just like my dad.

My childhood was what I consider idyllic. Long peaceful days and nights of wheat fields, hard work, and breathtaking sunsets melting a huge open sky. The winters were a frozen, white tapestry of bitter winds and treacherous snow banks, giving a sense of serene calm even in harsh circumstances. And the short summers—my favorite—were overflowing with ripe strawberry paths in what seemed like an endlessly large garden, magnificent black cattle herds dotted the countryside, and mild temperatures caressed your skin with the elusive prospect of getting a tan in 70 degree sun.

It was in this place that I first began to hear God, though I didn't recognize His voice until many years later. I developed a keen appreciation of nature, from the smallest blades of grass to the farthest diamond clusters of light in the deep of night. Many evenings in solitude, I would climb up to the roof of the barn and lay watching the kaleidoscope of galaxies swirl in slow motion. I would talk to God, asking Him a million questions, thanking Him for the beauty of His creation, and simply breathing in the wonder of it all. I never expected to hear His reply. But I secretly wanted to hear Him, deeply, quietly… afraid to even let the desire bubble to the surface.

Rejection was my biggest fear. You see, I had always secretly thought that God didn't want me as much as He wanted men to be on the earth. I thought He made men because He wanted them and He made women just to please men and that although He loved me, I was just an afterthought, a servant, a thing. It would be many years before I learned the truth.

And yet, in those dark nights of stargazing, in the colors and smells of dew drops on wild prairie roses, in the awe and wonder of the Dakota plain's deer and flatland creatures, I felt an intense stirring inside. There was something swirling, burning, speaking, and I could not explain it.

At a very young age, I began to have vivid, gripping dreams. They would stay with me upon waking and I couldn't shake them. Different than other fast-fading dreams, I could always tell the ones that were heavily outlined in saturated color and emotion. They were written in permanent ink on my mind. I would stumble down the creaky, wooden stairs in the dead of night to find my parents and they said it was just nightmares and not to worry. I didn't understand until many years later that dreams were one of the ways that God would speak to me through my entire life, warning me, giving me seeds to activate, revealing battle plans, and inviting me to partner with His vision.

Looking back, I can see that God was actively speaking to me from infancy. He speaks to all of us, at all times, in different ways. Whatever we have the faith for, He's right there, engaging us in the way that we can believe in. And He always pushes us to go further, believe more, and expand our vision to match His.

WHAT DOES HE SOUND LIKE?

The Bible says His voice is like the sound of many waters rushing (think Niagara Falls), or like thunder booming. Just as my own voice sometimes yells, sometimes sings, sometimes rushes, and sometimes slowly whispers, God's voice lifts and falls, roars and coos, shakes the earth, and vibrates the core of our hearts. When He speaks to us individually in secret, He's not roaring like a lion. There's no need to shout when He's living on the inside of us. He roars at the enemy. He roars at death and corruption. He declares a thing and it's done. His voice is released and the created things in the universe respond. Once you become more familiar with recognizing His voice, listen for the different ways that God's voice sounds to you when He's speaking to you privately, when He's speaking to groups, and when He's speaking to creation. A Father's voice has different tones, volume, and depth, depending on who He's talking to, what subject He's talking about, and His intentions.

In the Old Testament days, the Spirit of God didn't live inside humans, so whenever a person heard the voice of God, it was always an external audible voice, which is why the Bible frequently speaks of a booming voice. But in these New Covenant days, we who have given our lives to Jesus have the Spirit living inside of our bodies. So we have the obvious advantage of being able to hear God speak through our minds, our thoughts, and even externally, if He chooses. It doesn't always sound like a distinct voice, separate from our own. For me, it's frequently a thought pressing into my mind... but not always.

I remember one evening when all of my household was asleep. I lay in bed thinking about God, the universe, heaven and hell. Suddenly I heard a male voice whisper my name, right into my ear, as if his face was a centimeter away. "Katie..."

In an instant, I had the awareness of intimacy. This was a closeness that no one but your spouse and children should dare to enter into. Even though I recognized that the voice was not my husband, I instinctually turned to look at my husband in surprise. He was fast asleep, on the farthest edge of the bed, turned away from me, just a tuft of dark hair peeking out of the covers.

The voice was gentle, tender, beautiful, calling me. Acknowledging me. He knows my name. And He calls to me in the night. Just that very thought gives me such joy.

FLEXING YOUR SPIRITUAL SENSES

In the physical world, we hear dogs bark, cars honk, and people sing. We learned, from the womb, to use our physical ears to hear physical sounds. Every time our infant ears heard a new sound, it lit up a new neuron cable in our brain, connecting and activating different regions of sound recognition. This allowed us to begin to instantly recognize sounds, become familiar with who or what it was coming from, and understand what the sound meant.

As new baby creatures in Christ, we start the process all over again, this time in the spirit realm. Just as human babies are perfectly designed to learn to hear physical sounds, spiritual babies are perfectly designed to learn to hear spiritual sounds. We're wired this way. It's normal, healthy, and easy for new creatures to learn to hear God's voice. If you've been taught that only the "special people" hear from God, change your perspective. In this New Covenant age, His kids hear His voice and learn to recognize it.

We are a spirit living in a human body, so we are both in the physical realm and also in the spirit realm at the same time. We practice learning how to use our spiritual ears to hear a spiritual God. There is a whole new realm opened up to us, because of the blood of Jesus. Remember, the physical world is modeled after the spirit world. We've already learned how to use our physical senses to navigate this world; now we must learn how to use our spiritual senses to navigate the spiritual world that we're a part of (God's Kingdom.)

God speaks to us and teaches us through dreams, through nature, through colors, sounds, shapes, textures, music, other people, animals, galaxies… the truth is that God can speak to us through anything that He wants to. We will see or hear something in the physical world and suddenly a thought is upon us that makes us wonder. Something profound. Something beautiful. Something that instigates awe, or a change of direction, a discernment, a warning, or a beautiful meditation. Sometimes He will speak to you about you. And sometimes He will give you a word that He wants you to say to someone else.

Anyone and everyone can hear from God, and anyone and everyone can hear from other spirits in the spirit realm. There are a few keys to getting a stronger "signal" to receive and recognize His voice:

DESIRE

If you want to hear from God, you will. At a young age, God placed the desire in me to want to hear Him and to want to know Him. So for many years, I pressed through wrong understanding and areas of unbelief, as He continually drew me into right understanding and clearer hearing. It's a process that continues to this day.

You search Him out. You look for Him in the everyday miracles of life. The clouds, the wind, the laughter of children—they are all miracles that echo His name and display His hands actively working, loving us constantly.

If you don't have the desire, or if it's waning, you simply ask. You say, "God, I don't feel a strong desire to hear You, but I know I'm supposed to. So fan the flame. Make my desire for You stronger and give me a deep passion to hear You. Give me grace and give me expectation." He will do it. You ask and you keep on asking.

UNIQUE VIBRATIONS

Everybody hears Him differently. Don't get hung up on hearing Him the way that so-and-so does. You have your own unique relationship with

Him and He will speak to you in a way that's deeply personal and fitting for you individually. There are often combinations of ways that people hear from God. Some people get God dreams, visions, and moments of clarity through nature. Some people hear Him speaking and teaching through color, texture, and sound vibrations. Some people read books or listen to songs and get instant revelatory downloads. God speaks through secular music, secular books, secular movies, and secular people—don't limit Him. He can speak through a donkey if He wants to.

He frequently teaches me through secular music, plot lines in books and movies, and even news articles and broadcasts, which oftentimes mirror spiritual scenarios. I'll be minding my own business, relaxing, and suddenly I'm hit with a wave of revelation or truth or even a funny joke He tells. It gently presses into my mind and touches my soul. Sometimes a split-second download of truth will spark a joy explosion that wipes away anxiety, frustration, or pain. Watch for His wisdom to come to the surface in your mind. You'll be amazed.

One of my favorite ways to intentionally hear from God is to simply begin talking to Him and wait for His reply. I like to get alone and read the Bible, find a gripping scripture, and meditate on it for days and weeks to see what new layers of revelation He'll give me. It's also exciting for me to observe and experience nature and simply enjoy it wordlessly with Him. We communicate without words in a way that's hard to explain, but it's infused with joy and wonder and curiosity, much like a small child exploring the woods for the first time. He will show you such beautiful secrets if you spend time enjoying Him, with no agenda, no schedule, and no demands.

Some people have surprise glory encounters where out of the blue, they're hit with a teaching, a meditation, or a single, power-infused, life-changing thought. Some people go for walks and converse with the Creator of all things. Some people hear Him through their work or daily tasks. Some people hear Him while they're brushing their teeth and others hear Him best in quiet, still meditation. One man I know said he frequently hears God while he's shaving each morning. Some people hear Him best when they're scaling a mountain or holding sick babies. Seek Him out in whatever ways work best for you. He'll meet you where you are, whatever you have the faith to believe for.

You will have a thought, impression, or a sense of something gently pressing into your mind. Sometimes it will be words, other times it might be phrases, a picture, a vision (like watching a video) or an emotion that He wants you to ask Him about. Sometimes, it might be a stirring, something that cannot be expressed with human words. When you don't understand what it means, ask Him to give you understanding.

Busyness is a good way to quiet His voice, pushing it to the corner. In fact, many people purposely construct busy lives, in an effort to distract themselves from the pain, frustration, and disillusionment they've experienced. However, if you have a busy life, and it's out of your hands, don't feel condemned. God will always meet you right where you're at, giving you grace to hear Him and enjoy Him no matter what your circumstances are. Your desire for Him will supersede any busyness that's out of your control.

IS IT GOD OR...

If the thought or sense invites you to embrace wisdom, hope, love, or other characteristics of His nature, these are God's thoughts. If the thoughts bring fear, hatred, hopelessness or other characteristics of the old, dead world, discard them; they are not from your Father.

Be careful to examine thoughts carefully, though. Not every scary thought is from the enemy. If you're afraid, it may just be that you're looking at God's message from the wrong perspective. Sometimes God will show you scary events, not to scare you, but to invite you to intercede, to expose the enemy's plans or some natural disaster, and to counter it with His vision for the future and together change the forecasted events.

Sometimes He will give you a weird or scary dream or vision that is symbolic. Don't discard these poetic God-thoughts; they're given to you for a purpose. When you're invited to partner with God to release revelation, wisdom, instruction or encouragement, or to change the future, it may not come in the form you were looking for. So we stay humble, ready to learn, ready to unlearn the things we thought we knew and to be schooled by the Spirit.

You've got to remember that God is not a human. Human words are not His first language and they're not ours either. We communicate Spirit-to-spirit in a spirit language and the message gets filtered through our human mind, understanding, and words. That's why everyone has their own unique way of expressing or translating what God has said to them. Some people speak in 17th century King James vernacular when giving a word from God. Other people use words unique to their culture. Some people use flowery, poetic words. Others sound very bland and abrupt.

So don't worry when people express things through their own filters of past experience, cultural vocabulary, and current belief systems. God's not worried about it and we don't need to be either. When we learn to hear people with spiritual ears, the words they say are just secondary.

SURRENDER

Love Him with all your heart, mind, soul, and strength. Many people are concerned about being deceived, hearing demonic voices, and getting swept off into some faraway cult activity. They want to hear God, but are afraid of deception, so they stick to only receiving His words as written in their favorite Bible version.

Let me tell you lovingly, the Bible is wonderful, but the Author is even better. God is not fully contained in the Bible. The Bible is an introduction to the lover of your soul. There is more.

If you want to hear His voice, but keep far away from deception, then ask Him to keep your heart and mind in purity. The quickest way to get into deception is by disobeying Him and harboring secret sins. This is what's known as "taking His Name in vain." If you say you love Him, say you want Him, but disregard His words, you're fooling yourself. And that's a dangerous path. This is truly where the rubber meets the road. You can fool all the people in the world, but you can't fool God. This is where your love relationship with Him gets real. You keep yourself accountable to Him. You keep yourself involved with His mind and His heart, daily, heartbeat by heartbeat. You press into daily intimacy with Him and you let Him probe you.

He's never reaching out to you to shame you or humiliate you. He doesn't get inside your personal bubble to hurt you, scare you, or yell at you. You certainly may feel scared or shameful if you're being confronted about bad behavior, but that's never His intention. He's a big, scary guy, but He's the most loving, gentle, tender, powerfully compassionate Father you'll ever encounter. When He confronts you about painful issues, or sin issues, it's always so that He can heal you, show you the Truth, and give you the opportunity to release all the lies, hatred, impurity, and wrong thinking. He has nothing but blessing, favor, joy, love, and peace waiting for you. It's never an emptying out without a filling back up of everything that's pure, good, and worthy of a royal child of God. He simply says, "That's not who you are. That thought you've been thinking, or that behavior you've been indulging... that's not who you are. You don't have to do that anymore. Let me show you who you are." And He gives you an image of your true, holy, beautiful, royal self, with overflowing grace to believe, to grab hold of it, and to walk in it.

So we say, "God, let me love You with all my heart, mind, soul, and strength. Keep my heart and mind turned to You always. Protect me from deception. Every time You bring something to my attention that needs repentance, give me grace to do it Your way. I can't do this thing on my own, God. Pour down Your supernatural power to walk in Your ways and to stay under Your wings. Thank You God! You are more powerful than the enemy. You are more loving than he is hateful. Your Truth is stronger than his lies. Let me always be enraptured by You and You alone, in Jesus' name."

WRITE IT DOWN

Your journey is unique. The things He's spoken to me might not be the same things He says to you. We are all on a path of growing up, in Him. We keep growing, keep discarding the old beliefs in favor of the new truths He shows us, and we expand our vision.

In my own journey, it has been immeasurably helpful to keep a God journal. In the beginning, I wrote down favorite scriptures or passages that were stirring something intense in my soul. I would write freely, expressing my thoughts and observations, and frequently found that the releasing of words on a thin piece of paper would heal all sorts of wounds, and bring clarity to all manner of confusion. Yes, God can speak to you and through you through your own personal act of writing. I would write and He would counsel me. I would jot down ideas; He was birthing dreams. I poured out my heart like tears; He was wiping away the pain and applying soothing balm.

Not only can God speak to you through private journaling, it can be revelatory to look back and finally understand what He was saying to you all those years ago. You had written about a dream, or a vision, or a confusing scripture, but now you see it with His eyes and you understand what it means. You get an immediate sense of your growth and it gives you faith and confidence for the next season, the next step.

GRATITUDE

A thankful heart has no limits.

One of the surest ways to stifle the voice of God is to grumble, complain and foster a "not enough" attitude. It's not that He stops talking or that He's angry at us and huffs off in a fit. It's simply one of those spiritual laws—you reap what you sow. God wants us to continually sow goodness, because He wants what's best for us. But He doesn't want a bunch of robots, we have free will to think and do and say as we please. So if we sow thankfulness, we will reap a huge harvest of things to be thankful for. If we suppress the natural desire of our new spiritual identity to be thankful, our spiritual senses get dull, slow, and corrupted, like strong muscles that begin to atrophy with disuse.

Think of the natural mechanisms in an engine. The machine needs constant lubrication to run smoothly, quietly, efficiently, and optimally. If the wheels, gears, and valves run out of oil, they quickly degrade and can become rusty and static.

Gratitude is the oil that keeps our spiritual senses functioning in peak condition and not only optimally, but even advancing, growing more fine-tuned and complex, more aligned with our spiritual senses day by day.

So we learn to cultivate a heart attitude that is always thankful. We look for things to be thankful for. On the best days, on the worst days, we search (and we don't have to search far) to find even one small thing to be thankful for. Even if it's just a small flower in a dirty patch of grass. Even if it's the tiny smile that a baby gave you in Wal-Mart. Even if it's that you have clothes on your back, or that you had food today, or that you just took a breath without pain. Anything. Find something to be thankful for and then say it. The action here is important. You say, either out loud, or in your mind, "God, thank You for such-and-such." And you pause a moment to say it with sincerity.

A genuine word or thought of gratitude is like a small wind on a vast ocean. Small shifts create large waves. When you purposely set your heart to engage God with gratitude, you enter into a conversation. Your intentional act of thankfulness, no matter how small, sets off a spark in the spirit realm. It ignites a flame that turns into an explosion of supernatural power. Suddenly, your attitude is different. You may only feel a small turn, but if you could see in the spirit realm, you would see demons repelled and angels activated.

When you release thankfulness, you are releasing the very nature of God and it's a warm aroma, His own breath flowing and delivering life and fragrance to every part of your atmosphere. Cultivating a heart attitude of thankfulness grows you up, helps shake off old, dead mindsets that you don't need here in this new day, and allows you to enter in deeper, to continue, with clarity, your conversation with the I AM.

Thankfulness invites the truths of the spirit realm, God's kingdom, to invade and displace the natural, physical components of your daily reality. Quite literally, thankfulness allows you to hear Him better, more consistently, and allows the heavenly realm to flow effortlessly out of your being and into the physical world around you.

Thankfulness is highly under-used, under-rated, and largely ignored. It's a powerful weapon to release the Kingdom and hear His voice in your everyday life. Be intentional with this. Throughout the day, look for things to be thankful for and then say it in your mind or out loud. If you're having a particularly horrid day, make sure to find something to be thankful for—it will change your life, instantly.

At the end of the day, or if you're a morning person and up with the roosters, go to some place alone, get out your God journal, and write out what you're thankful for. Doesn't matter how small it is, no one's looking but your Daddy. You let it flow, without judgment, without editing... you release whatever comes to mind and suddenly you're feeling very blessed. This activity, by the way, is an excellent way to activate the spiritual fruit of joy, that supernatural, impossible fruit that only God can manifest.

THE NEW NORMAL

In conclusion, remember that you are designed to hear God. It's part of your inheritance, part of your spiritual DNA, your destiny, and part of your new daily life in Christ. It doesn't matter what your background is, where you came from, or what you were taught. Hearing from God is normal. Not hearing from your Dad, is not normal. Change your perspective and anticipate this new awareness, this new level of Kingdom living. Then celebrate, with thankfulness and excitement, each new sound you hear echoing through His heart.

What I've written about here are only my own experiences and observations, and perspectives thus far. Be free to explore His voice and His world in ways that no one else has experienced yet. There is more. There is always more. Be ever mindful that He's on your side and He wants you to hear Him even more than you do. Each step of the way, God will give you grace to keep moving forward, advancing and improving and expanding. Praise God! Enjoy the journey, my friend, my sibling. He's a good Dad and whether you're a new Christian or a seasoned warrior, I'm glad to have you in the family. Grace, vision, sharpened senses, and fresh awareness to you, in Jesus' beautiful name.

Katie Regan is an American author. She grew up on a farm in the grassy plains of North Dakota and now enjoys living in lush, green North Carolina, USA with her husband and children. To see a current list of her publications, visit her Amazon author page: *amazon.com/author/katiereganauthor*

Twitter: @katiereganauthr

Hearing God in "Knowing"
Laurie Bruesehoff Hilgers

STILLNESS IS A PRECURSOR to rest in the Lord, drawing us into a continual experience of His Presence. Put simply, we have to hear God's silence before we can listen to His voice. A silence exists in God that is so knowing, so healing, so releasing, and so embracing, that all kinds of things can be communicated to your heart.

The silence is almost deafening:

> *"Deep calls unto deep at the noise of Your waterfalls; All Your waves and billows have gone over me."*
> PSALM 42:7

Here are the words of Graham Cooke from *Approaching the Heart of Prophecy*: "That capacity to enter stillness can release an unbroken communion with God and bring us into a place of being God-conscious."

How do you explain the wonder and awe of hearing God's voice? How do you describe the intimacy and friendship that we're each invited to share with Him? I've spent a considerable amount of time sorting through my memories in various seasons of my life. Many of the times I "heard" Him speaking to me were pivotal, life-changing events.

Sometimes, He speaks with His still small voice in my spirit. Other times, I've heard it audibly. Most often, however, He will speak to me through impressions or visions, a "knowing," if you will.

This "knowing" is an anchor that gives me confidence. It helps me hear Him in His silence. I can trust that He's still with me and will never leave me. This truth leads me to ask who He wants to be for me in every circumstance. I have a quiet confidence that He leads me in silence, since we are One. Here's my personal paraphrase of Isaiah 30:15b: "In quietness and confidence shall my strength be."

I've come to the conclusion that there are no limits to hearing His voice, especially if your ear is continually tuned to hear what He is speaking in the moment.

My relationship with Him has been on the fast track since that beautiful day of deeper surrender when I somehow found myself in a sobbing heap on the floor of my closet. It was a safe refuge for me after I'd retreated to my bedroom to escape the enemy's tormenting words through a loved one. I was in my 30's at the time.

God was waiting up there for me that day and His intent was clear—to capture me with His love. When I ran into the room an emotional train wreck, there was no fight left in me and nowhere else to run. I stood there, tears streaming down my cheeks. I was weary and worn out. I looked up with resignation to the inevitable, it seemed, and said, "I don't even know what you want with me, but if you want to do something with my life, you can have it."

Then I crawled into the small, dark closet, moving shoes out of my way so I could sit down. I wrapped my arms around my knees, buried my head in them and cried some more. When my tears were exhausted, I emerged from the dark closet. Something was different. Now, I had peace.

Hearing God in "Knowing"

While that was a moment of a deeper surrender, it was far from my first encounter or conversation with Him. Although He didn't speak to me with words that day, He began to show me in greater detail how He had always been with me. We really had been communicating all along.

We'd been in relationship since the beginning; I just didn't know how to relate to Him, and I didn't believe He loved me. If you don't believe someone loves you, it's difficult to trust his or her words and good intentions. Circumstances, choices, and lies from the enemy had caused my thoughts and mind to be out of agreement with His heart toward me. Those things, however, were subject to radical change.

Over the years, He's taken me back to places in my childhood and shown me where He was, and how He made His presence known in so many ways. I'd like to share them with you. As we walk through these memories together, you'll likely begin to see where He's always walked with you in your own life. Grab something good to drink (and maybe some tissues) and get comfortable. Here we go.

In one memory, I see my oldest brother and I playing in the woods where the cow paths wove through old oak trees high up on the bluff. The creek ran down below, and over time, it had carved out a little island perfect for childhood play and imagination. Trees had fallen over the water from the island to the pasture, giving us bridges to cross. It was our paradise, 15 minutes from the farmyard, a place where we would take picnic lunches and play make believe for hours. He played with us those days, walking the paths with us, keeping us from falling off the hill.

My next memory goes back to grade school, and our teacher, Mr. Clausen. I was in the fifth grade. I was a misfit in my class of nine kids. I had already experienced some great traumas in my young life, and they had caused me to turn inward. Occasionally, I would experience brief moments of peace. Now, I realize this was Holy Spirit comforting me.

At the time, I was reading about what our behavior toward others was to be. I was reading I Corinthians 13, also known as the "love" chapter. In my heart, I sensed God showing me His way of doing things.

A light bulb switched "on" in me as I silently observed that what I was reading was not being demonstrated in the Christian school I was attending. I felt the Lord's heart and presence that day. I felt His sadness when I was taken to the principal's office for staying in from recess to read rather than go outside. It was safer than being mocked and bullied by my classmates.

I knew that Mr. Clausen saw what was going on. It turned out that our new teacher was a misfit, too. Conflict arose when he challenged the leaders of the church and school. I sensed it had to do with standing up for me but I never knew for certain.

These tender years were awful. I didn't have any safe place to be. Home wasn't safe; school wasn't safe. Even riding the bus was awful. I could count on being punched and spit on several times per week. The bus driver only laughed at the boys. I had no one to defend me.

Eventually, Mr. Clausen was forced to leave his position for reasons that weren't clear to me. I remember crying. He was one person who "got" me. I looked up to him, and he cared for me. I fondly remember roller-skating with him during a school outing at the roller rink. He smiled down at me with his gentle, kind eyes. He was a true gentleman. He showed me the heart of Father God, the love of Jesus and the comfort of Holy Spirit.

As life moved forward, our family became unraveled for many of the same reasons so many others do; we weren't getting what we really needed from our Dad in Heaven. We each turned to harmful, wrong things to fill the voids. As the voids in my life grew and my emotional wounds became more painful, I turned to smoking, drinking, and a few other things to numb the pain.

Several years later, my spiritual experiences and my "hearing" Him went to another level. My first real job in the world was working in a nursing home. This was a pivotal, life-changing experience and I'm still grateful for it. I learned love and compassion while caring for elderly and sick people. Many of them had no one else to love them. I learned to be with them in their brokenness and dying, to cry with them, to hold their hands.

Hearing God in "Knowing"

My old friend Otto was in his eighties. He was the grandfather of some high school acquaintances. Both of his legs were amputated above the knee from the effects of diabetes. I looked forward to taking care of Otto, which I did often. We loved each other. I remember him saying to me, "Girl, if you were a few years older, I believe I'd ask you to be my wife."

I laugh now at how he would grab my face with both hands and kiss me goodnight with no teeth in his mouth. Oh, how we laughed and had fun together! When he had a massive heart attack one night arguing over a card game with the ladies, there was no bringing him back. I cried and cried. We all did. He was beloved, our Otto was.

I'd worked in this particular nursing home right out of high school, and then left to pursue private care for several people with greater needs. It was interesting that as my own wounds were influencing my decisions in negative ways, I began caring for people who couldn't walk, some who couldn't feed themselves. These were paraplegics, quadriplegics, and one person with MS. Eventually, I realized I was in over my head in caretaking at this level, and I returned to work at the nursing home.

It was in my second stint of employment there when I met a co-worker named "Jim." He was a few years younger than me. We enjoyed working together, and became infatuated with each other. I was in an unstable relationship at the time, which had grown more tenuous after I watched him do a line of cocaine in front of me. Jim was pure and untainted by the world, and we laughed a lot. He was refreshing to be around.

One Saturday night, Jim had made plans to go to a midnight showing of the movie, "Dawn of the Dead." I was uneasy with our choice of movies, but I didn't know why. I was sensitive to darkness and had been all of my life. I just didn't understand what I was dealing with. Religious school didn't teach me about Ephesians, chapter six, and our battle against spiritual entities.

Before the movie, we went to a place called The Lion's Tap for their famous hamburgers. We each had a beer, burger, and fries. The beer was okay for me, but Jim was not of age yet. I recall that I felt something unsettling in my gut as we ate. I didn't understand what it was, so I did my best to suppress it. After dinner, we drove to the theatre. All through the movie, I wanted to get up and leave. Something in me was screaming to get up and run out of there. I was afraid of offending Jim, so we sat through all of it. When the show was over, it was almost two a.m. While we were in the theatre, the sky had opened up outside. The rain pummeled the pavement so hard it bounced back up. Fear had taken a firm grip on me in the movie, and now driving home in the torrential rain compounded it.

The windshield wipers were unable to keep up with the rain as we drove west in the old Ford Fairlane. We approached a town called Chaska. The downpour hadn't let up and visibility was poor. Through the rain and windshield wipers, we both saw another vehicle begin to make a left turn in front of our car. As the distance between cars decreased, I heard myself screaming, "Oh, God!" Jim was screaming, too. There was a crash and then everything went dark. In retrospect, I believe Holy Spirit would have had us simply go home after dinner. There was an assignment set against us. He was trying to protect us from the eventual outcome.

I woke up in excruciating pain. Jim called my name to see if I was okay. I couldn't answer him. When the vehicles had collided, I'd been sitting next to him. The 1965 model wasn't equipped with seat belts, so there was nothing to hold me back except the steering wheel. My body had flown up and got caught on it, collapsing both my lungs. While my whole body was prevented from going through the windshield, my head was not. So through it went, and then re-entered the car. After the initial impact, and after everything stopped moving, I was lying in a heap on the floor of the passenger side of the car.

I next remember paramedics coming to assess and help me. I heard myself screaming in pain as they were moving me. Remember that I worked in healthcare and I knew some things about spinal cord injuries. As the paramedics worked on me, I asked them if my neck was broken. My mindset at the time was that if my neck was broken, I didn't want to live. I was making my choice to live based on their response, or so I thought. They ignored my question at first. I can only imagine their thoughts at being asked the question. "What do we tell her?" I asked them again and maybe a third time until they asked me if I could wiggle my toes. Much to my surprise, I could, and as soon as I did, it happened; I was gone.

In an instant, I was standing about 50 feet west from the scene of the crash. Everything was in black and white. There were flashing lights everywhere, police and State Patrol cars, the rescue squad. The State Patrol was directing traffic. I couldn't hear anything, but I could see it all.

As I observed the paramedics working on me, I also became aware of this man standing to my right. He was dressed in white. It was Jesus. I don't know how long I stood there with Him watching emergency personnel work on me. I heard Him say, "It's not your time. You have to go back." My next memory was the ambulance ride to St. Francis Hospital in Shakopee for stabilization. From there, I was transported to Fairview Hospital in Edina, a facility better equipped to both handle traumatic injuries and facial reconstruction.

Even now, years later, these memories take my breath away. He showed up to save me and to send me back. My recovery would be long, spanning one and a half years and multiple surgeries. My life was devastated, my body broken in pieces.

After spending nine days unconscious in the hospital, I awoke. When I was able to walk to the bathroom for the first time, I did not recognize the face in the mirror. My thinking was fuzzy for a long time, and somewhere in my mind, I recalled an encounter with a man in white.

I went home to my two-story apartment with the spiral wrought-iron staircase. It was a beast to navigate with broken ribs and my right ankle in a walking cast. After going home to recover, I spent the majority of my time alone. Those closest to me had no capacity to give me the right encouragement, and told me to get over it. I'd been attending modeling school, but my dreams of a modeling career were over due to the obvious injuries on my face and head. I recall one day in particular when I was in deep depression with no hope for the future. I looked out over the balcony of the loft bedroom to the floor below, wondering if I would die when I jumped. I heard Him answer my thoughts. He said, "It's not far enough to commit suicide. You'd only be hurt badly. You don't want to do this."

In tears, I walked around the bed to look in the mirror on top of the dresser. My broken ribs grated against each other with every breath I took, and I couldn't bear weight on my right ankle at all. The left side of my face was full of stitches and glass fragments. My left eyebrow was gone. My badly damaged nose was reconstructed using a graft of skin from behind my left ear.

It was surreal. The only identity I had clung to was in my appearance, and that was gone. I saw no other value in me in that moment, but Jesus did.

"I will heal you," I heard Jesus say as He stood next to me. We both looked in the mirror. I touched my face, still in disbelief. Glass fragments would work their way to the surface for months. My left eyebrow could be grafted back in if I wanted to use tissue from an armpit.

As I surveyed my condition, I told Jesus, "You're going to have to heal me. I have no one else."

This was my first experience of God using healthcare professionals to minister to me. Even in the chaos and destruction, He'd made a way for me to have one of the best reconstructive surgeons available at that time. My surgeon was Dr. Allen Van Beek, the world-renowned surgeon famous for reattaching John Thompson's arms after a farming accident in North Dakota.

Dr. Van Beek was a kind, gentle man. His staff was sensitive to the nature of their patients' injuries. Over time and several surgeries, his gift and expertise had me looking nearly new. God also used my injuries to bring hope and healing to others. My case became part of his teaching curriculum as he traveled and taught other medical professionals. As we walked through the stages of healing and surgeries, we explored various options. With his encouragement and support, I agreed to become the first patient to have a balloon tissue expander implanted in my face. The purpose was to expand and stretch my healthy, unscarred facial skin on my left cheek.

When enough new skin was created, he would cut away much of the scarred skin and replace it with the new skin. It was a great plan and it worked. However, I didn't realize what I signed up for in the interim. After several weeks of filling that balloon with saline, my left cheek stuck out from my face several inches. People stared at me like the Elephant Man when I went out in public. I found it easier to bandage my whole head when I went out. But in my physical and emotional pain and discomfort, Father was not only using this for my good, but also for the benefit of many others. He whispered encouragement to me and gave me strength to persevere through this time.

My character was rebuilt and refined in this season of my life. I came through it with deeper compassion for others, more patience, more long-suffering. Sometimes, I stop and look in the mirror. I look at my scars. I sense Jesus looking at my reflection with me.

These moments take my breath away. They're intimate moments when His love washes over me like a flood. He often reminds me of what He said to me years ago; "Scars are proof of healing."

Then we smile at each other and I tell Him, "I love you." He says, "I love you, child," and we carry on.

Until recently I've only shared a few of my spiritual experiences with friends I could trust, those that wouldn't tell me I was crazy. I share them now to validate others' personal experiences with God.

One day recently, I was thinking about His words, "I will never leave you or forsake you," in light of all I have walked through in my life. Then He dropped this into my spirit: "'I will never leave you or forsake you,' did not begin when you got saved. It began in the beginning."

He knew us from before the foundation of the world. When we were born into the Earth, our spiritual senses were dulled by circumstances, events, and the lies of the enemy. We come full circle when we recognize that He has already reconciled us back to Him through Jesus' death, burial, and resurrection.

He's always been with us, never separated from us. We just weren't tuned to the right frequency to hear Him. He speaks to us in His still small voice in our spirits. He speaks to us through nature, through movies, through music, through art, through writing. There is nothing on this Earth that He is not present in.

> *For by Him all things were created that are in heaven and that are on earth, visible and invisible, whether thrones or dominions or principalities or powers. All things were created through Him and for Him. And He is before all things, and in Him all things consist.*
> COL 1:16-17

Since I moved across the country a few years ago, I'm finding those verses are key for me. I ask Holy Spirit to lead me in all truth regularly, and Jesus' words in the Gospels have new life and meaning to me. We were made in His likeness for His pleasure, to be in relationship with Him. Every relationship develops and grows through conversation and communication. His communication with you is specific to how He made you. He initiates the communication and pursues us until we remember who we really are in Him. When we awaken to our true identity, we no longer search for anything else to fill the voids or heal the wounds. We are One with Him, and in Him, we live and move and have our being.

> God knows everything about you and He totally gets you. He's the one who understands you most because He is the one who loves you the most. So everything is laid bare for God to see. There is nothing in our life that is hidden. You can't have a thought that He doesn't listen to. He knows everything about us and it's His love of us in everything that He knows about us that empowers us to love Him back. ~ Graham Cooke, *Growing Up in God*.

> **Laurie Hilgers** describes herself as an energetic, lively, passionate woman living out her dreams on the west coast of the US. She maintains a 'perpetual tourist' status to live life fully engaged every day. She loves a good road trip, loud music and writing stories to pair with her nature photography. Laurie has one son she adores in addition to many others who fondly call her 'mom.' She's known to love well and laugh infectiously. As you read her writing, healing and hope join hands to show you relationship with Father God. Laurie reminds us that, "He loves to take the broken pieces of our lives and build something beautiful with them."
>
> Email: janedoewritesblog@gmail.com
> Blog: http://www.thejanedoechronicles.com

YOU <u>CAN</u> HEAR DAD'S VOICE
Cherieann Radiant

WHEN I WAS a little girl, roughly five years old, I was a pastor's kid and I spent a lot of time sitting through church sermons. In my boredom, I would read the stories in the old and New Testament. One day, I was reading stories about how God spoke to Moses, and David, and Elisha, and these people would talk back and have conversations with God, and I looked up from my reading and realized we didn't do the same in our church. We had one-way conversations to God, but not back and forth conversations. We definitely didn't have the same kinds of adventures happening that I saw in either the old or New Testament with God in today's times. At five years old, my questions started with, if God really is the same yesterday, today, and forever, then where is the voice of God today? And it became my life's mission to search this out.

Today, hearing the voice of God is one of the things I am most asked to speak and write about. People are so eager to hear the voice of God, which is wonderful. They see what I have and they want it right now! Yet, all they tend to ask me to speak or write about is on technique. Beautiful ones, I am here to tell you that concerning hearing the voice of God—frankly, there is no technique.

This is all about relationship. And relationship cannot be reduced down to technique. It is not how relationships work.

This is about a wonderful, amazing Dad who *loves* you. He created you to hear His voice. It is not something you have to work hard for. He said, "My sheep hear My voice." It is a given.

When a child is born, that child has a voice. That child also knows how to hear the voice of their parent. They did not have to work to obtain that. It is a given. But that child also has things to learn in those areas and ways they can grow.

They need to learn language for one thing. You can tell a newborn, "I love you." They *can* hear that voice. But they do not comprehend the voice and understand what it is saying right away. That comes with time. That grows as the relationship grows.

The parent is not worried that the child will never understand or comprehend what they are saying. The parent understands this process takes some time. The parent also understands that building a deep relationship with that newborn will require time to cultivate. Real relationships built on foundations of trust, communication, and mutual understanding takes time. The parent is prepared to put in that time. The parent is confident that the day is coming when that child will not only hear "I love you," but also will understand and comprehend it, and that the day will come when they can return that love back.

Right now, you *can* hear Dad's voice. You are His child. He is your Dad. You *can* hear His voice. It is a given. You may not be comprehending it in all the ways you would like. You may not be hearing it to the degree you want to be hearing it. You may not be hearing it in the specific ways you would currently prefer. You may not be able to tune out the voices of others right now as well as you would like. But you *can* hear His voice. You will get better at it. You will grow more in this area. We do not doubt this about any other child. Do not doubt this about your own self, as a child of God.

So we have established that you can hear Dad's voice, but you want to grow in that area. Remember that this is all about relationship, it is not about technique. It cannot be about technique. It is something that is designed to be messy on purpose.

Do you know what happens if we think we can reduce the Gospel down to technique? Do you know what it means if we reduce hearing the voice of God down to a technique? We have created a situation where we don't need the Holy Spirit. We will just go about the technique, do steps one through five, rinse and repeat them, and we don't actually develop a real, vibrant relationship with God that has depth that can enable us to withstand and overcome anything we may face. Then we encounter a circumstance in real life and we don't know how to hear the voice of God and partner through the circumstance together. That typically leads to the line of thought that we need someone else to hear the voice of God for us. We then say to ourselves, I can't hear the Holy Spirit speaking to me, even though I am in Jesus, and He is in me, and I need some other person to interpret the voice of God for me in this circumstance, going back to an Old Testament prophet type of situation.

It is a beautiful thing indeed when others come to you and confirm what God has been saying to you directly. Part of the good news of the Gospel is that you are in Jesus, He is in you, and you don't have to go through anyone else to hear God in the everyday. You have every invitation to hear Him yourself, directly, one on one. You don't need anyone else to be your shortcut. You don't have to live off someone else's relationship with Dad. You get to step right up to the table yourself and dive right in. That is beautiful and brilliant good news.

Others can come alongside you and encourage you in your journey. Frankly, the Holy Spirit can do a far better job than any mere person can, of teaching you, encouraging you, comforting you, whatever it is that you may need. It is what He lives for! He is excited about His job. He loves that job. Don't let anyone else take His place in that for you in your life. If you do, I guarantee you that you are missing out.

Do you understand, beloved ones, what will happen if I sat here and taught you technique? I can give you tips, of course, but if I dare reduce hearing the voice of God down to a technique, here is what will happen. The Holy Spirit will set up circumstances in your life in a specific way where technique won't work at all for you, so that you will have to go talk to Him directly. The Holy Spirit is smart. And He knows that a direct line of relationship and communication between you two is what will change your life. He knows exactly what you need for what you will face next. How He talks with one person, it may be completely different in how He talks to another person. He wants to set it up that you both can connect clearly, anytime, anywhere, no matter what. He wants to be the first person you run to in any situation. He is the One with the brilliant answers and solutions.

So you know you can hear the voice of God, you want to grow in that area, and you realize it is not about technique. But where do you go from here? Let me ask you this. What do you do in your other relationships? How do you grow them? How do you take them to the next level? Do those things with Dad. Do those things with the Holy Spirit. Yes, it really is that simple.

Let's say you had the ideal best friend. What would you do with that person? You'd spend time with that person regularly. You'd share about yourself, your likes, dislikes, hopes, and dreams. You listen to the other person as they share those same things. You have conversations. You may write letters, emails, and texts back and forth. You hear that person tell you about their heart for you and you respond likewise. You hang out. You may watch movies together. You may read books or go have fun at a park together. You may just sit and have a cup of coffee or tea as you start your day together and hardly speak a word to each other at all, mostly enjoying each other's presence. You may tell that person a secret and laugh or cry together. You may tell that person your thoughts, your fears. You may just sit under a blanket and watch the stars twinkle. You may chat while out running basic errands and while you gas up your car. Go do these things with Dad. Go do these things with the Holy Spirit. I guarantee you He's interested. Just start somewhere. Start a conversation. You may be a talker or you may be a writer, but whatever works for you, your personality, how you like your friendships and relationships to be, start doing that with Dad, with the Holy Spirit. It might feel weird. It might feel awkward. Just start somewhere. And do it again, and again, and again. It will grow.

Some of my best times with Dad have been our dates over coffee or tea. I especially LOVE that He always runs my errands with me. We have inside jokes together. I can walk into a store, and one of "our" songs is playing, and I smile, and sometimes start crying, good crying. We talk about the past, present, and future. He will read books with me and even watch a TV show or movie with me. He is always loving on me. Always encouraging me. I love our intense conversations and I love when we hang out silently, just soaking up each other's presence. I am never, *ever* alone. I have forgotten what it is like to be bored, as even the normal everyday things with Dad, because of who He is, have ceased to be normal, everyday, or boring.

This relationship with Dad is meant to be the easiest relationship you are ever in. You've got the Creator of the Universe, with unlimited power and resources, who also happens to be your Dad, and He is completely in love with you. Everything He is, everything He does, He has made it about relationship with *you*.

You were not created primarily to serve God. He already had the angels to carry out His every command. You were not created primarily for worship. Again the angels were already taking care of worshiping Dad 24/7. You were created for relationship. God is Love. And Love must Love. It cannot do anything else. It is who Love is, it is what Love does. God can do anything, but He desired someone to lavish Love upon, someone to rule and reign with. This is where you came into the picture.

In relationship with God, at some point do we serve? Yes. In relationship with God, at some point, do we worship? Yes. We do these things inside the context of relationship, with a Dad who looks upon us with massive favor and immense Love. At some point, in a marriage, we serve our spouse. At some point, in a marriage, we praise our spouse. But we would never say that the main point of marriage is primarily centered around serving or praising. Marriage is primarily about two people partnering together and loving each other intensely, more than any other. Why would we see relationship with God differently? He wants to partner with us in incredible, endless, and astonishing ways.

Do you understand, beloved, that the voice of Dad changes everything? Do you?

The Creator of the Universe wants to tell you how He created everything. He wants to show you the inside secrets He put inside each and every thing and how it all works the best. He wants to show you wisdom that would not just give you favor in your circumstances, but cause an acceleration to make up for past years where you missed out on *all* He had set aside for you that you didn't quite pick up yet, didn't understand, didn't know how to take advantage of at the time, and more.

So much *more*.

I'm talking about the One person who can teach you how to overcome every circumstance you could ever encounter. I'm talking about the One person who can and will be the most consistent towards you in their nature and in the intention of their heart towards you. I'm talking about the One person who has every answer you could ever need or desire, and they won't simply spit that answer at you like a vending machine, but will give you that answer in the most intimate relationship you could ever imagine. I'm talking about the One person who doesn't want to just *do* these things for you, who doesn't want to just be these things for you, but the One person who has given you the invitation to become just like Him, in all of these ways, in all of this Goodness, in all of this Majesty. It's not Him staying way up there, and Him being good enough to shower things over you way down below. It is God extending His hand out to step up to where He is, to become like He is, and in that becoming, to partner together in relationship to do incredible, what most would say is impossible things. This is the *Good News,* beloved.

The adventure starts with a voice. His voice. A voice you already know. A voice you can already hear, whether you realize it or not. A voice where you can have the rest of this side of eternity and the next to keep getting to know more and more and more, and better and better and better, for there is no end to it. Come and join in the wondrous adventure, loves! The adventure of being loved and to Love. The adventure of being known and to know. This is your destiny, love. Rise up and meet it. What are you waiting for?

You Can Hear Dad's Voice

If you are still struggling, try this tip. Write Dad a letter. Tell Him your heart. Tell Him how you feel. Tell Him your fears, your hopes, your desires. When you are done, let Him write a letter back to you. Start in an area where you know His heart for you just to get you started and see where it goes. I am including an example letter of Dad writing back to you, to help you get started and to visualize the process.

A Letter from Dad to You:

My Sweetheart! The one My heart loves! How I love *you*! I thought of you today, and I just couldn't stop smiling. Every day now, you see a little bit more like how I see. Yet there is still so much that you do not see. I have so much good planned for you, for your life. Even now, you could not handle seeing or knowing it all. It is that good! Rest today, in My Love. Let it cover you today. Let it fill every hole inside. Take My Joy. It is not what the world offers and it will sustain you in places where you previously thought you could not go. You can have strength where "they" tell you it is impossible to have strength. And that will enable you, as you practice that Joy every day, where you can partner with Me to do things that "they" say are impossible. And yet, impossible is our destiny together. Don't settle for anything less, My love.

As a child, you wanted to soar, to fly. And My heart is to show you how to do that in real life, this side of eternity. Let's run that way together, beloved. I have waited a long time for these adventures with you. And you have been so worth the wait! You will understand more in time, you are the best and My greatest investment. I don't invest in worthless things. I invest in great things and I patiently wait till My investment matures well. YOU are the pearl of great price that was worth selling everything I had to get. I don't regret it, not for a second. I am wise in what I invest in, and I pick to invest in you. Thank you for letting Me invest in you. Just wait and see what comes of it! You're gonna love it! Till then, practice Joy. And see what I do in you and through you as you do so.

All My Love,
Dad ❤

Loves, just take a step or two every day in practicing and growing in hearing Dad's voice. I guarantee that if you do, you will get to where you want to be in it and your heart will ever be satisfied. Baby steps, every day. Yes, it really is that simple. And one last piece of advice for you on this journey: Dare to be confident in His Love towards you. If there is one thing you can safely be confident in, it is in that truth. For God so Loved you, and God *is* Love.

Cherieann Radiant is a worshiper who lives fascinated by the nature and majesty of God as a lifestyle. Her heart is to be about Dad's business of Goodness on the earth, and that no one would be safe from a blessing around her. A speaker, blogger, writer, teacher, and coach, it is evident that her favorite gift of the Spirit is Wisdom. She has coached and mentored many in areas such as health, finances, family building, team building, and is sought out for wisdom on numerous topics such as hearing the voice of God, breakthrough, and living out the impossible in everyday life. She has operated as a consultant for the individual, the family unit, the entrepreneur, and for multiple businesses. Her "Mama heart" shines through all she does. Cherieann is married to Joseth Radiant and currently has one daughter named Fearless Trust. She blogs transparently about her own personal journey with Dad.

Blog: www.blacksheepprincess.com

Thank You for Purchasing This Book

More from Inkity Press

Divine Healing
Made Simple

Seeing in the Spirit
Made Simple

Hearing God's Voice
Made Simple

Traveling in the Spirit
Made Simple

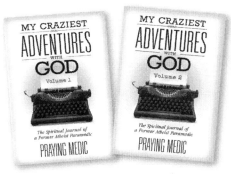
My Craziest Adventures with God
Volumes 1 and 2

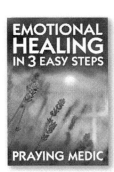
Emotional Healing
in 3 Easy Steps

Defeating Your Adversary
in the Court of Heaven

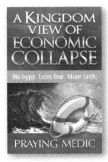
A Kingdom View of
Economic Collapse

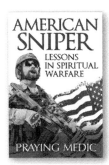
American Sniper: Lessons in
Spiritual Warfare

Idee:
2 Brilla mit Polarisationsfilter:
mit der einen sieht man nur das Positive,
mit der andren "   "   "   " Negative

Tafel mit positiven und negativen statements:
getrennt durch Polfilterfolie